Daddy Wouldn't Buy Me a Bauhaus

Daddy Wouldn't Buy Me a Bauhaus

Profiles in Architecture & Design

Janet Abrams

Princeton Architectural Press · New York

To my mother and father, Anita and David Abrams,
in their ninety-second and ninety-third year

Contents

Foreword

Deyan Sudjic

Janet Abrams began her career as a critic at what, in retrospect, seems a very particular moment in the 1980s, a time when there seemed to be a major shift in attitudes toward architecture and design. The first whispers of a reaction against an ascendant postmodernism were already in the air, sometimes with paradoxical results. Feeling insecure, SOM put itself on the couch—and on the lookout for alternatives to corporate modernism. At the first Venice Architecture Biennale, held in 1980, postmodernism's defining moment, the Strada Novissima—an installation of twenty facades by twenty architects—put Rem Koolhaas on show alongside Michael Graves. Everything was in play, and future directions were still to be defined. Meanings and context seemed as important as plans, appearances, and techniques.

The upstart London monthly *Blueprint*, founded in 1983 by a group of journalists, photographers, writers, and designers—of which Janet was one and I was another—vigorously attempted to play its own skeptical, Anglo-Saxon part in this process. The magazine set out to be both iconoclastic and disposable, while aiming to root architecture, design, graphics, fashion, and their visual representation in the popular culture of the time. We thought we were going to turn design and architecture upside down. As is usually the case, this took the form of doing all that we could to champion a new group of names, drawn from among our contemporaries. As they rose, so would we. (Now that print has lost much of its authority, we wait with more or less resignation for another generation to dispatch us, in electronic haiku, 140 characters at a time.)

Fashion cycles are the natural means for edging out one generation to make room for another, but they don't always make for the most reliable of critical judgments. Janet, however, has never been interested in adopting fashionable attitudes. What drives her is the exploration of ideas, and that is what makes her writing compelling reading today. She combines endless curiosity and erudition with a fascination for observation and detail across the broadest cultural spectrum, in a way that might reflect an early interest in the work of the trenchant English critic Reyner Banham, who, like Janet, combined a sharp wit with a determination to extract every scrap of meaning from the smallest of details. Banham, too, made the decision to move to the United States, but his influence was still pervasive at the Bartlett School of Architecture in London when Janet arrived there as an undergraduate student immediately after his departure.

The breadth of her writing shows her ability to engage with some of the most formidable voices of our time, dealing with Peter Eisenman's bicoastal psychoanalysis and Koolhaas's first significant completed buildings on her own terms. She has found herself in Los Angeles, talking to Disney's Michael Eisner, and in a casino designed by David Rockwell, exploring the nature of mapping, play, and craft. Writing, for Janet, is a voyage—a mission to understand, to explain, and sometimes to hold to account. She has the ability to frame complexity in pursuit of clarity.

Janet's perspective over the years has grown beyond architecture to encompass the wider horizons of design, technology, and their meaning for the world. It follows her professional trajectory, from journalism in London to a doctorate at Princeton

University to directorship of the University of Minnesota Design Institute, and then on to an MFA at Cranbrook Academy of Art—with interludes at the Netherlands Design Institute in Amsterdam and the Canadian Centre for Architecture in Montreal. It's a list of institutions and actions like no other, one that reads like a timeline of most of the key developments in design culture over the past four decades. Her writing also reflects the impact of the digital explosion, and the subsequent renewal of interest in the physical and the mark of handwork. That interplay between thinking and doing is what makes her uniquely qualified to explore the nature of the material world against the background of accelerating change.

THE LEADING MAGAZINE OF ARCHITECTURE AND DESIGN MARCH 1986/NUMBER 35 £2

BLUEPRINT

**HIGH TECH
SEX IN
LONDON**

**THE BIG APPLE
PHILIP
JOHNSON
AT 80
SURVIVING
NEW YORK**

Blueprint, March 1987 (despite the
error in the date on the cover):
Philip Johnson, photographed by Phil
Sayer, for a special issue on New York

Introduction
Tightrope Walking with the "Circus of the Perpetually Jet-Lagged"

Janet Abrams

Have you ever wandered down a street in a familiar city, noticed a new building asserting itself in strident aesthetic contrast to the surrounding urban fabric, and asked yourself: "What were they *thinking*?" Or navigated a cumbersome website and wondered: "Isn't there a simpler way?"

These are the kinds of questions that drove me from the 1980s to the 2000s, as a critic on architecture, design, and digital media. Early in my journalism career, I gravitated toward the interview as a mode of inquiry; the extended profile soon became my preferred format. I wanted to get beyond press release platitudes, to dig into the ideas, theories, and even *emotions* underlying the work of contemporary architects and designers. Their creative choices—writ large as buildings, interiors, urban spaces, mass-produced objects, everyday information design, and commercial software—play a profound role in shaping our lives— then, as now, even if the dominant aesthetics today are quite different from decades past.

———

Daddy Wouldn't Buy Me a Bauhaus gathers twenty-six profiles, the majority of which originally appeared in two design magazines:

Blueprint, the London-based monthly established in 1983, and *I.D. Magazine*, the New York–based bimonthly founded in 1954.[1] Others were published in the UK daily newspaper *The Independent*; in *Building Design*, a UK trade weekly; and in books, exhibition catalogues, and limited-edition publications.[2]

Collectively, they form a portrait of an era: the cusp between analog and digital, in which the solid objects of architecture and design were beginning to face significant competition from the distributed virtual experiences of the Internet and other new media platforms.[3]

It was also the era in which certain architects began to garner international celebrity. During the 1980s and 1990s, the expansion of networked electronic communications and adoption of computer-aided design made it easier to design buildings in one time zone and construct them in another, transforming architectural practice into a multinational enterprise. Architects based in the United States and Europe became increasingly sought-after by clients around the globe, who, thanks to a bevy of international architecture magazines, clamored for buildings that would become cover stories (or today, ready fodder for Instagram). Suddenly, signature styles were an export commodity—modified somewhat to acknowledge the specifics of site and local culture.[4] Hence Rem Koolhaas's wry expression, which I have borrowed from our conversation (pages 97–108) for the title of this essay.

My role as critic and outside observer, especially as US correspondent for *Blueprint* in the 1980s, enabled me to select individuals for interview whose work and opinions were not yet widely known, particularly on the other side of the Atlantic. (It should be noted that few of them worked alone; if their practices then consisted of just a handful of people, today they may employ dozens, even hundreds, in multiple offices around the world.) Some were already renowned veterans of their discipline at the

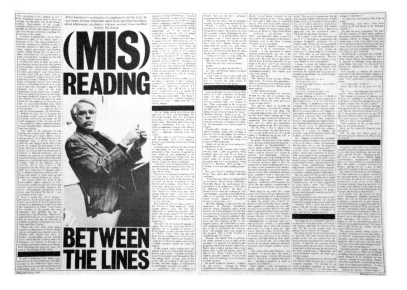

"(Mis)Reading Between The Lines,"
my first profile for *Blueprint*, on
American architect Peter Eisenman,
February 1985

"My Tea With Andrée," on French
designer Andrée Putman, *Blueprint*,
October 1985

"Call That a *Fish*, Frank?," on American
architect Frank Gehry, *Blueprint*,
September 1988. The opening spread
showed a model of Gehry's building

for the Chiat/Day advertising agency
in Venice, California, incorporating
Giant Binoculars, an artwork by Claes
Oldenburg and Coosje van Bruggen

time of my interview (architects Berthold Lubetkin and Philip Johnson; graphic designer Paul Rand); others were on the cusp of international fame (architects Frank Gehry and Rem Koolhaas). Information designers such as Muriel Cooper and Ben Fry were barely known beyond a tight circle of fellow specialists, but would come to be recognized as pioneers who laid the intellectual and aesthetic groundwork for the digitally mediated culture we now inhabit.

———

A through line connecting many of these profiles is the exploration of spatial experience and its visual representation. In my earlier profiles of architects, the subject at the heart of each conversation is *real* space: its commissioning, design, visualization, construction, and eventual occupation. When I joined *I.D. Magazine* in the early 1990s as its writer-at-large, my focus shifted to design for digital communication. But here, too, I found that certain innovators were using three-dimensional space to navigate data—laid out in a Cartesian grid so it could be viewed from different vantages, and zoomed into for extra detail. This represented a dramatic shift from the hitherto dominant metaphor of static, superimposed windows (another borrowing from the language of architecture).

It is no accident that two of the leading exponents of information design profiled in this book have backgrounds in architecture. Richard Saul Wurman studied at the University of Pennsylvania, where he was a disciple of architect Louis I. Kahn; in our conversation, Wurman recalls Kahn reassuring him that he would *always* be an architect, no matter how diverse his subsequent activities, which have included the creation of the TED conferences and the Access travel guides. Lisa Strausfeld earned her MArch at Harvard's Graduate School of Design before completing a master's degree in Media Arts & Sciences at the MIT Media Lab.

Ben Fry, the youngest person in this collection, earned his doctorate at the Media Lab in John Maeda's Aesthetics + Computation Group (effectively the successor group to Muriel Cooper's Visible Language Workshop), and acknowledges his design lineage in our conversation about his visualizations of genomic data.

The shift from the printed page to the screen is a central concern in several profiles. It was not yet obvious in the 1990s which aspects of the culture of print could be successfully transferred to electronic media, which ones would inevitably be lost, or what new affordances the latter might offer.

After discussing the challenges of interface design for the financial data industry, Michael Bloomberg argues that newspapers "will be around for an awfully long time. They're random-access, have multiple displays like our [Bloomberg] TV screen, and are very portable. You'd have to replace those characteristics electronically before you could replace a newspaper." (This was the era of hulking desktop computers, before the arrival of handheld smartphones that can relay news 24/7 from myriad sources.)

Muriel Cooper says she is "always trying to push some more spatial and dynamic issues into a recalcitrant medium" (print). She argues that "electronic media are malleable. Print is rigid," before quickly reversing herself: "I guess I'm never really sure that print is truly linear: it's more a simultaneous medium."

Meanwhile, Bob Stein is so convinced that traditional books are the best medium for conveying ideas that he goes to great lengths to create interfaces for Voyager's CD-ROMs that are as book-like as possible—rather like designing a car that faithfully emulates a horse-drawn carriage. In contrast to Stein, April Greiman expresses her frustration that early 1990s interface design is being done mainly by "nerds" mostly coming from engineering backgrounds, "who know nothing about typography. People are treating the multimedia interface like pages, instead of trying to get 3D and motion, more like a movie."

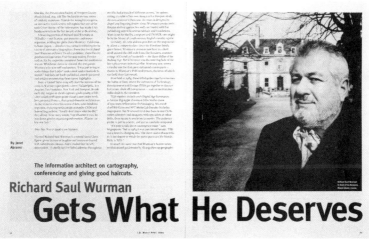

"Muriel Cooper's Visible Wisdom,"
profile of the director of the MIT Media
Lab's Visible Language Workshop, *I.D.
Magazine*, September–October 1994

"Richard Saul Wurman Gets What He
Deserves," profile of the creator of the
TED conferences and Access guidebooks,
I.D. Magazine, March–April 1994

Another theme is the push-pull of ideas across the Atlantic: the lure of America for European architects and theorists, as a paragon of modernity and advanced technology; the reciprocal attraction of Europe for Americans hungry for history, and eager to immerse themselves in its palimpsest of architecture and urban design precedents.

This theme surfaces in my remembrance of British architectural historian Reyner Banham, who, in his *A Concrete Atlantis*, had described his pilgrimage to Fiat's Lingotto car factory (1923) in Turin, with its iconic rooftop test-track, as "a kind of homecoming for one partially Americanized European." Phyllis Lambert, who persuaded her father to hire the German architect Mies van der Rohe to design the Seagram Building in New York, discloses that she wrote her undergraduate thesis on Henry James because she was interested in "the problem of the American in exile, relating to his or her culture. That fascinated me because I was an exile in the United States, and was deeply attracted to European culture myself." My conversation with Rem Koolhaas took place shortly after he had begun to build in the Netherlands with his practice, OMA, having returned from a sojourn in the United States, where he had studied at Cornell and achieved early acclaim as the author of *Delirious New York: A Retroactive Manifesto for Manhattan*, published in 1978. "In America," Koolhaas observes, "even if current architecture tries very hard—or pretends to—it is still grappling with the problem that it doesn't have a real context, doesn't have a real relationship to history. In Europe, history is a given and remains in many cases a serious obstacle."

Transatlantic cultural exchange inevitably surfaces in my interview with the king of theme parks, Disney CEO Michael Eisner, whom I met at the company's Burbank HQ shortly before the launch of Euro Disney outside Paris. Arguing that Disneyland is "a kind of definitive urban planning," Eisner tells me: "I feel similar walking through Siena as I do through Disneyland." And architect Michael Graves, whom Eisner hired for several Disney commissions, explains how his abiding love of classical architecture and landscape design was shaped by his time as a Rome Prize Fellow in the early 1960s.

———

I was particularly attuned to this tug of culture and ideas, having left my native England for the States at age twenty-four, after three years as a trainee journalist, following my bachelor's degree at the Bartlett School of Architecture, University College London.

There, I had narrowly missed having Banham as an architectural history professor—he had left the Bartlett for SUNY Buffalo the year before I arrived. But Adrian Forty's course on the Social History of Architecture and Robert Maxwell's seminar on Semiology and Architecture were both formative, shaping my awareness of architecture and design as symbolic artifacts— and, as I came to think of them, the tangible outcomes of conflict resolution among competing cultural, political, technological, and economic forces.[5] By my third year at the Bartlett, I knew I was more interested in *writing about* the designed environment and its relationship to social organization than in *designing* or *building* it. In my final semester, in place of another studio design project, I wrote a collection of short essays on various contemporary artifacts, to self-imposed word-counts and time limits, under the supervision of Steven Groák—a practice run for my next phase.

After graduation, I entered an on-the-job journalism training scheme run by trade publisher Morgan-Grampian, whose titles included such gems as *Travel Trade Gazette*, *Laboratory*

Equipment Digest, and *Tunnels and Tunneling Incorporating Muck Shifter Weekly*. My sights were set on joining *Building Design* (generally known as *BD*), its weekly newspaper for architects and construction professionals. But first, a stint on *Estates Times* would give me a very different, and useful, perspective on architecture from my Bartlett education.

As a novice reporter on this real estate weekly, I was introduced to the arcane culture of City of London property agents and their Sloane Ranger assistants (in Peter York's inimitable term for the young ladies of England's upper classes) who fed me lavish lunches in wood-paneled private dining rooms in the hope that I'd feel morally obligated to write about the shiny new office block they had just shown me around. Back at Morgan-Grampian's HQ in down-at-heel Woolwich, I was taught to compose parsimonious picture captions on these interchangeable heaps of square footage, which had scant architectural qualities besides the variants of their curtain wall systems, lobbies, and lavatories. The names of Le Corbusier, Mies, and Wright—never mind Laugier or Ledoux—rarely disturbed those decorous lunchtime conversations. My eyes were peeled open to the commercial aspects of building design, and how architecture was often just a minor player in the complicated game that is urban development.

With three training stints and two invaluable skills—touch-typing and Teeline shorthand—under my belt, I joined *BD* as a "sprog," writing news stories and compiling its events calendar, and rising to features editor after a year.[6] On Fridays, we'd come up to still-dusty and mostly vacant Clerkenwell, to watch as ladies with impossibly long, polished talons somehow input our copy into their typesetting machines, then we'd repair to a salt beef sandwich bar (the neighborhood's sole dining spot, now the site of Herzog & de Meuron's London offices) to celebrate the issue "going to bed."

The earliest piece in this collection, my 1982 interview with Lubetkin, dates from this period. By composing a written-through narrative, rather than a Q&A, I could incorporate relevant backstory about his achievements, personal history, and the context of our conversation—his first with an architectural publication in decades. I began to sense the potential of one-on-one dialogue, which would evolve into the core of my journalistic practice.

———

In early fall 1983, I crossed the Atlantic to begin my studies toward a doctorate in Architectural History, Theory and Criticism at Princeton University, on a Fulbright Scholarship, taking a student standby ticket on the QE2—mainly because I could bring more luggage by boat than traveling by plane. My family waved me off from the dock at Southampton; my mother later told me she was quite convinced she'd never see me again.

———

Arriving at Princeton was a jolt. Journalism versus Scholarship: suddenly the lines were drawn, and it was very clear which type of writing doctoral students were supposed to deploy in their coursework and dissertation. I immediately sensed subtle disapproval of the kind I'd been practicing thus far.[7] Fast, responsive writing about contemporary artifacts and practitioners was not exactly appreciated by my professors; scholarly writing was superior, even if—or precisely *because*—it reached a smaller, more rarefied readership. Texts lacking the obligatory genuflections to the critical theorists *du jour* would count for nothing on an academic résumé.

Undeterred, I moonlighted as a journalist for *Blueprint*, which had been launched in the fall of 1983 by a group of London-based journalists, led by publisher Peter Murray, editor Deyan Sudjic, and art director Simon Esterson. Spanning all

"Information Overlord," profile of
Michael Bloomberg, CEO and cofounder
of Bloomberg L.P., published in *Rethinking
Design 4: Medium*, 1997. Photography by
Adam Bartos

"Delirious Visions," profile of Dutch architect
Rem Koolhaas, cofounder of OMA, published
in *Blueprint*, February 1988. Opening spread
featured OMA's Dance Theatre in The Hague,
photographed by Peter Cook.

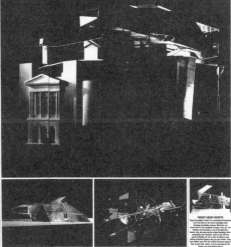

Austrian architects Wolf Prix and
Helmut Swiczinsky, partners in Coop
Himmelb(l)au, *Blueprint*, December 1988–
January 1989. Cover portrait by
Steve Pyke

"When the Sky Falls In," profile of
Coop Himmelb(l)au, opening spread,
Blueprint, December 1988–January 1989

aspects of design, from architecture to fashion, its extra-large pages allowed for lengthy articles with huge accompanying images, often full-bleed across double-page spreads; its commissioned cover portraits elevated architects and designers to celebrity status—equivalent to those featured on the cover of Andy Warhol's *Interview* magazine.[8]

A breakthrough in both format and editorial content, *Blueprint* became an immediate force to be reckoned with amid the fusty publications that had long dominated the British architecture and design scene, such as *Building*, the *RIBA Journal*, *Design* (published by the UK Design Council), *Building Design*, *Architectural Review*, and *Architects' Journal*. The latter two, stablemates of the Architectural Press, were published from offices in Westminster that were more like a gentlemen's club, complete with a private bar, the Bride of Denmark, on whose mirror famous architects autographed their name using a diamond-tipped stylus. *Blueprint*, by contrast, operated from the leaky top floor of a standalone building in Marylebone, shored up on both sides with giant struts; the floors below housed the studios of industrial designer Sebastian Conran (son of Terence Conran, one of *Blueprint*'s early backers) and architect David Chipperfield.

My assignments for *Blueprint* provided welcome excuses to escape the university campus and travel to various parts of the States, facilitated by Princeton's proximity to Newark airport and cheap airfares on People Express. Deyan would call me on the wall-mounted phone of the architecture school's PhD room (this was pre-fax, pre-email—the early dawn of the Apple Macintosh 128K) to ask me to go see a new building or interview someone and write it up for the next month's issue. Hence a day-trip flight to Louisville, Kentucky, to review Michael Graves's Humana headquarters; a hair-raising initiation to Miami's I-95 in rush-hour traffic, to meet Laurinda Spear and Bernardo Fort-Brescia of Arquitectonica, and Andrés Duany and Elizabeth Plater-Zyberk

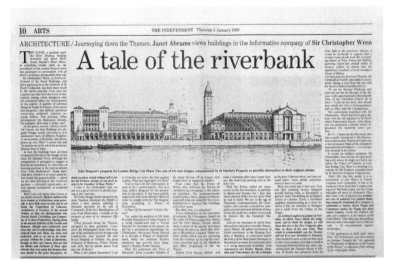

"A Tale of the Riverbank," my interview with Sir Christopher Wren, published in the British newspaper *The Independent*, January 5, 1989

"Britischer Architekt," interview with James Stirling and Michael Wilford, of Stirling Wilford Architects, *The Independent*, June 26, 1989 of Duany Plater-Zyberk & Co.; train rides to New York to interview architects Peter Eisenman and Philip Johnson, the latter on his eightieth birthday (there would be a follow-up ten years later). At first, I dispatched hard-copy text and 35mm slides to London via international courier, counting the minutes until the rep showed up at my dorm room. Later, a friend working for Graves would sneak me into his Nassau Street studio to use the firm's brand-new fax machine—taking extra care not to accidentally speed-dial my copy to one of his clients.

Returning to London in 1987, I took breaks from writing my dissertation[9] to interview French interior designer Andrée Putman, Phyllis Lambert, and Frank Gehry, catching them on UK visits. I made trips to the Netherlands to meet Rem Koolhaas and to Austria to meet the partners of Coop Himmelb(l)au and, with heavy heart, wrote an obituary for Reyner Banham, whom I had met on my first trip to the States in 1978.

I got my foot in the door to write on architecture for *The Independent*, the recently launched British newspaper, with a cold call to Tom Sutcliffe, editor of its Arts page, to which I contributed regularly from 1988 through 1991. Writing for a daily publication was a new challenge, especially using Atex software that put page design and copy editing into the journalists' hands.[10] With much tighter page real estate than at *Blueprint*, my features could only run to about twelve hundred words—still a positive tome in a newspaper. Reference to stylistic categories such as "postmodernism" or "classicism" was forbidden—any such jargon was immediately sniffed out and jettisoned, while the identities of architects I had assumed to be household names were regularly queried. My profiles for *The Independent* included conversations with James Stirling and Michael Wilford and an "interview" with Sir Christopher Wren about developments along the River Thames, using excerpts from the 1750 *Parentalia*, the Wren family memoirs, as his responses to my questions.

Prince Charles began to weigh in on architecture during this period; in his 1984 speech to the RIBA, he infamously described Ahrends, Burton and Koralek's competition-winning proposal for an extension to London's National Gallery as "a monstrous carbuncle on the face of a much-loved and elegant friend."[11] In 1989, he published *A Vision of Britain: A Personal View of Architecture*, accompanied by an eponymous BBC documentary. It became increasingly difficult to practice architectural criticism for a general readership in competition with the heir to the throne; whatever one wrote became de facto either an endorsement or rebuttal of his latest proclamation. At an opportune moment, I switched to writing photography criticism for *The Independent*, and later took a full-time position as features editor at *Punch*, the century-old humor magazine. When a job came up in the States in 1991, I left England once again.

After fourteen months in Chicago, I moved to New York and joined *I.D. Magazine* as writer-at-large, under editor-in-chief Chee Pearlman, making my debut with a profile of Paul Rand, recently retired from his Yale professorship. This was followed by pieces about pioneers of information and entertainment design: Bob Stein, cofounder of Voyager Company, publisher of educational CD-ROMs (then the cutting-edge digital platform); David Rockwell, designer of themed environments from casinos to restaurants; and the aforementioned Wurman and Cooper, the latter then the only female professor at the MIT Media Lab. I also wrote on graphic designer April Greiman, for the catalogue of her solo exhibition at arc en rêve centre d'architecture in Bordeaux, France; on architect Julie Snow, for her first monograph; and on Michael Bloomberg, then CEO of the eponymous financial data and media business he had cofounded in 1981, for Mohawk Mills' *Rethinking Design* series.

It was a propitious moment to be in Manhattan, with the burgeoning of digital media: the era of *Silicon Alley Reporter* and

The International Design Magazine
September October 1993 $7

I.D.

Biosphere's Utopia Under Glass
Changing Identities at the Walker
Fast-Track American Trains

Paul Rand

The master of Modernism on art, graphics, and other devotions

Profile of Paul Rand, the modernist
graphic designer, author, and educator,
published in *I.D. Magazine*, September–
October 1993

the New York New Media Association's networking gatherings in vast corporate lobbies, of meetings with twentysomething web design CEOs before buyouts or IPOs obviated the need for them ever to work again. As a writer, the challenge was to convey the surprises and sensory allure of efflorescent new-media platforms—websites, CD-ROMs, laser discs, digital stock trading devices, early (clunky) "electronic books"—while analyzing them as harbingers of new kinds of social and economic behavior.[12]

———

Given the average word count of online articles today, it is hard to imagine how lengthy profiles of the kind I wrote in the 1980s and 1990s could find their way to publication. Five-thousand-word pieces are hardly the stock-in-trade of architecture and design magazines these days—at least, the few that remain in print.[13]

Meanwhile, the technological forces that have decimated print publishing have also reshaped the practices of architecture and design. Sadly, the forms of many contemporary buildings often seem to have been determined by the algorithms underlying the software used to design them, rather than by humans; long gone are the drawing board and T square—tools of the trade when I studied architecture in the late 1970s. Rand's skills at creating two-dimensional corporate logos enabled him to rise to almost godlike status in the twentieth century; how would he have fared in today's fast-moving culture of time-based interactive design and the plethora of other categories—game design, service design, social design, critical design—that have recently arisen?

These are issues for the rising generation of architecture and design critics to explore, albeit they will likely do so online rather than in print. Internet-based publications can reach a much bigger, global readership than the titles for which I wrote these profiles, but the culture of journalism has fundamentally changed.

While I was gallivanting around the world to meet particular people and see specific buildings, I always felt a tangible connection to a place-based community of writers and editors. The offices of *Building Design*, *Blueprint*, *The Independent*, and *I.D. Magazine* served as hubs not only for their regular editorial staff but also for their network of freelance contributors—intense, bustling, and (despite their avowed championship of design) incorrigibly messy marketplaces of images and ideas, and their rapid throughput into print. I felt privileged, as a member of these ecosystems, to be "in conversation with writers...who were way beyond the hack journalists in powers of thought and expression, and in their intellectual reach," as my fellow-contributor Robin Kinross, the historian of typography, recalls of *Blueprint*'s early years.[14] Today's critics probably see their local baristas more often than their editors; some are willing to break what I consider a cardinal rule by reviewing buildings without going to see them in the flesh.

Just as the publishing and design industries have undergone dramatic change over the last few decades, so have my own interests. After many years paying close attention to *other* people's creative endeavors, it was time to delve into *my own*, and by hand.

In 2008, I went back to graduate school to earn an MFA in ceramics at Cranbrook Academy of Art in Michigan. Since then, I have focused on my studio practice as a sculptor, working in ceramics, bronze, and other materials. I continue to write and edit, now mostly about the visual arts, the relationship of the handmade to other modes of making, and how the ongoing dialogue between analog and digital shapes contemporary material culture. But that, as they say, is another story—for another book.

———

I once read a description of journalism as being analogous to the exposed wires at the end of an electrical cable that gradually merge into the sheathed cord of history. Looking back at this body of work, thinking about the individuals with whom I spent a few hours in intense conversation many years ago, I see a kaleidoscope of characters—the majority still alive, but several now departed—who are inexorably becoming historical figures. As with all collections of interviews with leading names from other eras and arenas of practice, some of these people will come to be seen as having made lasting contributions to their field, while others will drift into obscurity—perhaps, one day, to be rehabilitated by future historians. My job was not to evaluate their significance in the long-term, but to convey the live-wire immediacy of each encounter.

Over the years, I developed strategies for making my own role explicit—at least as a critical dilemma—within the formal structure of the piece, rather than smoothing away the traces of my active engagement in the conversation or by adopting the false neutrality of the transcribed Q&A. Across the span of these profiles, I also see my own evolution as a writer and thinker about architecture and design. For this opportunity, and for the pleasures and challenges of the dialogues from which they were distilled, I am grateful to all of the people you are about to meet.

Santa Fe, New Mexico
February 2020

NOTES

1. *I.D. Magazine* was founded in 1954 as *Industrial Design*, but in its final decades, its initials stood for *International Design*. Not to be confused with *i-D*, the British fashion and culture magazine founded in 1980 by Terry Jones.

2. The profiles in this volume retain their UK or US English spelling, corresponding to the country in which they were originally published.

3. The shift from analog to digital is the core theme of my previous books: *If/Then: Play: Design Implications of New Media*, editor (Netherlands Design Institute, 1998); *Else/Where: Mapping—New Cartographies of Networks and Territories*, co-editor with Peter Hall (University of Minnesota Design Institute, 2006); and *WWW Drawing: Architectural Drawing from Pencil to Pixel*, editor, with Mehrdad Hadighi, project director (Actar, 2020).

4. The phrase "the Bilbao Effect" came to signify the potentially transformative impact on the local economy of a culturally successful building, exemplified by the Guggenheim Museum Bilbao, designed by Frank Gehry, which opened in 1997.

5. Architect, theorist, and educator Robert Maxwell (1922–2020) subsequently became dean of architecture at Princeton University, where he was a member of my doctoral dissertation committee in 1989.

6. At *Building Design*, I worked at first under editor Paul Finch and, later, Martin Pawley (1938–2008), who had recently returned from teaching in the States and encouraged me to apply for graduate school there.

7. One of my final pieces for *Building Design* was an interview with Princeton professor Michael Graves, during a London lecture-trip. Asked what he thought of Britain's hi-tech heroes Richard Rogers and Norman Foster, he answered that their approach was "antithetical to what I do. If I had to practice architecture like that I'd rather practice law." He and Foster almost came to blows over that comment when they crossed paths at a London restaurant—or so Graves told me, in my first week at Princeton. Janet Abrams, "Digging Graves," *Building Design*, June 10, 1983, 2. See also my "5+10: The New York Five Today," *Building Design*, July 9, 1982, 12–17.

8. *Blueprint* introduced to the British design publishing scene the A3 format (equivalent to 11-by-17-inch tabloid) established by *Skyline*, the monthly newspaper of the New York–based Institute for Architecture and Urban Studies, for which I wrote several "Letter from London" columns before leaving to study in the States. Edited by Suzanne Stephens, *Skyline* was designed by Massimo Vignelli from 1978 to 1980, then by Michael Bierut, from 1981 onward; Vignelli also designed the IAUS's scholarly journal, *Oppositions*. See Kim Foster, "Massimo

Vignelli: *Oppositions, Skyline* and the Institute," *Places,* September 2010. The majority of *Blueprint*'s cover portraits were by photographer Phil Sayer; other regular cover photographers included Steve Speller, David Banks, and Steve Pyke.

9. My 1989 doctoral dissertation—"Constructing the Corporate Image: Architecture, Mass Media and Management at the National Cash Register Company, Dayton, Ohio, 1894–1906"—explored how the early US multinational corporation defined its identity, using architecture, design, photography, and print communications to articulate the growth of its managerial structure, physical environments, and global markets.

10. Atex was a newspaper industry precursor to desktop publishing software such as QuarkXPress and Adobe InDesign. See Michael Crozier, *The Making of The Independent* (G. Fraser, 1988).

11. Prince Charles delivered his "carbuncle" speech on May 30, 1984, at the Royal Gala celebrating the 150th Anniversary of the Royal Institute of British Architects. Ahrends Burton and Koralek's proposal—with an office tower to fund its private development—was ditched after the Prince's remark. Following a £50-million donation from the Sainsbury family, obviating the need for a commercial tower, Venturi, Rauch & Scott Brown's design was selected through a second, closed competition; the Sainsbury Wing opened in 1991. https://www. princeofwales.gov.uk/speech/speech-hrh-prince-wales-150th -anniversary-royal-institute-british-architects-riba-royal-gala.

12. I continued to track these developments as director of the University of Minnesota Design Institute in Minneapolis (from 2000 to 2008), where I commissioned several digital design prototypes and undertook research into the cultural shifts occurring in response to electronic communications, particularly in the field of mapping.

13. *I.D. Magazine* closed in 2010, after fifty-five years in print. *Blueprint* and *BD* are still going, but both have changed ownership several times; the latter has been online-only since 2014. The *Independent,* launched as a broadsheet in 1986, went tabloid in 2003, and has been exclusively online since 2016. Among the publishers of the books in which some of these profiles originally appeared, several have gone out of business or been absorbed by multinational conglomerates.

14. Robin Kinross, *Unjustified Texts: Perspectives on Typography* (London: Hyphen Press, 2002), 13. See also Alice Twemlow, *Sifting the Trash: A History of Design Criticism* (Cambridge, MA: MIT Press, 2017), in which she devotes her third chapter to the evolution of the British design media in the 1980s, including an extensive discussion of *Blueprint*'s early years.

Lubetkin Speaks

Berthold Lubetkin

Building Design, March 12, 1982

Berthold Lubetkin has been up since 8:00 a.m. being interviewed by the local radio station and, later, a television company. The BBC came round yesterday. The Sundays are due tomorrow.

This audience is purely a matter of chance, he informs me, shuffling painfully on crutches to his chair: I had simply been the first of an "avalanche" of calls from the architectural press on the announcement of his Gold Medal, awarded by the Royal Institute of British Architects.

"I told the others I was in Barbados," he confides with a twinkle in his eye.

———

He is weary and not a little disdainful of his dramatically revived popularity. Old colleagues have suddenly rung to renew acquaintances that lapsed more than thirty years ago. Lubetkin withdrew from architecture in the 1950s because he foresaw its demise into the kind of fashionable merry-go-round of which my very presence is a symptom. He regards the belated accolade as paradoxical.

"On the one hand I am very grateful, but on the other I am very surprised. It seems to me that what is now being done in architecture, and in art in general, is hysterical irrationality, which is diametrically opposed to what our architecture purported to be. Therefore, to grant the medal in these circumstances for something which is so out-of-date is puzzling." A couple of things temper his skepticism. He was encouraged to discover a party of students had travelled from London recently, to meet him at the exhibition of his work with Tecton at Oxford's Museum of Modern Art. "I was amazed to find how many young people are enthusiastic about the whole thing and wish to pursue the rational. I thought it was mummified."

Besides this glimmer of hope, he looks forward to the Gold Medal address in June—"if I am still alive"—which promises an opportunity "to be sting-y, satirical, though I mustn't be too rude."

He quickly dispenses with most of my intended questions: "the modern tendency toward biography" is not something he supports. "After the war, I went to Auschwitz, and there was a road as white as the paper you are writing on. White with the bones of people. That shows how unimportant biography is. One should be interested in architecture, not architects."

It is a conversation heavy with despair, gloomy as the cluttered Clifton room in which he passes the hours writing his memoirs in dedication to his late wife and reading philosophy. György Lukács's book *Goethe and His Age* lies between us, next to a Rubik's Cube and this week's *New Statesman*.

Eyes cloudy with disillusion and poor health, chin on hands on wooden stick, he explains in a firm, authoritative voice why he gave up architecture. There are many reasons, he says, but to put it briefly: "I was disappointed with the development of modern architecture as I understood it and practised it. To me, and incidentally to my partners—I'm concerned that it's a bit egocentric—speaking collectively of the partners, we imagined the new architecture as a sort of symbol, a metaphor of the new world. I abandoned architecture because it had lost its line. It

was the harbinger of a better world and it turned out to be like…
miniskirts.”

Coming to England in 1931 from France, “where everything
was sleepy,” Lubetkin perceived the resentment for all the unful-
filled Homes for Heroes promises following World War One.
“People were appalled. After the sacrifices—having their guts and
lungs hung on the barbed wire…” He detected a swell of feeling
for change, especially among the working class. “That was what
was so inspiring: searching for new ways and new roads to it. But
don’t make any mistake,” he raises a finger, “I was never a member of the Communist Party.” The mid-1930s was the period of
greatest change, he recalls. Since then “things have settled into a
sort of routine; the world as it is now is in a tragic state.”

Fundamental to this malaise, Lubetkin is convinced, is the
universal abandonment of reason, evidenced in the lack of interest in theory. “If any theory was available, then there would be
some hope of putting it into practice. It is a fact that we have no
theory of modern architecture.” Empiricism, as a theory, “has a
grip on this nation,” which, though progressive in the days of
John Locke and Thomas Hobbes, Lubetkin now believes to be
“regressive.”

The recurrent theme of our conversation is this ubiquitous
tendency in art and architecture toward “irrationalism.”

“People attack reason because reason leads to understanding and understanding leads to change. Plenty of people have a
vested interest in what there is, for one reason or another, and
don’t want to recognize the supremacy of reason, which dictates
and organises. They want to give chaos a favorable interpretation. Even modern science is being used simply to bamboozle us,
which is an extraordinary affair.”

Lubetkin thinks the socioeconomic situation today is “very
much more severe” than his heyday in the 1930s, with which
there are many parallels. “The decay has gone so far that it is hard

to mobilise any hope. Look at the atomic question. There is no doubt about it: we are all going to be pulverised in Europe. People don't think, or don't want to think. It's the same for architecture. Some prefer things as they are now because the effort to change is so big and complicated. Change is no longer a question of preference. It is a question of survival. You have to espouse reason and not, as Hitler said, 'think with blood.' People don't want a reasonable architecture because, as I said before, reason is the enemy."

He remains steadfast in his convictions about what architecture is. "The instant emotional impact, lyricism of... [*appassionato*] WHITE sharp-edged geometric regularity. Geometry is so precious because it gets rid of ephemerals, of whims."

He despises "the domination of the arbitrary. An artist who just does something because he says 'I like it' is not a creator but a consumer. He is consuming his own work."

Lubetkin cites examples of this rampant decadence: "The ICA exhibiting used nappies; artists filling tins with human excrement; buildings wrapped in WC pipes—I think we know which building we're talking about"—excesses which have ceased even to rouse most people's indignation.

Why then has the ordered discipline of modern architecture been so spurned and colour and decoration resurrected? Lubetkin regards this as "simply a manifestation of the tendency which we have talked about. That's why you have Venturiism, or whatever he's called, apparently building houses from tea chests and filling them with concrete. And those supermarkets with a wall designed to lean, or a missing corner, or you have to jump through a window or God-knows-what, provided it is all unreasonable. They are not architects. They are clowns." His contempt for the degeneration of modern architecture is such that when he and his wife went on driving holidays through Europe, they planned routes and often undertook huge detours to avoid known examples.

A second phone call interrupts, from a Parisian trying to get the Oxford show across the Channel. One of Lubetkin's remarks singes the airwaves: "Ce n'est pas le post-modernisme. C'est le Stalinisme." It is impossible to fix the discussion on architecture past or present. Never a member of RIBA or ARCUK (Architects' Registration Council of the UK), he spent almost the last thirty years farming in Gloucestershire and swears he hasn't read an architectural publication for nearly twenty. "I can tell you about stock breeding, pig breeding, various diseases, but to tell you exactly what an architect can do requires knowledge of the circumstances under which it works."

Still, he admits he views the growth of bureaucracy as a parallel evil to irrationality. "When we started, I was one of the main advocates of town planning regulations to give some control over appearances, neighbourliness. Now we've got it, I don't like it."

In an effort to tie the subject down to something more manageable than life itself, I rattle off some unambiguous questions. Of Peterlee, he gets as far as saying it was "one of the biggest tragedies of my practice" before he remembers some earlier matter unconcluded, and returns to it. Often, instead of speaking, he selects from his autobiographical papers some trenchant, telling extract. I cannot help thinking of the impassioned letter he wrote to Dr. Monica Felton, chairman of the Peterlee Development Corporation, in July 1943:

> I have the unfashionable conviction that the proper concern of architecture is more than self-display. It is a thesis, a declaration, a statement of the social aims of the age. Its compelling geometrical regularities affirm man's hope to understand, to explain and to control his surroundings. By thus asserting itself against subjectivity and equivocation, it discloses a universal purposeful order and clarity in what often appears to be a mental

wilderness...It can be a potent weapon, a committed driving force on the side of enlightenment, aiming, however indirectly, at the transformation of our present make-believe society, where images outstrip reality and rewards outpace achievement.

———

What, if anything, does he think of the Peter Palumbo/Mies van der Rohe proposal? "It's a financial matter, that's all. The City's been so buggered up anyway. The issue is, of course, the society which allows such defacing of the landscape." Does the fact that it is a Mies building make any difference? "I don't think so. I'm not an admirer of Mies."

Who, then, *does* he admire? This question unleashes a torrent of enthusiasm.

"I'm still very fond of early Corbusier. His original thoughts, not necessarily the buildings. Garches, Citrohan, certainly not that fungus, Ronchamp. The bold way they sat in the landscape without the bother of that preacher—Frank Lloyd Wright. The straightforward affirmation of the independence of the building from outside, like ships on the sea. That is, after all, what inspired Whipsnade. They are just put in, each of those buildings, as a statement.

"The Pavillon de L'Esprit Nouveau was a revelation, just opposite where I was working on the Russian pavilion [translating Konstantin Melnikov's design]. It produced a vision of what life directed by reason and sensibility could be. He exorcises in his early work all the irrationalisms, comes as near as possible to functionalism, in what he was saying if not in his buildings. He was reflecting certain necessities he was intellectually convinced about.

"But there was a built-in contradiction: he was talking about techniques and function but in reality he was aware this was not enough. He was advocating the physical, but he welcomed the sun on his roofs. Although he didn't acknowledge that lyricism in his writing, it was there because he was a damn good architect. The organic unity of the physical and the spiritual, which is the secret of existence, is lost. That's what's wrong with architecture today."

What can be done to redeem it? Is it any longer possible to "build socialistically"?

"We not only can, but *must*. Otherwise we will drown in the juice of publicity-sniffing. The only weapon at our disposal is classicism; cool repose and grandeur of eloquence without gesticulation and emotional crisis and hysteria." He points out that Dadaism and derivative nihilistic art forms have only been subverted by the very establishment—"which landed us in this horrible mess"—against which they were intended as a protest. "You have to be as cool as you possibly can, because that's the only enemy which the establishment can't stick."

A vein of stoic cynicism relieves the general despondency. "When I am asked about the future, I always remember Bertolt Brecht saying: 'If you see a light at the end of the tunnel, jump aside: it's the express train coming in the opposite direction.' My dear, I am sorry to say I am very pessimistic about our survival, let alone about architecture. To the point where I am writing all these things and I know they are going to be cinders. But that is the privilege of being more than eighty years old."

I leave him to his work, my copy of *Lubetkin and Tecton: Architecture and Social Commitment* (the catalogue of the recent Arts Council touring exhibition) now inscribed with a quotation from the dying Emperor Vespasian: *Ut puto deus fio*—"I believe I am becoming a god."

(Mis)Reading Between the Lines

Peter Eisenman

Blueprint, February 1985

"Are you going to do a number on me?" Peter Eisenman inquires when I phone to arrange this interview. One of the distinguishing characteristics of Ivy League architect-academics is to veil their rapturous delight in publicity with feigned outrage at the mere prospect; Eisenman is perhaps the archetype of the genus.

A master of double-talk, even his firm's Manhattan office is not exactly where it purports to be. The Eisenman/Robertson practice, designated at 560 Fifth Avenue, is actually entered on Forty-Sixth Street, under a dingy canopy proclaiming Lazar Brothers tailors. When I finally arrive at the correct floor, Eisenman says we'll go next door to talk. I already know to expect that this will not be a straightforward matter.

I follow the shock of white hair back to the elevator, down to the lobby, through the revolving doors, outside to the neighbouring entrance, into another lobby, up another elevator, and along to a grey door down a corridor lined with grey doors. This circuitous preamble is but a foretaste of the interview to come. Talking to Peter Eisenman, I frequently feel like Alice down the burrow, confronting characters with a logic all their own. Substitute a pipe for the hookah, and a chair for the large mushroom, and he could be the Caterpillar. When he succeeds in leading his questioner up some intellectual impasse, he grins like the Cheshire

Cat; but the gap in his front teeth and the round metal spectacles give him an overgrown-schoolboy look which reminds irresistibly of Tweedledum or, "Contrariwise…"—as when he does a volte-face in mid-sentence—of Tweedledee.

Behind the grey door I recognise the somewhat scruffy space in which I had previously interviewed Eisenman, on the tenth anniversary of *Five Architects* in 1982—the publication which established him and his fellow Fivers, Michael Graves, Richard Meier, Charles Gwathmey, and John Hejduk.

Like most of his colleagues (though perhaps less conspicuously than Graves or 1984 Pritzker Prize–winner Meier), Eisenman has moved on to bigger things than the numbered series of private houses with which he was engaged at the time of the book. He resigned the directorship of New York's Institute for Architecture and Urban Studies in 1982 in order to concentrate on teaching at Harvard University, and on architectural practice in partnership with Jaquelin Robertson, who is also dean of the architecture department at the University of Virginia. One of the practice's major successes was to beat Graves to the commission for the Visual Arts Center at Ohio State University in Columbus, Ohio, in a limited competition held in 1983, a large-scale model of which takes up the table in the room in which we are talking.

This project forms one focus of the conversation, which constitutes a free-associative ramble through such divine and cosmic topics as theology, geometry, *Star Wars*, psychoanalysis, metaphysics, Léon Krier, and The End of the World—not necessarily in that order.

Krier is clearly the "absent presence" throughout, the intended target for Eisenman's meditations on such ostensibly nonarchitectural phenomena as the Torah and the mathematics of Chaos. "Léon Krier, I've decided, is the person who most epitomises the problem for me in architecture," says Eisenman. "What I can't understand is why no one in England takes him on. Krier says that the main line of English thought now is Quinlan Terry, Léon Krier, and Prince Charles."

(When the *New York Times* finally reported on *that* speech by Prince Charles and its aftermath—not relayed across the Atlantic until October last year—its London correspondent quoted Quinlan Terry's belief that the Classical orders are God-given as evidence of Britain's increasingly reactionary architectural climate. Peter Eisenman has apparently taken this story as The Writing on the Wall.)

———

If you're wondering what Judaic scriptures have to do with architecture, all will be revealed in the five-thousand-word Open Letter that Eisenman is currently preparing for a forthcoming issue of the revamped *AD* magazine (L. Krier, D. Porphyrios, and C. Jencks, editors; Eisenman declined an invitation to join this illustrious board). If, however, you tend to sympathise with Krier's contention (interview with P. Eisenman, *Skyline*, February 1983) that "the problems of Jewish intellectuals are of no interest to architecture as a fine art," then you should probably skip the next few paragraphs.

What seems to be happening is that Peter Eisenman has been "discovering my roots," largely as a consequence of his psychoanalysis, and of his recent first visit to Israel, of which more in a moment. He's also been doing "a lot of reading in first-century literature," presumably as a change from the Deconstructionist lit crit that has been in vogue among aspiring *architectes parlants* in recent semesters. Derrida is de rigueur, and no drawing board is properly equipped these days without well-thumbed copies of Jean Baudrillard's *Simulations*, Jean-François Lyotard's *The Postmodern Condition*, and sundry sexy texts by literary critics of the Yale School.

In case you hadn't noticed, architecture is no longer a question of mere buildings. Architecture, according to the gospel of St. Peter, is now "about Text." Indeed, "It is the Archi-text. The ARCH-Text, if you want." Furthermore, lest you be misled by the excesses of PoMo, it is not about making images either. "The Image is not an Hebraic notion," instructs Eisenman, adding, sotto voce: "'Build Unto Me No Graven Images.'"

———

The two things that most interest him right now are Texts, and Misreading. Ah, but tread carefully here. For Eisenman, misreading is not the duplicitous activity it might sound. "Misreading doesn't have any negative connotations. You see," he explains, in supremely Looking-Glass fashion, "error to me is as truthful as truth. But there's a difference between Error and Lying."

So what makes it error? "Error is dealing with misreading. Error is not negative. Error is a provisionality on the way toward Not-Truth."

Eisenman finds authority for this pursuit of misreading in his Jewish heritage, particularly in the "structure of interpretation" which he sees manifested in the interpretive relationship between the Talmud (the compilation of Jewish Oral Laws) and the Torah (the written scriptures). "And then comes the Kabala, which is the Interpretation of the Interpretation. That is, the hermeneutic Reading Between the Lines of the Torah."

Eisenman is categorically *not* interested in the Torah per se, and sees no conflict in restricting his attentions to the meta-linguistic levels of debate constituted by the Talmud and the Kabala. "Since there is no Jesus figure and no resurrection in Judaism, the word comes before Nature and before God. And if the word comes first, then playing with the word—rather than with Nature or reincarnation or whatever symbols come out of Graeco-Christian tradition—is very important."

Eisenman thus seeks to stake a claim for the Text as "a Jewish homeland," citing George Steiner's essay "Our Homeland, the Text" as supporting evidence. The target, once again, seems to be Léon Krier, who, says Eisenman, "goes on about the need for the expression of homeland in architecture."

The tone of the discussion is beginning to suggest that he has missed his vocation. Shouldn't he be studying to become a rabbi? Plenty of texts to get one's teeth into as a rabbi. "That's where you miss the point. I'm not a religious Jew. I'm a *cultural* Jew." He identifies with Walter Benjamin, "someone for whom Jewishness was a state of mind, somehow outside the reality of religion."

If this sounds rather remote from the normal domain of architectural discourse, there is cold comfort. "You don't just have to be Jewish to understand the position that I'm talking about. Though many of the people who are working in this area, like [Jacques] Derrida, probably happen to understand Jewish thought, since they're Jewish."

A supremacist tone is creeping in. Doesn't that give the Jew a privileged position in this discussion?

"The Jew has always had the privileged position. According to my psychoanalyst."

Prepare, O Reader, to depart at this juncture for an excursion into the uncharted terrain of Eisenman's unconscious. It is not fair to assume, as many English people do, that all Americans are in psychoanalysis, but in Eisenman's case, it seems pivotal to his intellectual operations. He has not one but two ("only two") shrinks. Woody Allen might think this greedy, but...well, Eisenman's a complex kind of guy. Besides, he only sees one of them in the flesh; the other one he talks to by phone, in Los Angeles.

"I think of the mind as a kind of fog. My shrinks are beacons on opposite shores."

Why does he need two shrinks?

"Well, because there are two shores."

Really?

"I'm convinced there are two shores."

Isn't that a problem he ought to speak to *one* of them about?

"I don't want to steer a course with only one. When bomber pilots used to fly, they used to intersect the radar beams to understand where they were going…"

———

Back on dry land, or at least on one of the shores, we're into a discussion of theology again, this time, in relation to the Ohio State University project—currently at working drawings stage, and destined to start $35 million construction in the spring for completion in 1987. Eisenman contends that the OSU project is "about an architecture which attempts to stand outside the Graeco-Christian tradition." Which is to say, "It's not concerned with Origins or Metaphysics. I'm interested in theology, because it talks about the condition of Diaspora, of wandering. Not necessarily with a need to return to Origins."

Paradoxically, Origins are a subject to which Eisenman cannot help returning at periodic intervals throughout the conversation. "Origins could be first principles, or could be a place. I think this Visual Arts Center at Ohio is placeless."

I point out that the previous sentence is a contradiction in terms.

"Placeless, in the classical sense: it does not deal with a realm of geometry which confirms place and root. If you were to examine OSU, one vector is a skewed line which could be plotted by Euclidean geometry, and one is an asymptote, which cannot be. Therefore, their crossing is a collision of two non-placemaking geometries."

But, given that he's building this project, doesn't that make these things somewhat academic?

"Yeah. Building. But we're talking about its *conception*. There's always a difference. Hopefully there's the manifestation of a conception in all architecture. That's what symbolism is about." He draws a distinction here between Architecture, and "Just Building," gesturing around him to the office as an example of the lesser breed, which "doesn't manifest a conception because it doesn't have one."

The OSU building "is about its *idea*: the breakdown of Classical, hierarchical, ordered, closed, Euclidean space...which has been the traditional means of conferring and representing Graeco-Christian thought in architecture." Eisenman anticipates that anyone—whether architect or layman—who enters the OSU building will feel "a very tangible anxiety, due to the lack of contact with traditional spatial integers which allow him or her to understand their environment." He patently takes some delight in this prospect. Why is it his objective to suspend people into anxiety?

"Because that causes them to question. All works attempt to set up and control reactions. I'm interested in redefining the programme which the audience comes with. That's what I believe art has always been about. Once you've felt anxiety, you'll be able to say: 'Wow. I know that this is comfort, and this is anxiety.' It's not a bad thing. After all, people go to horror films to be made anxious."

He recalls having sat "riveted"—much to his own surprise—through the Philip Glass/Robert Wilson opera *Einstein on the Beach* at the Brooklyn Academy of Music. This he regards as "four and a half hours of controlled anxiety. There was an incredible amount of risk-taking in an era of New Romanticism."

On the subject of modern music, Eisenman says he listens to "early David Bowie...Kraftwerk...Joy Division...New Order," and John Zorn, whose *Locus Solus* piece will be the soundtrack to Eisenman's upcoming work in the Milan Triennale (February 22 until mid-May).

"They asked twenty-one architects from around the world to do an environment, with furniture—it was sponsored by Italian furniture manufacturers. The title of the show is *Elective Affinities*. We were given a space where the room had an upper level, and the lower level was supposed to be the origin of the piece: how it was conceptualised. Twenty of the architects designed furniture, because they were very smart and consumption-oriented, and realised they could make money."

Who are these twenty?

"Oh...Michael Graves, [Arata] Isozaki, [Hans] Hollein, Superstudio...You know, the usual lumberjacks of architecture. As Claude Rains said in the last line of *Casablanca*: 'Round up the usual suspects.'"

So what did Eisenman do?

"A box. An inaccessible void. You look through the top, and see L-shaped fragments spinning in space. Then you look through the bottom and realise that you're seeing through mirrors."

Thus, mirrors. which are normally the agents of illusion, reveal that the assumed reality (above) is no such thing. The L-shaped fragments turn out to be pieces of the Fin d'Ou T Hou S, broken up for this subsequent project in an act of architectural cannibalism. They don't literally spin in space: they are, rather, seen sequentially through peepholes in the twelve-by-twelve-foot volume.

The Fin d'Ou T Hou S, which is the subject of Eisenman's one-man show at the Architectural Association, was first displayed at the Leo Castelli Gallery in Manhattan during late 1983, as part of the group show *Follies*. The project was presented via the familiar series of arcane transformational diagrams—here described as "decompositions." A cursory glance at these drawings prompted in this viewer the kind of sinking feeling which would be induced by a request to perform three-dimensional computer-programming in one's head.

Perhaps it is the *process*, rather than the physical object that it ostensibly describes, which is what this architecture is about: challenging the viewer to master certain geometric rules, manipulate them from step to step in the sequence, and not end up with a brainful of unrelated parts. Eisenman's work is concerned with the elaboration of strategies that demand a certain competence—"literacy," one might say—on the part of the audience; the reward for such tenacity is membership of the Masonic elite of initiates who can follow it.

What sticks in my mind (for I must confess not to have devoted sufficient time to the accompanying wall of dense-packed verbiage) was the palette of pink and green in which the project was rendered.

([A discussion of this particular colour combination engenders an amusing spat over who was first to use it in their projects; the same kind of teasing altercation erupts at another point in the interview over John Hejduk's alleged influence on Frank Gehry's latest buildings. Such a concern for precedent, for establishing lines of genealogy, takes on a disproportionate intensity in conversation with Eisenman. He is, above all, an agent provocateur: it is not so much the "right answer" which he is after, but the fun of the quarry, the sheer sport of dialectic. He likes to enmesh the questioner in an hermetic argument; arbitrarily declares most logical escapes as out-of-court; and having thus closed off all retreats, performs rhetorical loop-the-loops around would-be contenders.)

"The reason I chose pink and green," says Eisenman, "is because they talk about a neutral axis of grey. I started with red and green in House VI: it signified that there was a topological geometry at work as opposed to Euclidean."

There follows a deft interweaving of hands, which would do a sushi-master proud. This serves to demonstrate that the pair of stairs in House VI (only one of which is functional, as you recall) is built in such a way as to confirm and deny, respectively, these two types of symmetry. The L-shape which figures in the Fin d'Ou T Hou S, is apparently "the one economical move" which has this geometric bivalency.

"An L-shape, a cube with an octant cut out of it, is topologically symmetrical and produces Euclidean asymmetry. It's as simple as that. What looks to be an unstable and open form is in fact topologically a closed form. If we carry around an expectancy of seeing things in a Euclidean way, then when we see something non-Euclidean, it's anxious-making. Whereas the topological geometer, looking at my work, thinks it's very conventional."

Curious to know the hidden meaning behind the project's cryptic notation, I ask Eisenman to write out the title in my notebook. He explains that there are nine possible interpretations, but, pencil in hand, falters after six:

Find Out Hou (*find out how*)
Fin D out (*find out*)
Fin D' Aout (*end of August, the month he designed it*)
Fin D'Où (*end of where*)
Fin D'Ou…ou (*end of either…or*)
Fondue (*this one for gourmets!*)

Anyone thinking of a trip to the Architectural Association in Bedford Square might pause to peruse a sample from the abridged version of the Fin d'Ou T Hou S user manual, as published in the *Follies* catalogue: "The Fin d'Ou T Hou S…is not projected from a known or classical origin. Rather it presumes that its own origins are unknowable and then guesses at or approximates these origins in order to decompose an object from them…Thus suspended between substantiation and ephemeralness, the condition of the object is part presence, part absence. It is an object-in-process which began nowhere and ends nowhere, existing in a present of absence and presence, suspended between reason and madness, between art and folly."

The computer-programming metaphor which this project brought to mind turns out to be not so far from its source of inspiration. The Fin d'Ou T Hou S was "the beginning of an investigation into fractal geometry," a relatively recent branch of mathematics/physics, which finds application in diverse fields, from esoteric hi-sci, to populist sci-fi. Thus, Eisenman endorses his latest enthusiasm by citing, in one breath, the mathematical plotting of chaos—spearheaded by the young Cornell mathematician Mitchell Feigenbaum—and the animation techniques of *Star Wars*—pioneered by George Lucas's Lucasfilm computer graphics department.

The real motive for his interest in fractal geometry lies in the possibility that it might undermine critical assumptions underlying classical theory. "It is in direct opposition to Léon Krier's notion that classical geometry is the geometry of nature. In fact it's the *reductive* geometry of nature, because most of nature cannot be plotted by Euclidean geometry."

Fractal geometry, says Eisenman, is also used to plot Brownian motion—the constant random zigzagging of microscopic particles—showing "where a point has been and where it will be, but never anything more than that. So it produces a geometry of 'were' and 'will be' within a present."

———

This brings us, in a roundabout manner, to questions of Past and Future, of Presence and Absence, especially the absence of the verb *to be* in the present tense in Hebrew—not to mention the Zeitgeist.

For those who last heard Eisenman when he gave the 1980 John Dennys Memorial Lecture at the Architectural Association, rest assured that the threat of nuclear apocalypse has temporarily abated—at least for the purposes of the Eisenman public lecture circuit. (One must always have a fresh message up one's sleeve for such contingencies.) Apparently, the "post-Hiroshima" scenario no longer governs his outlook.

"Why am I not interested in The End of the World? Well, because that's a kind of Zeitgeist argument. I've decided it's as much a Zeitgeist argument as Not-the-End-of-the-World! I've no care where the Zeitgeist is any more."

So what *is* he interested in? (*Da Capo al Fine*.)

"Misreading. And Texts. That have nothing to do with Geists at all. Timeless concerns."

He cites his essay-in-progress, "The End of the Classical," of which pirate editions have leaked from his enclave at the Harvard Graduate School of Design. This essay dwells upon certain ideas culled from our old French friend Michel Foucault, and our newer French friend Jean Baudrillard, and takes great pains to distinguish The Classic, The Classical, and Classicism.

"In this article, I articulate the Truthful, the Meaningful, and the Timeless as states of the *Classic*. That is, when buildings *were*, as opposed to buildings being *messages about* things that were. I'm interested in turning my architecture into a state of 'were-ness.'"

Until recently, as witness the (pirate) transcripts of his Harvard studio seminars, Eisenman has been promoting something called "As Is" architecture. I inquire as to its demise.

"'As Is' has gone. 'As Were.'"

Surely that's just in the past? It's the same.

"No. *Is* is a verb which does not exist in Hebrew. *Were* and *Will Be* exist."

Why should its presence or absence in Hebrew have anything to do with it? If he could find a verb that was missing from, say, Sanskrit, wouldn't that be just as good?

"No. I'm interested in Hebraic thought. Why the word takes its dominion the way it does. The fact that Hebrew has no verb *to be* in the present tense starts to key the difference between these two conceptions. There is no presence; only absence."

Well, no: there's past and future.

"That's absence, in the present sense. Since we live in the present."

Surely we live suspended between past and future?

"OK. I'll take that. That's good. A suspended position between 'As Were' and 'As Will Be.'"

———

Eisenman is busy with a new project in Jerusalem (suitably enough) which is/will be "a non-place from which you can view the Were and the Will Be." Standing on the hill next to the former British High Commissioner's headquarters (looking down over both the Old City and the Dead Sea), this edifice is entitled *Gateway to Destiny*, "though it's not a gate in the traditional Triumphal Arch sense of a gate."

The desire for simultaneous dual vantage—having it both ways, so to speak—seems to be a recurrent theme with Eisenman; in the last interview, he told me he was writing a retrospective of his oeuvre to be called *Eisenman-Amnesie*, using the last letter of his name as the fulcrum, on the spine of the book. (Like his long-awaited monograph on Giuseppe Terragni, this has yet to materialise.)

In a similar vein, his project for the Berlin International Building Exhibition (IBA), *The City of Artificial Excavation*, constitutes a simulacrum of past history. Eisenman builds anew a grid of catwalks the same height as the Berlin Wall, and thereby "reveals" courtyards in which "emerge" the (newly constructed) foundation of the historic Friedrichstrasse grid. This "Open Art Surgery" carves through layers of the urban flesh, exposing a war wound—not by digging in, but by superimposing embodiments of topographical notations. The latest word is that all but one "corner" of this project will now be built.

The question remains. What exactly *is* As Were architecture? Or for that matter, As Will Be architecture? And how does Eisenman approach these problems on a pragmatic, day-to-day basis, over the drawing board, with contractors baying at him?

"That's what I'm working on."

Eisenman gestures vaguely toward the OSU project next to where he is sitting, twiddling a thin, transparent cane which is no doubt destined to be chopped up into "absent" columns in some future scheme. The OSU model looks—by the knock-kneed angle of its lattice-grid walkway—to have undergone some sort of failure testing.

"There it is," he says. "I don't know."

My Tea with Andrée

Andrée Putman
Blueprint, October 1985

Andrée Putman has a habit of losing things. But, more importantly, of finding them. The silver necklace she wears—and has done every day for the past twenty years—she found in a gutter. Her silver scalloped cigarette case, into which she empties the Gauloises that account for her rich-roasted voice, has been recovered three times after assorted robberies. This lucky trait she owes to her mother, who once found a long-lost purse deep in a forest, drawn to the spot by Andrée's sister who had urged her to come and see a remarkable frog...which just happened to be sitting on the purse.

Certain objects, then, exert some kind of magical influence on Putman, luring her to them through time. France's leading interior designer has made it her mission to find and restore to recognition seminal works of design history, hitherto condemned to obscurity by their creators' heirs (or "hares" as she says).

Putman has just exhibited a collection of the furniture which she has rediscovered and "edited" for reproduction, at Liberty, under the enigmatic title *Positive Negative*. The allusion to monochrome is apt: Putman's interior design palette is, like Henry Ford's for the Model T, anything you like so long as it's black...and white, and occasionally grey and silver. She dresses in this colour combination (mainly in Azzedine Alaïa and Thierry Mugler), and the objets d'art of modern design which she has reincarnated are likewise variations on this minimalist theme. Putman's company, Ecart International, is now in one hundred countries, although she steadfastly refuses to sell in South Africa, where the issue of black and white is no joking matter. To be "à l'écart," she explains, means "on the side," not belonging to the world.

The designers included in her collection were all solitary people, so much so that when she first became interested in "the detective life" of tracking down the rights to their work, most people couldn't spell names like Robert Mallet-Stevens, or René Herbst, and put an "e" in Gray (Eileen, of the lovely leather armchair and mirror and rugs). Mariano Fortuny—coincidentally the subject of a show at Liberty featuring the crumply silk gowns for which he is best known—"was a *couturier*, full stop," until Putman showed the world his great black umbrella of a studio light, designed to illuminate his own photography sessions.

"I look at myself as a very naive archaeologist of the future," she says. "I have been very interested all of my life by the loss and mystery of some major pieces." She never actually met Ms. Gray: a rendezvous was arranged by a mutual friend but "while walking along rue Bonaparte, she had a run in her stocking and said she couldn't come." Having just started work with Zeev Aram on reissuing her furniture, Ms. Gray later died of a chill.

Putman was not always destined for a life in design. She trained to become a composer for six years at the Conservatoire de Paris, but at an important exam the chief juror took her aside and advised her that if she was prepared to sit in a room with paper and erasers for ten years she *might* turn into an "interesting" composer, perhaps along the lines of Alban Berg, Anton Webern, and Béla Bartók, her favourites. "I said, 'Thank you so much. I want to talk, to hear people; I want real life.' I'm not someone who can, of my own choosing, become the prisoner of something I'm not certain to be the best at."

Right now, she seems to have achieved the desired status. Her clientele includes famous and infamous names from fashion and what one might, in Eileen Gray's day, have described as "high society." She has done *all* of Karl Lagerfeld's houses (in Paris, Rome, and Monte Carlo), as well as his Paris offices; Valentino showrooms in Italy; ten Yves Saint Laurent boutiques around the world; and sundry shops for Mugler and Alaïa. She has just redesigned the women's departments in Barneys, the upmarket Manhattan store; elsewhere in New York she has assisted Arata Isozaki on Steve Rubell's Palladium nightclub, refurbished Morgans Hotel for the same client, and is all set to transform his latest hotel, the Royalton. Putman also selected the furniture for the Park Avenue apartment of Stephen (Knoll International) Swid and his wife, Nan (Swid Powell), recently renovated for the *second* time in seven years by Gwathmey Siegel. There are, of course, innumerable other private clients who simply can't be named.

Her philosophy is clear. Black and white, as a strong but neutral background, allows objects "of any period to create, by their differences, a kind of vibration." Particularly so when the objects are works of art, but it is "very distressed in a place where many colours are used: it creates conflicts, loss of concentration. I see places more like envelopes for people to live in. Not as décors [*tone of basso profundo disdain*]. Design is the envelope. Décor is something which is stuck forever. Everything should be moved. Flexibility for me is a sign of civilisation."

Putman believes that environment has succeeded fashion as "the obsession of the world." But, just as she despises those who are slaves to fashion, she believes people should "find the style which is them and stick to it in their environment. It helps to ignore all these laws and rules."

She will soon launch a collection of her own furniture designs: a console, a chair, a desk, a couple of tables, all in laminated Formica. Just for a bit of adventure, there will be some beige and a pinstripe of electric blue in them. She has also designed fabrics, china, mosaiclike tiles, stationery, and rugs, manufactured by various French and Italian firms. Having completed the interior design of French Minister of Culture Jack Lang's office ("It's a room full of tricks"), and the library, film theatre, and conference room in the new Bordeaux Museum of Modern Art, she is working on the interior of the *hôtel de région* (local government headquarters) for Bordeaux, in a new building designed by a local firm of architects.

The young designers in her team (the Putman design firm is also called Ecart "as I believed neither of them was going to succeed") are plucked straight from school whenever possible. She feels it's better if they are not sullied by experience in other offices. Putman has an eye for young talent—Philippe Starck and the upcoming Patrick Naggar, for example.

Perhaps her instinct for nurturing such designers—and for vindicating the forgotten greats—is a defensive response. She still remembers being ostracised by her friends "in the very serious world of art" for her eclectic interests in fashion and design. "They were so hostile to the arts and crafts, because these were things people could use for their lives. You know, in [Samuel] Beckett's play *Waiting for Godot*, Estragon calls the other person 'Architect!' It's like *salaud*."

Miami Vice Versa
1: Of Vice and Vixen

Bernardo Fort-Brescia and Laurinda Spear /
Arquitectonica
Blueprint, September 1986

Don Johnson's face is on the cover of the health fitness magazine in the local whole-food store. He has given his visage gratis
because he wants to share with us his commitment to a drink-
and-drugs-free existence. Don Johnson's face on the cover of *US*
magazine at the Newark airport newsstand. Inside, a sultry pose
with cigarette, the text effusive on how he's just quit smoking.

"In five minutes we'll be landing at Miami International.
Please extinguish all cigarettes and kindly don't unfasten your
seatbelts until we've come to a complete and final halt at the
gate." Down below it's the long bar of Miami Beach. Hotels
attempt topography on this inexorably flat terrain. Radiused
intercoastal islands, blue sky, big boats, and white-horse tufts
upon the greenish water.

4215 Ponce de Leon Boulevard. A nondescript building in
a semi-industrial zone just north of chic Coconut Grove: headquarters of Arquitectonica. An appointment to meet Bernardo
Fort-Brescia and Laurinda Spear, husband-and-wife head hon-
chos of the practice famed for ostentatious condominium blocks
along Miami's bayfront Brickell Avenue.

Grandiose names: the Palace, the Imperial, the Babylon,
the Atlantis—this last, at least, well known throughout the

tele-literate world, a mirror Gouda with a palm tree and a red spiral stair, seen every Friday night in the title sequence to this year's favourite inter-ethnic male-bonding coke-busters detective series, *Miami Vice.*

The secretaries are studiously disinterested; they confuse *Blueprint* with *Blueprints*, a newsletter put out by Washington's National Building Museum. Not much less than client-catching *Wall Street Journal*, *House Beautiful*, or *Vogue* can pique the interest of this practice, to judge from the hefty press dossier which I eventually extract from the PR, a character who takes her screening role literally.

She stands in the doorway, announces with unflinching smile that Mr. Fort-Brescia will not be able to see me after all. He's got a more important meeting, about some mega-dollar marina. Behind the bulk of the PR, a tall, taut woman appears, her long brown hair tied back like a prefect from the sixth form at St. Mary's. Proffers long fingers in a handshake that could chill Chernobyl. I recognise Laurinda Spear from the photo in *Esquire* magazine's 1984 register of Men and Women under Forty Who Are Changing America.

The division of labour is quite distinct. Spear is the design-brain, commander-in-chief of the coloured crayon. Fort-Brescia, scion of a prominent Peruvian dynasty, is the jet-setting deal-maker who gets their outré concoctions realised. Loquacious by reputation, with Ivy League connections and South American savvy, he scoops commissions from big shots like developer Harry Helmsley.

We repair to the conference room, a sequestered cubicle graced by a few renderings of monstrous monuments and a framed advert for *Money* magazine featuring the "Pink House." Spear originally designed it for her parents while a graduate student at Columbia University, studying with Office for Metropolitan Architecture principals Rem Koolhaas and Elia Zenghelis.

Many credit Koolhaas for the suave sophistication of this cool house: progressively paler planes of pink toward Miami's Biscayne Bay. "*Money* readers live a Little Better, a Little Smarter," reads the caption, under a scene of cocktail drinkers around the pool.

Spear explains her hometown's hospitality toward Arquitectonica's buildings. "Historically, Miami has been relatively courageous. Developers take a chance with things that look new; attitudes are different. It's not so stodgy as cities in the Northeast. It's always been a resort town, like Rio, Brighton even. There's a lighthearted atmosphere, especially with this being the tropics. It gives architecture a lot of latitude."

Is lightheartedness a key ingredient, or would they have their work read differently? "Well, of course we want it to be taken seriously, because we're serious about our work. But there's not a lot of angst in it. It's not cynical," she says, citing a current project, the Miracle Center—a not-quite-faith-healing temple containing a health club, theatre, pool, shopping mall, and parking, along the Miracle Mile stretch of Coral Gables' Coral Way. A rather ordinary slab below the health club tower is dressed up with jagged panels of patterned concrete, apparently affixed at random. "Part of the facade has these pieces that are just floating around, very casually appliquéd."

The wilfulness of this ornamentation recalls SITE's Best Showroom Strategy: good for a smile, but palling on repeated viewing. What do they feel about doing such commercial projects? "I think it's great to do shopping centres. We build anything. We're not selective about the kinds of projects we get. It's great to do a commercial project. Who wouldn't?"

Spear hands me over to one of her vice presidents for the official slide show. The VP tries valiantly to enthuse as a successively more depressing array of office parks, marina/condominium developments, luxury townhouses, and car dealerships hits the screen. We have reached the Turtle Kraals marina / condo scheme in the Florida Keys, when a gentleman in tie and round brown glasses bursts in through the back door of the conference room. The "unavailable" Fort-Brescia hovers on the threshold, grins apologetically, and withdraws.

An alarming disparity grows ever more apparent during the slideshow, between the smooth, abstracted glamour of the house-style axonometrics and their crude commercial doppelgängers. On the one hand, the drawings destined for the architectural glossies: monadic monuments absolved of context that could taint their purity. On the other, the sales-pitch scenarios for clients: up-tempo/sunny-sky/kids-with-balloons/lush-lawned/yachts-asail fantasies conjured up by T. Howard & Associates of Texas. The vice president helpfully explains that the latter images are what they show non-architects: "They're not so educated."

As the litany proceeds, any lingering suggestion of architectural or even graphic logic behind Arquitectonica's disposition of triangles, kidney curves, and other exo-gizmos falls away before the singular imperative of late-capitalist lettability.

Thus, the yellow balcony protruding from the north face of the Atlantis is not mere aesthetic affectation, but actually raises the value of the lower apartments. The "skycourt" is primarily justified as the means for stacking equivalent volume higher up, commanding better views and corresponding prices. The Porsche-driving tenants must be disappointed to have paid extra for their pad only to find that the local foliage and the shadow cast by the balcony diminish their outlook; the mirror glass may be telegenic, but insiders say its reflectivity obliterates the ocean view by night. Still, the residents are wised-up to their commodity: the condominium association charges members of the press royalties to view its interior spaces.

The North Dade Justice Center, a $4.5-million boomerang
on stilts in a mangrove wildlife preserve, will be Arquitectonica's first public building when it is completed in July 1987. Honda
Carland, an automobile dealership in Georgia, finished working
drawings stage in April.

The Banco de Credito, in Peru, a 430,000-square-foot
fortress in the foothills of the Andes, looks even more worrisome
in its commercial rendering than the widely published
axonometric led one to expect. This vast square doughnut
exemplifies Arquitectonica's fondness for forms crashing
into each other, for shears and skews which supposedly
constitute meaningful articulation. The lucky-dip assortment
of embellishments serves in this case not to amend but rather
to amplify the ungainly proportions and essential banality of
the idea: a conventional modernist box with strip windows and
pilotis. Take away the surface excrescences and you're left with
the sort of staggeringly mundane edifice that graces places like
Croydon. Topped out in the spring, and now a year or so from
completion, Peru's largest public bank is "subject to terrorism,"
hence the huge elliptical elevator shaft through which everyone
must ascend to the building proper.

Arquitectonica's New York office is headed by Spear's
younger sister Alison and *her* husband, fellow Columbia graduate
and 1984 *Men of the Ivy League* calendar pin-up Campion Platt.
They have been kept occupied doing working drawings for the
Fred the Furrier fashion concessions in Bloomingdale's department stores around the Northeast; the actual designs are produced in the Miami office. (Owing to the politics of reproduction,
none of the four aforementioned projects can be shown here,
as they have all been promised to other magazines "on an exclu-
sive, first-publishing basis.") A second branch office was opened
in Houston four years ago, but closed earlier this year after the oil
price plummeted.

"Architecturally, Texas is dead," the vice president tells me, a situation confirmed in a recent *New York Times* business news report. The 1983 Capital Park West scheme, a three-million-square-foot office park of various non-Platonic solids, which the architects like to describe as "an idyllic garden," will thus not be going ahead.

Arquitectonica is currently doing a house for *Miami Vice* star Don Johnson in Miami, reportedly on the same island as Al Capone had his mansion. But the architects are very tight-lipped about the project: "He's very sensitive…" Spear reckons, "It was just a natural. He'd been filming in so many of our buildings that he decided he would have us as his architects when he built here." Arquitectonica's buildings are regular locations for the show, their flamboyant forms and cocktail colours fitting its aesthetic formula perfectly.

Asked whether they are more concerned with making objects than creating space, Spear distinguishes between their domestic work (they have recently finished another private house, in Lima, Peru) and commercial structures. "If it's a house, we're very much concerned with the interior space. In office buildings, the floor plan is pretty much laid out. They don't want wild shapes that aren't leasable. You have to deal more with the exterior. Frankly, we design buildings from the outside in. We don't want some horrible surprise by designing the plan and then ending up with a facade we don't like."

She approaches the plan "like a graphic design. Some of the time we design as if the elevations were paintings and then put the four together. Sometimes we have more leeway and can do a painterly plan that gets elevated in three dimensions. We always work from the standpoint of the building's artistic content, we always care that there's something about it that looks good to us. Which is completely subjective. In addition, of course, it has to be functional."

She maintains that "unless you're really historicist…which our buildings never are," it is not possible to pinpoint specific sources of formal inspiration. "Since we're fairly well-educated people—we've been to college—any sources are internal. There are millions and zillions of things that influence us, from going to Rio, to Egypt, to looking at Piero della Francesca. There are millions of things that influence anyone who's an artist."

She emphatically distances her practice from current debate. "Oh, we're not postmodernist. We're just straight, normal modern architects."

―――

Miami Shores: thick grass like greengrocers' turf, the balmy warmth of late afternoon. Drive into the forecourt of the "Pink House," front facade a rusty pink à la Barragán, shaded by a row of royal palms. Call over the wall as directed, reluctant to rupture the silence of affluence. Ring the bell. No answer. Wander round and stare in through a window: a blind eye of eerie blue returns my gaze, a porthole filled with water. Even the lawn conforms to geometry: a semicircle terminates the raspy grass. Call from the Biscayne facade, a baby-pink punch card of different-size squares. Peer from the patio into the kitchen: pristine like a scene from *House & Garden*, cupboards wall to wall.

A girl is sunning herself on the wooden jetty next door. Go back inland, up the neighbour's drive, ring the bell. Through the metal gate to an inner courtyard, I watch a woman furtively unlatch her door. No, she doesn't let anyone in; no, I cannot use her phone. Drive to the nearest shopping mall; call Mrs. Spear. She apologises for not hearing me, says she'll leave the front door open. Drive back.

Inside, the first layer is the indoor-outdoor lap pool. Two white lounge chairs idle on the patio. Enter the second layer, a tall white slot with many windows, their opening latches far up and out of reach. No one around. The only sound the distant rumble of a tumble dryer.

Climb the stairs. Mrs. Spear appears, looking lithe and tanned, in shorts and curlers, barefoot. My shoes suddenly seem conspicuous, trespassers. "We are Japanese style here," she says, pointing to several pairs of sandals.

"My great-grandmother travelled in China in the 1880s," she says, "that's why we're all so interested in the Far East." She unveils the antique silks, flattened jackets, framed in Perspex under white sheets, Miss Havisham style. She presses a button, and the hurricane shutter draws back, flooding the living room with the aperture of Biscayne Bay beyond the gridded window. "We have little art," she says, "because every window is a painting."

I follow her to the guest suite, tucked in by the front door, opposite the lap pool. "Doug Davis [*Newsweek*'s architecture correspondent] stayed last weekend," she says. "He's too long for the bed." Baths have sloped tiled backs à la Villa Savoye. Mrs. Spear tells of her battle with the neighbours, who have placed an order to limit her use of the house for location filming or commercials to a number of days per year, at certain intervals. She isn't pleased and will press the case. Location fees offset her taxes, which are "onerous," so she says.

Now she must go, been on the phone to Washington all day. Pours me an orange juice, tells me to take my time, take any photographs I like, show myself around. Mrs. Spear disappears. Look down from the balcony across the cubic living room, out beyond to Biscayne Bay. Press my nose up against the glass block wall at the top of the stairs. Marvel at all the gridded windows, wonder how they get up there to do the dusting. Cool and quiet. Handwritten signs in plastic frames implore guests not to sit on the glass countertops. *Miami Vice* calendar in the kitchen. "Don Johnson's a great chum of mine," she had said.

Spartan and clean. The sitting room: capacious chairs in pink and grey, some books, antique apothecary jars, one-legged wooden birds on the top shelf. Outside, the sun has sunk behind the pink front plane, glass block reflects in the lap pool's still blue water. Put my shoes back on, pull the door to, drive off.

2: Town Kriers

Andrés Duany and Elizabeth Plater-Zyberk / Duany Plater-Zyberk & Co.

Blueprint, September 1986

Andrés Duany is wearing a smart suit and an incongruous round lapel badge bearing a tiger and the data "Class of '71." He is short and sharp-witted, and right now this Cuban-born Princeton graduate is pacing the podium with Napoleonic swagger, extolling the virtues of Haussmann's Paris.

The audience of middle-aged middle-Americans—or so they appear, though their tiger-emblazoned beer jackets and bald patches give them away as elder generations of this Ivy League school, migrated back for reunions—responds appreciatively when he describes a certain developer as "leading a life analogous to a Renaissance prince, laying out streets, knowing all his fellow residents by name, and making lots of money…"

He is referring to Robert Davis, patron-speculator of Seaside, the Florida panhandle new town which Duany and his wife-partner Elizabeth Plater-Zyberk (Class of '72) urban-designed between 1978 and 1983. Blonde and demurely elegant in a white sailor suit, Plater-Zyberk adroitly tackles questions from alumni on sewers and streets, picket fences and parking, persuasively arguing the couple's creed and advocating with firm charm the advantages of the American Small Town.

She explains that, having arrived in the Sunbelt after education in the Northeast, they both wondered why low-density cities such as Miami—where their practice is based—could not enjoy the same amenities as the high-density metropolises of the Boston–Washington corridor. They set about improving America's sprawling backyard, Suburbia. Their mission—in direct contrast to that of Arquitectonica, of which they were founding partners—is to make and mend the urban fabric, not build yet more monuments.

At first it is hard to believe that they could ever have been associated with the brash Arquitectonica, as their current work and concerns are diametrically opposite. But it soon becomes apparent that the present distance between them and the better-known Miami practice is just part of a process of intellectual development; what Duany and Plater-Zyberk represent is not just superficial rehashing of past formal precedents, but informed and sophisticated application of selected historical typologies.

Their work is a blend of European—especially English—urban models, with Mediterranean classicism, flavoured with Latin tropical culture. Their fervent allegiance to American free-market ideology is probably not unrelated to the fact that Duany arrived from Cuba aged ten in 1960, while Plater-Zyberk was born in the States two years after her parents left Poland in 1948.

Their current work does not have a social commitment in the sense that Kenneth Frampton would presumably advocate, though Duany says they are "trying desperately" to get commissions for low-income housing "by doing the various manoeuvres it takes to get that kind of government job." What they *do* do, "over and over again," is middle-class housing. "Some people criticise us, saying, 'They're not in a crisis…' But Florida is the fastest-growing state in the union, where middle-class housing is being built in the tens of thousands of dwelling units. Most architects of any ability have abdicated this bread-and-butter work in favour of doing very small high-art pieces like New York lofts."

This sector, they suggest, is extremely difficult to satisfy. "This is the one country where there's housing waiting for people—you have to court them. The middle class can actually afford to exercise their taste and pretensions, and they always have extraordinarily high aspirations and demands in terms of convenience—they must have the bathroom next to the bedroom, for instance." Below this sector is the class which is "grateful for a bathroom anywhere and a roof over their head." Above, the upper class can afford to commission monumental one-offs from star-architects like Richard Meier, Robert Stern, or Michael Graves.

Duany and Plater-Zyberk claim no ambitions to join that league: "They're almost the last generation of hero-architects." While professing great admiration for the work of James Stirling and the Office for Metropolitan Architecture (from which Arquitectonica was a direct descendent), they are convinced that isolated monuments are not the priority in the American Sunbelt in the 1980s. "This doesn't need masterpieces, it needs fabric."

They have identified the middle class as a neglected sector, usually catered for by urbanistically illiterate speculators concerned only with the bottom line and oblivious to the amorphous trails with which they litter the American landscape.

Evoking turn-of-the-century ideas of Civic Art and the City Beautiful Movement, they emphasise the traditional principles of Beaux-Arts composition: axes and vistas culminating in landmark public buildings, carefully dimensioned streets and sidewalks, attention to the scale-giving qualities of trees and walls or fences, adherence to building lines to confer overall coherence on separately designed structures, height-to-width ratios to preserve a consistent public realm, and kerbside parking rather than vast, distant lots.

Duany and Plater-Zyberk were still with Arquitectonica when the practice was recommended to Seaside developer Robert Davis (who had inherited the land from his grandfather) by an editor at *House Beautiful*; they took the job with them when they left. Of the "divorce," Duany reflects that "at the moment it happened, it seemed to be personality problems. In retrospect, we didn't get along because we felt very differently about architecture. In the early days, Arquitectonica's work wasn't so intensely wilful and arbitrary. But later it became extremely personal, it ceased to be a matter of discussing things; it was 'I want this.' Laurinda and Bernardo became the powerful partners—they brought in the work—so it was no longer among equals. We weren't that far apart at one point but now in terms of architectural syntax and urbanism we stand at entirely different poles." He contrasts Arquitectonica's "monumentalism" with their own architecture, which is "so self-effacing we don't even design the buildings."

At Seaside, indeed, they leave them to other architects entirely. Believing that one practice could not, by itself, produce the diversity which they recognised as a key factor in their favourite small towns, Duany and Plater-Zyberk dedicated several years to developing an urban code which would generate "controlled heterogeneity" without their direct intervention. They produced a succinct document including a zoning code distilled into a single page of easy-to-follow graphics, so as to avoid deterring would-be buyers. So far some sixty buildings are complete, and the code's authors take pride in the fact that only two variances have been requested in three years, and above all, that many of the buildings have been put up by interior designers and drafting services without detriment to the public realm.

The zoning code designates eight building types: three mixed-use, four residential, and one for light industrial workshops. It specifies the dimensions for yards, porches, out-buildings, and parking, and mandates maximum roof and porch heights to maintain consistent proportions. A certain minimum percentage of lot frontage must be built on, to conserve street lines, and towers of two-hundred-square-foot footprints are encouraged for sea views even from the most landlocked site. A supplementary building code stipulates such minutiae as hidden hinges and porcelain fixtures on kitchen cabinets—the kind of tender-loving-care extras which self-building buyers might not be expected to adopt. But they do.

The master plan allows for some 350 dwellings, 100 to 200 lodging units, a retail centre, conference facility, and recreation complex, to be built over ten to fifteen years depending on the economic climate. Following the example of the many Southern towns which Duany and Plater-Zyberk researched, Seaside is organised formally around a central square on the shorefront; a concentric pattern of streets evolves around this tight geometric core and dissolves toward the periphery in response to natural topography and landscape—two large gorges, high ground, and woods.

Apart from the post office, which recently opened in a mini-temple designed by the developer, most of the public build-ings are to be designed by "name" architects known for their sym-pathetic aesthetic. "We help the client develop a taste for certain kinds of things; he selects the architects from periodicals, people who are comfortable with the ideology."

Steven Holl's commercial block was due for completion this summer; Walter Chatham, another young New York architect, is doing a lodging house; Robert Stern is designing a hotel. Other architects involved are John Massengale, Stuart Cohen, and Deb-orah Berke, who has done several houses and the cabanas for the summer outdoor crafts market run by Davis's wife, Daryl. So far, the best-represented firm, with some dozen units, is the New

Haven practice Orr & Taylor, whose Victoriana Rose Walk cottage estate is now Seaside's dominant idiom.

Duany & Plater-Zyberk admit that their interpretation of what constitutes a typical American small town is purely intuitive. They were paid in Seaside real estate for the four years spent researching, developing, and testing the code. (Duany is wistful about having sold their land in the meantime: land in Seaside is now selling for at least twice the price per square foot of property in Seagrove, the adjacent town. "Our draughtsmen who kept theirs are becoming millionaires, as far as I can tell!")

Davis and his wife toured the South in a red convertible for two years, pinning down worthy prototypes; the architects were equally empirical: "We would drive up to a street or square and say, 'We like this' and measure it," says Duany. They were particularly inspired by Key West in Florida, certain "beautiful small towns in Texas," and Jackson Square in New Orleans. Only the latter will Duany concede as being miniaturised Europeanism. "The others are too large by European standards. Léon [Krier] thinks American streets are too wide, but he doesn't count on trees. Building-to-building dimensions and height-to-width ratios can be wider than a European street because the vegetation maintains it."

This is the situation Duany & Plater-Zyberk seek to remedy. Though they have only a few built demonstrations—Seaside and Charleston Place in Boca Raton, principally—the elements of their urban design philosophy are already clearly articulated. It is an avowedly classicist approach, strongly tinged by Léon Krier's attitude, stressing morphological rather than numerical issues, aesthetics not statistics.

So far, they acknowledge two "failings" in the real thing: first, that it is "excessively pretty—nobody allows anything to age with dignity. They're always painting things over. We're constantly fighting off the Disney World syndrome." The other problem is that the development's economic success has made prices prohibitive, especially for younger purchasers. As a result, Seaside doesn't have the kind of sociological mix that Duany & Plater-Zyberk fondly anticipated. They admit that their vision of the town is essentially nostalgic, and that—as a vacation resort without a primary productive economic base—it is "very privileged," idealist if not exactly utopian (the latter being more applicable to plans with an explicitly socially reforming motive). "There was a society which existed throughout this country, which achieved some kind of normative form at the end of the nineteenth century and was intact until around 1940: the American Small Town."

Duany & Plater-Zyberk juxtapose their vision of Main Street, USA, against that of Robert Venturi, who argued in *Learning from Las Vegas* for an appreciation of just that commercial kitsch from which architects had hitherto kept their gaze averted. Venturi's Main Street is "ugly, ordinary…and messy," according to Duany, who adds: "Ours is plain, but dignified and rather pretty."

Duany talks in apostolic tones of their declared mentor. "You have to consider us within Léon Krier's bunch of people. We're part of the Rationalist movement. We've never had any problems with Krier. He has never led us astray, either in his personal advice or in his writings. He has never been proved wrong. How can there be any anachronism? Nothing sells for more per square foot than the projects we do! It's awfully nice when the critics like our work, but the real test is the market. Ours is an entirely different ambition: to build America."

Now We Are Eighty

Philip Johnson

Blueprint, March 1987

Leaving the lifts on the third floor of Fifty-Third at Third—a stepped pink granite ellipse that cabbies call the Lipstick Building—one confronts a pair of glass doors. The left is etched *John Burgee Architects*, and, across the alignment, the right-hand door adds the insubordinate clause *with Philip Johnson*.

"John Burgee and I are partners," Johnson tells me. "But I graduated on the first of January. I'm now design consultant." One's heart sinks for the receptionist who will have to recite the revised mouthful every time the phone rings. From the caramel-coloured lobby, lined with anaemic Andy Warhols, we pass through a veil of "shattered" glass partitions into Johnson's private office. The curvilinear cubicle (nicknamed the Rumpus Room by his minions) is furnished with Ed Ruscha prints on the wall and Robert Venturi oxblood chairs around a circular table.

The *éminence blanche* looks spry, debonair, a model of monochrome elegance. Unlike his architectural wardrobe, the Emperor's sartorial style remains a constant. White hair stands like toothbrush bristles a quarter inch from his scalp. The signature black glasses adhere improbably to the sides of his skull— less spectacles than cranial cutlery, ebony chopsticks for the mind. *All the better to see you with, my dear...* "I had them custom-made forty years ago, because no one would make a round pair of glasses," he explains. "It came from the Machine Aesthetic. Car wheel hubs should be cylindrical, but they cut them with a flat top. It drives me crazy! To me, glasses are round. They make a pair now with a little 'Philip' on the side. Awfully silly, but that's the way I'm caricatured, always."

When he speaks, in a soft, mellifluous baritone, his teeth show small and separate, like premature peas in a pod, a child's milk teeth in a grandfather's physiognomy. Sharp as ever at eighty, Johnson talks animatedly, the conversation darting from Ledoux to Lloyd's, (Krier's) Speer to Spitalfields, Mies to McDonald's, Times Square to the Tate Gallery extension. Effusive on other current practitioners, he generally refrains from commenting on buildings he hasn't seen, and grows aloof when it comes to questions of his current design projects. His practice, which had $2.5 billion worth of work on its drawing boards, according to the 1985 Rizzoli monograph, is actively involved in schemes in Boston, Washington, London, and Los Angeles, to name but a few.

"The figure eighty never seemed much to me," says Johnson, shrugging aside his octogenarian status. "I go right on working, just as always." Despite the disclaimer, he is evidently not unaware of his distinguished age. Citing "intimations of mortality," he announced the donation of his New Canaan estate to the National Trust for Historic Preservation just before last Christmas. The thirty-acre property has six buildings, including the 1949 Glass House, a design inspired by Mies van der Rohe's Farnsworth House in Plano, Illinois, with whose plans he was familiar. "Mies called my house a rather bad copy of his. He never liked it," Johnson says candidly. "I wasn't trying to do the same thing as him, though I was certainly vastly influenced by his work." Under the terms of the donation, he will live at the Glass House for the rest of his life, and thereafter it will be managed for public tours by the Trust, as with several other important homes around the country. "It puts it in good hands, gives back to the community some of the things I've done, even if the architecture is very simple."

Johnson never saw the original Barcelona Pavilion and is now unlikely to see its simulacrum, since he travels less these days. "Ninety nine point nine percent of us remember it only as pictures," he notes, adding that "under normal circumstances" he would oppose the reconstruction of an "extinct" work such as this, known primarily through reproductions. "But this is not normal. It's one of the monuments of the twentieth century. The building is apparently much better than the photographs, absolutely superb." But he has a couple of minor reservations. "The glass is clear, and it's supposed to be dark green. That stops the sense of enclosure in the main room, lets it seep out into the court with the [Georg] Kolbe sculpture that it should have been cut off from. But on the other hand, they did succeed in getting the spatial feeling, which is the main point of Mies's work. So in this case, I think we'd make an exception to the idea that you can't rebuild monuments."

He professes to be "delighted" with the outcome of the Mansion House Square saga, having written in successive letters that he felt this Mies building, commissioned by Peter Palumbo, was "most inappropriate for London. Palumbo bought the Mies house here, as you know, so we're pals, but I thought that building should not be built there, and said so." He declines to comment on James Stirling's designs for the site, having only seen a couple of drawings, but moves rapidly into an encomium of Big Jim's work elsewhere, emphasising his ability to produce great architecture while cramming complex briefs onto tight sites. "What Jim can do so marvellously is to adapt the feeling of the street and the neoclassic building next door, and weave it into the programme, which was so unbelievably difficult," Johnson remarks of the Stuttgart Staatsgalerie. "You have to snake through the building because you want to get to that little *siedlung* at the top of the hill. I would have said, 'Go change your brief, Mister, and I'll be back!' But he got all of that in, and made that beautiful circular court. All you can do in this Vale of Tears we call the world is to get the greatest architect you can and let him work against the restraints," he says, pointing to the Sackler Museum (Fogg addition) at Harvard University, for which Stirling also produced alternative solutions.

"I'm crazy about the Fogg, but then I'm so totally devoted to Jim. Who else could make a staircase so it's a pleasure to walk up three or four floors? And he's a genius with the rooms at the top, where you walk through in an interesting, though logical and simple way." Then his tone changes to that of a benevolent headmaster scolding a favourite pupil for his latest prank: "The facade does not please me, needless to say. Jim made out that this was what the States was building in the 1920s and 1930s. 'Fake Banding' as we called it in our first book. Where you take two bands and emphasise them using two bricks, and just pop the windows in wherever function tells you to do. Jim can do better than that," he chides. "And has, in many buildings. I like the new Tate," he adds quickly, mollifying the rebuke. While in London for his first British commission—a 1.6-million-square-foot office complex at Hay's Wharf—Johnson was quick to catch a glimpse of Stirling's latest. "Well, I crept under the hoardings!"

Johnson's own project is similarly under wraps, allegedly still at yellow-trace conceptual stage. At first he divulges only that it will step down toward the river, in black granite and Portland stone, and refers darkly to its forthcoming scrutiny by the Royal Fine Art Commission. Later, however, pointing out the sample slabs of charcoal stone ranged on the carpet in the corner, he crooks his right thumb and forefinger into a C, flashes a mischievous grin and murmurs: "We're doing Greenwich."

If Stirling's London building was a predictable delight for Johnson, the same could not be said of Richard Rogers's Lloyd's.

In fact, it knocked him off his feet. "I'm *amazed* I like Lloyd's," he says fervently. "But I admire it more than I can say. I was surprised because my own interests are so neoclassic, or historically minded." He had anticipated that Lloyd's was "messy… out of place in London, especially the City of London… anti-urban… the wrong direction for us, anyhow… That kind of mechanolatry certainly ought to be over by now."

Instead the building proved "quite the contrary. This is a superb example of a technology carefully done, artistically done. To me a machine that perfect had never been created. And it should have been. It expresses one direction of modern architecture—the Machine Art attitude—that has never been carried out so well."

He checks his enthusiasm with a few reservations. The main entrance was, he says, "not grand enough for such an expensive object. You don't crawl into mouseholes to get into such a superb, important building. I could say that a tall vault the height of a cathedral doesn't do any good unless it's a lot longer, that Beauvais is too short because it's just an apse. Lloyd's atrium is too tall: it doesn't count any more, it's too far up to see. Now, in a real Gothic cathedral, like Notre Dame, you can see all the way to the altar. The relation of height to length works.

"But I don't see any point in talking about those things, since they're mere details. If I criticised Lloyd's as I would a neoclassical building, I would be using the wrong set of criteria. In terms of what he was trying to do, it was unbelievable." Suddenly, Johnson is intensely animated. "I admire anyone that can make 4,400 drawings or whatever, and work out that handrailing, those fittings in the toilets, those elevators with the parts all visible, the light coming through them, the way all those parts cling to the building, the elevators all polished, and a single piece of glass for the roof. You cannot carry that direction through more successfully."

He pauses on a note of pragmatism—"I hope they can clean it, in a few years' time"—then shifts again to higher gear, buried passions bubbling to the surface. "I remember vividly when I was young going into the great engine room of an ocean liner and watching the pistons going in and out. You expect people in oily rags to go around wiping those pipes and pistons all the time!" The metaphor evokes Fritz Lang's sinister underworld in *Metropolis*. "Nothing wrong with *Metropolis*. That had a great influence over us."

But the film was meant as a criticism…

"At that time. But you see, ever since the Futurists in 1911, the machine has been a great symbol. We had a show at the Modern in 1933, called *Machine Art*, which celebrated the machine, the wheel, the ratchet. Most of the movies were against it—[Charlie] Chaplin's *Modern Times*—but they didn't seem to affect our sense of worship."

And now? Does the technical impetus still pertain? Two recent shows, at the Whitney and Brooklyn Museums (*High Styles: Twentieth Century American Design*, 1985–86, and *The Machine Age in America, 1918–1941*, 1986–87), have indicated a revival of interest in that era.

"It's really messy to call all that Machine Art," Johnson retorts. "The interpretations were all over the place. If I were still a machine idolator, I would be a purist and not go in for stream-lined pencil sharpeners!" But he is far from dismissing the machine as a force in culture. "To me, it's one of the mainstreams of our times, as is neoclassicism. You see, I'm a great admirer of Léon Krier."

Recently appointed the first director of the SOM Foundation Institute, to be based in Chicago, Krier's name crops up repeatedly in the course of the interview. "I think Krier may be brilliant," says Johnson, hastening to add that he does not share Krier's views on Albert Speer ("I don't think Speer was a very good architect") nor his attitude to the contemporary condition. "I don't agree with his analysis of the industrial and commercial and consumerist world, because I think that's where we are. It doesn't do any good to fight against what's happening. But on the other hand," he says, in a reversal which appeases all positions, "if people didn't fight against what's happening, we would never make any progress at all. Like [Claude-Nicolas] Ledoux, sitting around making books instead of helping on the Revolution."

Krier's contribution, according to Johnson, is as a theorist: "Not necessarily a designer that is caught in the actual web of building. There are all kinds of architects, like [Frederick] Kiesler, like Ledoux, Krier, that become leaders without necessarily building. What Krier's done for drawing, for urban conceptualism, for the reappreciation of [Camillo] Sitte in modern times, is enough for one man to create. He's created a whole school." By way of illustration, Johnson says he just awarded first prize in the McDonald's hamburger corporation's student design competition to a scheme that "looked exactly like a Krier sketch."

Tadao Ando's work is another point of departure from Krier. "He's one of the best of the Japanese. I wouldn't want to go live in one of his houses, but I understand the line of design better than I do [Arata] Isozaki's. It's so chop-chop! I don't even pretend to understand in Iso's work what I conceive of as a lack of conviction. I like the building in LA, of course"—the "of course" a tag whose habitual use tends to undermine the phrase to which it is appended. Johnson is alluding to Isozaki's new Museum of Contemporary Art, seen while on reconnaissance trips for his own speculative office development in downtown Los Angeles. "But I've never been to Japan, and I've never seen Ando's work, so I shouldn't talk about his either. Nor have I seen Léon's—very symptomatic, don't you think?"

I interject that Krier is supposed to be building at Seaside, the new town on Florida's Gulf Coast.

"Oh no he is not!" comes the riposte. "That building has been 'being built' for five or ten years. But he seems to me to get to the essence of what cities are: the city square, the relation of dwellings to the country, to the street, and to the water. His redo of Washington: Boy! that is urban design. That's the highest form of our art. A man like Krier can vastly help form-making by focusing attention on the urban scene. Maybe he wouldn't be any good at making foundations," he chuckles, "but then, he's just a chicken."

Krier's influence is detectable in Johnson's PortAmerica scheme, a mixed commercial and residential project on a site along the Potomac river outside Washington, DC, for the developer James T. Lewis. A waterfront structure shown in the renderings of Johnson's scheme bears more than a passing resemblance to the pyramidal portico in Krier's *Roma Interrotta* project of 1979. Johnson and Burgee's proposed World Trade Center tower, a lynchpin of this scheme, will now be smaller than originally proposed, following criticism that it would overpower Washington's monuments and might endanger National Airport traffic. But the project's luxury "Georgian" residential quarter will probably go ahead much as planned, in a series of crescents that Johnson describes as "pretty classical. We picked the English street names out of fun. It's very Brighton, very Bath. What's wrong with that? No one's ever done better."

Talking of domestic architecture, I raise the question of New York's grave housing crisis, its alarming homelessness statistics. What is Johnson's position regarding the architect's social responsibilities? How should the architect intervene to promote such concerns? His answer is unequivocal. "I'm not in politics," he replies. "Whoever promises the most housing is the most interesting from a social point of view. We can't design unless we're told what to design. The architect is not the instigator of social policy. Maybe there are some that think they are," he continues, his voice tinged with impatience, "but it doesn't do them any good, because they never get it built. Never did, except in Vienna in its great socialist period. But that was a unique situation politically. We don't have that situation. We don't choose *not* to do workers' housing. We'd like very much to. Since the aim of all architecture as such is habitation and cities."

Johnson is temporarily stumped when asked which recent New York buildings he would recommend to an architectural pilgrim. "Let's see," he murmurs, gazing out of the window at the mêlée of International Style boxes in the vicinity. He enumerates the Helmsley Palace hotel, Edward Larrabee Barnes's Equitable Center, and developer Harry Macklowe's black glass wedge on West Fifty-Seventh Street, among others, before citing Helmut Jahn and Kohn Pedersen Fox as the two most interesting practitioners in the tall building category, "one that is not much regarded by architectural historians, but certainly by those of us that have to build them." I. M. Pei's Jacob K. Javits Convention Center is potentially "very good, sui generis, because of its inexorable battle of the space truss—using it on walls, ceilings, and everywhere." But he declines a firm judgement, since he "just drove by" and hasn't thoroughly inspected its interior. I venture that perhaps the Convention Center might be deemed a trifle *retardataire*. This innocent turn of phrase triggers a moment of unexpected reverie.

"*Retardataire*...," he echoes, savouring the term as one might a vintage cigar. "Haven't heard that word for years. [Henry-] Russell Hitchcock and I used to apply it to most everything," he chuckles with the knowing amusement of one who has lived to see the pendulum swing both ways. The aroma of the past not yet entirely dispelled, he concludes his list on a predictable note of loyalty. "I don't think we have anything really striking in New York." He demurs: "I mean, we have the Seagram Building. It's the greatest. Still."

Why then the change in his own work, and that of the "younger generation"? What accounts for the renewed attention to the skyline, to the sculptured massing of the tall building? "It is *very* interesting," Johnson begins, only to entirely abdicate an explanation. "I have no idea what influenced me. Boredom, I've called it many times." Jahn and KPF he diagnoses as "trying to express the skyscraper in different modes from the flat-roof-plop-plop-indistinguishable International Style." How much are they following his lead, say at AT&T, in this respect? "I don't know how much. But it's in the air, dear."

Is this the Zeitgeist creeping in? "Oh, I hope not," he retorts, as if it was an idea whose time had passed. "I don't think one needs Zeitgeists to explain changes in periods."

As in earlier remarks, such as those recorded in *Oppositions* in 1977, Johnson explains his retrospective appreciation of precisely those architects whose work he'd implicitly disparaged in his famous polemic. "It wasn't until we could shed the whole mystique of the International Style that we could start appreciating what Raymond Hood and especially Bertram Goodhue— my idol—were doing. At the time it seemed inevitable—the way the world was." Only later could he acknowledge that "our International Style book was talking about the decade *before*, the decade that had already passed. You see, in the old days when Hitchcock and I wrote that book, we had blinders on." His pitch rises theatrically, as if tangibly pointing out something that was obvious all along and only now was being confessed. "And quite rightly. How would you make a propaganda statement, a declaration of religious conviction, if you could see the good parts of the other side?"

But to make such a declaration, one must surely be aware of the opposition, to define one's own position with respect to it.

"We knew perfectly well about Hood. Rockefeller Center was being built at that moment. But we said, 'This is not the true revelation of the skeleton of the skyscraper.' Only the Seagram Building—only really the PSFS [by Hood and William Lescaze in Philadelphia], which we exaggerated out of all proportion—had the right religion, if not the beautiful look of the Hood building."

Louis Sullivan is another architect to whom Johnson has become converted. "I used to dislike Sullivan so strongly because he strengthened the corner by leaving out every other pier. Every other pier had a column behind it. That was very annoying to us purists, you can imagine."

Johnson makes a revealing slip when asked why, in his view, the climate changed. "I put the blame on…" He corrects himself: "I mean, I give the credit to the preservation movement. But why did people all of a sudden want to save every damn church on every street corner in every city in the country? It's the same impulse that makes people want to live in a house that looks like a house, the way a child draws one—whereas a Mies van der Rohe house doesn't.

"I remember when I was first teaching at Yale, I put on the wall 'You cannot not know history.' You're reacting to it whether you think so or not, so you might as well know what you're doing. Back in the old days it was simple. There were rules. Mies believed you could teach architecture. There are no such illusions anymore." Johnson maintains that architecture can't be taught except "by example, by apprentice to genius, by finding a Goodhue or a Wright."

This leads into precarious territory, the prickly issue of genius and the problems of its identification. "It manifests itself. Take the time of The Five. You have a guru talker, like Peter Eisenman; a type of genius, maybe, like [Michael] Graves; people like [Richard] Meier, a very clear-headed chappie. We don't know which of them will be great. They didn't think [Pablo] Picasso was very good—you can't tell genius till later." But genius alone cannot guarantee success; a capacity for adaptation is also essential. "Like an animal in the Darwinian system. Take [Henry Hobson] Richardson, a very great adaptor. He was the man who said: 'What's the first principle of architecture? Get the job.' Now that is a very American remark, very consumerist. But, you see, getting a job takes quite a different mental apparatus from doing great design work. Richardson did both. Some people can, others can't."

Schools, he contends, are "not very helpful for learning architecture. I don't know what they really are good for. I tell people not to go to school, but then my advice is to go just the same—the snazziest one you can get into, Big Five, Big Ten. When the church is running things, you make the right genuflections. These days you make them to the system which society has set up for you: the schools."

He traces a genealogy of past masters whose education was necessarily less institutionalised than today. "Richardson, the greatest we have, went to the Beaux Arts since there were no schools in this country. Wright stayed in Wisconsin and went to engineering school for a while. Where did he get the idea he could be good? Working with the big man, Sullivan." The latter, in turn, "went to the Beaux Arts and didn't learn anything. He learned it all from [Frank] Furness. I often asked Mies why [Hendrik Petrus] Berlage was his god," he continues, talking of his mentor. "I guess he didn't get along with [Peter] Behrens. But that's in the mists of history."

Questioned on current projects, Johnson slips into the polished opacity of a press release. He describes the Times Square development, for Park Tower Realty, as "a developer's submission to the city for a type of subsidy to enable business rents to be paid in an unfavourable area." The office stopped work on the scheme some time ago, he says, pending discussions regarding the prospective merchandise mart/hotel site at one end of Forty-Second Street. Johnson lists the various interested parties and refers me

to Park Tower Realty boss George Klein or Burgee for the urban
planning and financial details. "Those I don't know. That isn't my
part of the work."

So what is?

"Design."

This he does at New Canaan, making freehand sketches
on yellow trace over the weekends and bringing them in for the
sixty-strong office to hardline and develop. "Then I take them
home and rework them."

Johnson describes the evolution of the firm's buildings: "It
goes in sequence. The first building we did was what [Charles]
Jencks would call 'late Modern.' Pennzoil [1974–76] had a Miesian skin, but we warped the entire building. Then we got more
interested in skins as such—in different colours of glass and
how they behave in reflection, and in history. Transco [in post-oil
Houston, Texas] was next, and that's very Goodhue. It looks black
and white, but it's actually all the same. Those lessons we learn as
we go along.

"When it came to the Republic Bank [in downtown Hous-
ton], they absolutely refused to let us do a modern building. They
didn't want to look like the one across the street. It's a new thing
on the part of developers…like a circus! At first we were livid. We
wanted a decent community of buildings based on the theme
we'd started there."

Republic's stepped-down gables were the result of Johnson's revised attitude to historical form, but were postrational-
ised by the fact that one of the site's owners had an office in the
Pennzoil building looking out across to where the new building would be. "We used that as an excuse. It wasn't a real reason." But he adds, by way of further justification, that "gables are
very expressive forms against the sky."

Johnson regards working with commercial clients as
an inevitable interaction. "You can't leave architects to do

architecture unless it's your grandmother's house in California, with Sheetrock and studding." This is just a gentle dig at the "wonderful free-style movement that's going on around Frank Gehry" on the West Coast. "I don't understand it, but I love the atmosphere in LA. That's a different generation from mine, less business-oriented. It's very admirable that they can be building that freely. But they're all children," he says benignly of architects such as Thom Mayne, Michael Rotondi, Frank Israel, and Frederick Fisher. Anyone younger than forty qualifies as a "child" in Johnson's eyes.

Perhaps taking a cue from the Californians, he says the firm's new approach is to mix materials: marble, granite, and terracotta. Johnson's Los Angeles building—a speculative office downtown for developer Robert Maguire—promises to be "in bright colours. Mostly we've been monochromatic and monomaterial through the Crescent," an office/retail/hotel scheme nearing completion in Dallas.

Commercial developers have changed, in Johnson's view. "Fifty years ago at the Modern we considered them speculators. They were just people who bought land cheap and sold it dear. They built a building on the wind, as badly as they could, and shed it as quickly as they could. Now it's quite the opposite. A man like Gerald Hines, he's the leader of the pack, doesn't want to get rid of his building right away. The aim now is to keep a building and make a name for it so it will rent for longer years. Even the people who were known as schlock are demanding quality."

Whether a building will accrue this kind of reputation is a question of its "reliability, the excellence of the product," a combination, says Johnson, of its external image and its internal functioning. But one thing he can't abide: "We in this office are very much against engineers who make the floors so they bounce. To me that's not good construction. I don't know why. They're not going to fall down, but it feels cheap. Bouncing floors!" he scoffs, as if it were a breach of etiquette, like entering one's club without a jacket and tie. "All you do is make that much more steel," ensnaring a couple of inches twixt two digits. "That kind of thing goes right through a building from the toilets to the lavabos to the front door."

Asked whether he finds contemporary information technology a source of architectural inspiration, akin to that once provided by the machine, Johnson shakes his head. "You can't see it," he says, quickly qualifying by reference to Lloyd's and its corresponding cost. "At AT&T they had information specialists crawling out of the walls. We left it to them. I'm sorry," he repeats, unapologetically, "it doesn't interest us. The only difference is that the floors have to be thicker."

But as to the formal appeal of exposed technologies: "It's too much work, too expensive. We'd rather put the money in the stone."

Johnson mentions that he is due to make a "final statement before the architectural profession in June ... a very formal speech, my philosophy." Asked which writers have been formative influences, he says he likes "different critics for different reasons." Explaining: "When I was young: [Lewis] Mumford, Hitchcock. Hitchcock affected me enormously, because we worked together on the first book. It was really *his* book. He was the leader. Then there was the generation of [Vincent] Scully. My favourite critic right now is Alan Colquhoun, he's brilliant. I am amused by Jencks, but he doesn't influence me in any way. Colin Amery I find acute, and I have great sympathy with Gavin Stamp, because he opened up the English Domestic school—absolutely fascinating and still not properly appreciated.

"American critics are so against me now, for obvious reasons," he continues, retrieving a square-inch silver snuff box from his left trouser pocket. With long translucent fingers, he idly flips and snaps its monogrammed lid and says: "I'm not Mies van der

Rohe. I've built too much, though we build very little compared to the big firms, like [Helmut] Jahn and KPF. That's something they don't like, so they take it out on me."

How does he think he will be remembered, as an architect or as an art collector? "My collection is very minor," he replies, "and besides, it's all given away." He declines to disclose his "little list" of possible successors to the late Arthur Drexler, curator of architecture and design at the Museum of Modern Art, and, as such, tenant of the post which he himself created.

"I certainly will be remembered as an architect, but only one kind," Johnson reflects. "As a person that's in the middle of the maelstrom, the whirligig that is architecture, rather than for my formal greatness. I'll never be remembered for the Seagram Building. I'll never be a 'Great Architect,' quote-unquote, capital G."

Delirious Visions

Rem Koolhaas

Blueprint, February 1988

The writer faces a dilemma. After a day spent driving around Holland, looking at buildings in Amsterdam's suburbs and The Hague, she still can't decide how to tackle the discrepancy between her expectations and her experience of the built work. Hours spent examining projects in the architect's office overlooking Rotterdam's industrial waterscape, and protracted conversations with him that have consumed two ninety-minute tapes, haven't yet solved the problem.

The subject is a Dutch architect in his forties who, relatively early in his career, achieved considerable reputation among those he calls the "circus of the perpetually jet-lagged," for an idiosyncratic study of Manhattan.

A former journalist and filmmaker, the architect has returned to Europe since the publication of the book to try his hand at practice. Now, with one building completed and another under construction, it is time to assess the transition from paper architecture to built architecture.

The writer's dilemma is based on the firsthand evidence, and focuses upon a word. A word that is released at some point in Rotterdam, and returns to haunt the second interview in a Marylebone basement, recurring with compulsive frequency, tainting the whole discussion. The word escapes from the writer's lips, and the architect latches on to it as a condemnation of his buildings, worries it like a bone that gnaws away at him, retrieving it from unexpected corners of the conversation, just when the writer thought perhaps they were on to something.

The word is disappointment.

———

Remember the scene?

The Empire State and the Chrysler Building lying flaccid on a king-size bed, the Goodyear Blimp a discarded condom to one side, the outrageous couple caught in *flagrante delicto* by the Rockefeller Center and a thousand skyscraper progeny.

This cover image set the after-the-event tone for Rem Koolhaas's book *Delirious New York*, published in 1978, which claimed to provide a "retroactive manifesto" for the city. It celebrated New York's architecture as the quintessence of metropolitan urbanism, and offered an ecstatic blueprint for a "Culture of Congestion."

After more or less documentary chapters on the pleasures of Coney Island, the history of the skyscraper, the building of Rockefeller Center, and on Salvador Dalí's and Le Corbusier's responses to the city, Koolhaas offered a fictional conclusion. This comprised speculative architectural projects done with various collaborators (principally Elia and Zoe Zenghelis and Koolhaas's wife, Madelon Vriesendorp) that took the exhilarations and tensions of Manhattan's hyper-density and raised them to a fever pitch. Designed during the 1970s at New York's Institute for Architecture and Urban Studies, these projects—with such pregnant titles as the City of the Captive Globe and the Hotel Sphinx— became the icons of a new urban mythology. Rendered in highly coloured and abstracted style, they gained a wide circulation, providing the initial inspiration for all those lurid beachfront condominiums that grace the opening sequences of *Miami Vice*.

Koolhaas set up the Office for Metropolitan Architecture (OMA) with Elia Zenghelis, and their work soon attracted a lot of attention, albeit through publication rather than construction. But that may now change. Koolhaas, forty-three, has finished the Dance Theatre in The Hague and there are other projects coming out of the ground. A long, *pilotis*-supported block of low-income housing is nearing completion outside Amsterdam, on an urban development for which OMA produced the master plan, and where the practice has also built a primary school and gymnasium and will design a social centre. OMA is also at work on a private house in Paris and an apartment block-cum-visitor centre near Checkpoint Charlie in West Berlin.

The internationalism of OMA's work reflects the cosmopolitan outlook of its principals. They first met when Koolhaas arrived in London to study at the Architectural Association from 1968 to 1972. Then Koolhaas won a Harkness Fellowship to the United States, where he studied for a year at Cornell, under Colin Rowe and O. M. Ungers, moving to Manhattan to begin research on *Delirious New York*. The success of the book was such that Koolhaas felt obliged to sever all connections with it. "My first decision after its publication was not to become its victim. I was in the paradoxical and idiotic position of being well known, but not experienced."

He came back to Europe determined to build, and gave up teaching around the same time, having found that "there's almost a chemical smell that you exude when you're teaching that turns away people who might give you work!" He chose to start construction in Holland, reasoning that "here, if the buildings didn't work out, I could hide them."

Koolhaas's work in Europe has been completely outside the once-fashionable preoccupations of the postmodernists. Despite his poetic language (and Koolhaas certainly is a superlative rhetorician, with a brilliant sardonic wit), he does attempt to face and deal with the realities of the contemporary city. And it is these issues that form the subject of the new book he is working on. Broader in scope than *Delirious New York*, it is tentatively entitled *The Contemporary City*, as if in ironic evocation of the sweeping vision of 1950s and 1960s planning tomes. Koolhaas says it will be a consideration of "how to deal with average contemporary ugliness," taking as case studies the mushrooming developments on the edges of such American cities as Atlanta, Georgia; the proliferation of socialist-inspired new towns around Paris; and an example from Japan, most likely Tokyo. "The 'Huh?' Cities," Koolhaas chuckles, already ahead of the game. "People always ask, 'Why those?'" He explains that his interests have moved on from an earlier preoccupation with Constructivist iconography, to an appreciation of the more recent past. The shift in perspective began when he returned to Europe in 1978, having decided that the life of an architect in America in the 1980s did not appeal.

What intrigued Koolhaas in particular was the rebuilding of Berlin then being undertaken by the city. He joined his former tutor Ungers there for a summer school in 1978, just when the official new Berlin master plan was taking shape. "It was clear that they were going to commence on a Krier-inspired project, the reconstruction of the European city. That whole movement to restore Europe to its original splendour alarmed me. The reason I came back was to challenge it, to show that there was another potential for the European city."

Ungers and Koolhaas together produced a theoretical model for the development of Berlin, entitled *The Green Archipelago*. This document represented the antithesis of the kind of contextualism advocated by most urban thinking at the time. "We thought it was irrational to take Berlin, of all European cities, and attempt its reconstruction. Firstly, in order to respect its history, it was insane to attempt its physical reconstruction. The areas of destruction there were part of very significant historical events and therefore had somehow to be, not 'preserved,' but at least maintained as a visible presence. With the dramatic slump in recent years in Berlin's population, the real question becomes one of how to sustain some sense of real metropolitan life in the city."

This attitude to the city as a large-scale objet trouvé, this commitment to working unsentimentally on its mottled fabric of splendour and dereliction, bears comparison to the work of the NATØ (Narrative Architecture Today) group led by British architect Nigel Coates. But Koolhaas, while sympathetic to the NATØ position, is perhaps more influenced by his transatlantic perspective.

He sees an essential difference between the historical contexts of North America and Europe. "In America, even if current architecture tries very hard—or pretends to—it is still grappling with the problem that it doesn't have a real context, doesn't have a real relationship to history. In Europe, history is a given and remains in many cases a serious obstacle." It is in this context that Koolhaas's realised work needs to be considered.

"I'm talking about 1960s planning schemes in my lectures now," he says. Boldly venturing where few architects of his generation have deigned to set foot, he is now reexamining a whole realm of endeavour written off as virtually taboo: the discipline of urban planning. "I stumbled across planning as an area that was entirely deserted. One of my mottoes is that the most recent additions to the slag-heap of history contain the greatest richness, and the only reason that they are not discussed is because of aesthetic prejudice." He is, for example, eager to rehabilitate Alison and Peter Smithson, whose work he regards as very advanced. "They were looking for forms of planning that were less rigid, less codified, and while they had a tectonic expression, were nevertheless indeterminate." At the same time, he sees evidence of a reappraisal of 1960s work in the designs of certain contemporaries, notably Jean Nouvel, who, he believes, "skirts the whole Archigram mythology, but tries to deal with some of the issues they raised."

Koolhaas observes a serious lacuna in recent architectural thinking. "My generation of architects, by being focused on the city centre and on housing, neglected a vast area of other demands, such as corporate headquarters, places of entertainment, offices—a fact I find both tragic and hilarious." He cites the fact that some of the largest architectural projects in Europe in recent months have been awarded to American architectural practices as an indictment of the current state of European architectural discourse.

For Koolhaas, this issue has been made particularly vivid by his own experience over The Hague City Hall competition. At the start of 1987, OMA's scheme was awarded first place by the architectural jury but, five months later, after a second tier of adjudication, this decision was overturned, and Richard Meier's scheme declared the winner. Koolhaas's proposal was for a large slab of curtain wall offices, profiled so as to appear as a composite of three vertical layers, each of them with an asymmetrical and irregular outline, and differentiated by three different coloured glass claddings. Koolhaas says that his design was an attempt to address the unresolved, indeed, rejected issue of how to tackle massive projects in the centres of towns.

In fact, Koolhaas's whole position recalls that of the Brutalists. It recognises that life in the modern city is not pretty, cosy, or comfortable, and argues that it is a cynical and ultimately self-defeating delusion to pretend otherwise through nostalgic architecture.

Koolhaas faces up squarely to the fact that giant schemes, of limited programmatic content, are being proposed for inner-city sites all over the world. And he believes that the architectural profession has so far failed to come to terms with this pervasive new phenomenon. "I find the tactics for dealing with them so far inadequate. Either the scale is disguised in some form of camouflage, like Meier's solution for The Hague City Hall, which through its scale tries to be as polite, humble, and nonobnoxious as possible, or, alternatively, it is a completely alien element, literally from another planet, that has no relationship with anything in its context, like Canary Wharf."

He maintains that architectural discourse during the past two decades has remained resolutely oblivious to what is actually going on. "Architecture has been on a totally different tangent, without a hope in hell of accommodating, or even stimulating, any of the real issues that have emerged with startling necessity over the past twenty years."

The impulse for Koolhaas's new book came during a recent visit to Atlanta, where he discovered that all the optimism about the John Portman–led revival of the downtown area, which had seemed so potent during a previous trip in 1973, had evaporated. What struck him this time was the building activity along the city's outer perimeter. This he found "exciting in a completely random way," being a mishmash of residential and commercial buildings that adds up to a genuinely new species of urban environment—"plankton and spaghetti cities," as he calls them.

Koolhaas recalls a visit to one Atlanta architect's office in which he found a model of a proposed development consisting of a slice of classical American tract housing, next to a Rockefeller Center, next to more spec housing. "The average age of the people in the architectural front line producing these kind of schemes is something like twenty-four, and the oldest partners are thirty-two. Through an accumulation of these kind of details, you find that you are dealing with a totally new phenomenon: complexes whose thoughtlessness is infinitely vast, and yet whose impact is also infinitely great."

Koolhaas finds these perimeter developments fascinating, despite their awesome lack of critical intelligence. He may not like them, but nevertheless finds them irresistibly intriguing, and significant beyond their immediate physical appearance. "It's typical now to find that there is almost nothing you can like wholeheartedly. You either have to wear your critical apparatus, and then almost everything is unbearable, or you have to swallow it, and then you are living on a dual level"—in fact, operating with the double vision of Roland Barthes's Mythologist. Koolhaas's "retroactive" analysis of the contemporary city sounds remarkably akin to Venturi, Scott Brown and Izenour's famous examination of the Las Vegas strip, and he acknowledges that there is some similarity. Venturi et al.'s *Learning from Las Vegas*, he agrees, serves as a paradigm with much wider implications than the specific example of a gambling resort in Nevada. "Ignore the fact that the place is all casinos, and imagine what it would be like if one building really was a Roman bath, the next a temple of learning, and so on. A strip that took you from Caracalla to the Sorbonne is something totally different, almost unbearably exciting."

In fact, the same kind of Borgesian Chinese encyclopaedia of adjacencies is what simultaneously fascinates and horrifies Koolhaas about the new towns around Paris. The whole region has, he says, been excessively planned, controlled, and bureaucratised, and is overly socialistic in terms of land values. "There, the Avenue Salvador Allende may lead to the Piazza Pablo Picasso via the Rue Fidel Castro, but aesthetically it all looks exactly the same as what is happening on the fringes of Atlanta. Any explanation of contemporary urbanism that concentrates simply on land values is inadequate if the opposite political ideology produces the identical landscape. What is happening is a prospect that you can condemn or regard as exhilarating if it is in the right hands."

In *Delirious New York*, Koolhaas identified a curious paradox: the Europeans had produced architectural manifestos but not the buildings to back them up, while the Americans had built, but not written their underlying polemic. He sees a strange process occurring.

"I think that the most secret ambitions of the original modernists have now become the vernacular and in a true sense, 'reality.' There is a picture of [Kazimir] Malevich that is very important for me. He is seated at this table, on which are towers: some big, some small, some leaning, made of asbestos, mica, plastic, and felt—very enigmatic things. It was clearly an arsenal of ideas to be launched onto the world. Right now, a lot of those ideas can be detected even in the context of those schlock offices in Atlanta. In many ways, we are living the actual implementation of all those ambitions that were inaccessible myths for the pioneers of modernism: the speed of production, of volume, and engineering. But while we weren't looking, architects seem to have lost almost all control over the potential of modernism, lost any ability to find a connection with it once again."

Koolhaas's theorising, and his architecture, attempt to plot a way forward for this new era of building. Yet for all the provocative intelligence of his ideas, a cloud of doubt hovers over the results of his work. OMA's aim—here expressed in terse plans, striking neo-Constructivist projections, and sequences of diagrammatic site analyses—is to confer upon architecture a stringent scientific rationality, while resisting the imposition of determinate physical form. Koolhaas's position in fact embraces a paradox. He declares that "one has to surrender the pretension that one can control the built," and yet retains a belief in the power of rigorous conceptual frameworks to hold the "nothingness" together. Such abstractions resonate powerfully so long as they are safely confined to paper, and presented in exotic axonometric, from inaccessible aerial vantage points. But how do these gestures survive the transition from the conveniently abbreviated scale of printed-page urbanism to the banal reality of the building site?

The firsthand evidence of the work to date, albeit constructed on bargain basement budgets, is not convincing, however photogenic it may look. The Hague Dance Theatre relies on whimsical shapes, colours, and textures—on close inspection, crudely detailed—to create momentarily arresting, but inescapably flimsy incidents in an underwhelming spatial envelope. The elevations of the Amsterdam school and gymnasium (though admittedly not entirely finished) have a flatness that's disquietingly reminiscent of the original drawings.

Koolhaas's real influence may yet remain more in the realm of the written and drawn than the built, diagnosing conditions retroactively, where others have remained oblivious to their broader significance. He himself conceives two possible roles as an architect. "One is to maintain, through a series of random questions, a certain level of integrity, intelligence, and aesthetic consistency. I don't want to do dead, worthless, or contentless projects. But I have also felt a very strong need to discover things, whether I like them or not, to enter into areas that are fraught with danger, with unlikeable things or ugly things, things fraught with the potential to fail."

———

The latter propensity does not protect the architect from dumbfoundment when the writer fails to see the virtues of his The Hague City Hall project. He enthuses that it could go up in a mere twenty-four months, would be incredibly cheap, and would provide a dazzling addition to the city's skyline.

"For me, it is really inconceivable that someone doesn't get excited about the scheme, doesn't see that it represents a leap in terms of issues that have been holding up development for a long time."

The writer sees little more than a clunky model of a kind of mini Manhattan, an amalgam of Seagrams, a cluster of Lever Houses, all carved at random from a monolithic block. "I think you felt it as ugly, lumpen, or uncontrolled or awkward," the architect volunteers. "All those conditions are there, and given a charge which is exciting," he claims. The writer confronts a worrying inability to register where this charge can be found.

The writer suspects that the nature of the dilemma is a matter of changed personal taste. And yet she is reluctant to dismiss the architect's built work, because much of what he has to say about the contemporary metropolis still sounds so compelling.

The architect is perplexed by the writer's unexpectedly equivocal response, preferring to attribute this to some deficiency in the latter's perception than to shortcomings in his work. Was it circumstantial? An empty stomach perhaps, the overcast sky, or the fact that the dance troupe was away, and the theatre empty?

Perhaps the writer has failed to appreciate the necessary reduction in ideological ambition entailed in switching from the pursuit of paper projects to real projects, with actual clients and conditions, and correspondingly circumscribed potential for tidy resolution. "If I were a psychologist," he ventures at one point, "I'd say that your disappointment was on an ideological level, and transferred to the visual level." The topic won't go away: like a fruit pip lodged in a filling, it is an irritant that becomes an obsession. "Once disappointment was your formulation, everything seemed to fall into place. You were not open to a certain shift," the architect argues. He looks for external causes. "Maybe you stayed in America too long...Did you become religious all of a sudden?...Are you depressed perhaps?...It sounds as if you have great problems with Western civilisation..."

The scene is a bus shelter-cum-transport inquiry pavilion outside Rotterdam Central Station. A large paraboloid roof, lifted on pilotis, sails up toward the elegant modernist facade of the main station. It shelters a low, greenhouse-like structure that meanders around a series of curved corners. The reader will immediately recognise it as an OMA creation.

Blueprint inquisitor (fingering a glitter-surfaced counter in front of the inquiries window): "Is this a good building?"

Bilingual transport information consultant: "Not very."

Blueprint inquisitor: "Why is that?"

Transport consultant (pointing to improvised Sellotape draught exclusion strip between panels of glass separating his booth from the passenger concourse): "It looks nice. But it doesn't work."

Reyner Banham:
A Past Master

Blueprint, April 1988

I never studied directly with Peter (Reyner) Banham, but without doubt he was my mentor in the truest sense of the word. His death from cancer on March 18, at the age of sixty-six, was a personal loss, and robs the world of a rare and wonderful writer.

My first encounter with Banham was in 1979, when I trekked with a fellow Bartlett undergraduate to Buffalo, in upstate New York, to meet the historian whom we had missed being taught by at University College, London, by just one year. We arrived at an unprepossessing industrial building (since given its due recognition in Banham's last book, *A Concrete Atlantis*) and asked where we could find the esteemed professor. "In there," we were told, and we boldly pushed open a brown door at the end of a corridor. We found ourselves suddenly the focus of a full raked amphitheatre of students and standing next to Banham himself, who was in full flight lecturing on—of all things—English castles. We squeezed into hard, unyielding wooden seats, and were soon seduced by Banham's inimitable rhetoric: full of sly puns, canny conjunctions, personal anecdotes that made the archaic structures in question ring with gritty immediacy. His voice, a mellifluous Bristol burr, was unexpectedly "country"—like gnarled bark whittled and steeped in apricot brandy. The lecture over, we approached the podium.

"What in God's name are you doing *here?*" was his first remark, when we introduced ourselves. We told him we had come to meet him. After an hour's chat, we left, armed with tips on what to see on our North American tour, who to speak to, where to study in the United States, and a sense of privilege at having made friends with the man whose *Age of the Masters* had switched me on to architecture, and the possibilities of writing vividly about it.

―――

I got to know Peter, and his wife, Mary, well in subsequent years, meeting them on both sides of the Atlantic. During a summer visit in 1983, shortly before I set sail for the East Coast myself, Banham came to address my Lonely Arts Club in my garret on Long Acre. People sat in the living room and crowded out into the narrow hall to listen enraptured as he spoke, whisky in hand, for an uninterrupted two hours on his years with the Independent Group. It seemed as if he knew everybody—the next day, I Hoovered up the dropped names along with the usual detritus of wine corks and spent matches that testified to an exceptional club event. Peter was always generous with his wit and wisdom: there was immediate rapport and a torrent of information as soon as you spoke to him. Even in hospital, these past few weeks—having been rushed home from the States as his illness rapidly worsened—he was full of new ideas, suggestions for my dissertation research, barbed comments on personalities in the world of architecture and its histories. He was reading Jean Baudrillard's *Amérique*—not yet available in this country—and was obviously chuffed by the name check and reference to his book on American deserts.

―――

I visited him in Santa Cruz, on the West Coast, at Christmas 1984 (my second winter in the States as a graduate student). He showed me round the campus where he now taught, pointing out

Charles Moore's Kresge College with his mix of enthusiasm and benevolent put-down. We went round the town—a sleepy place a bit like Bournemouth, with its low bungalows and out-of-season funfair—and took in the sights, like the cove to which surfers flock for the most challenging waves and the eucalyptus tree on which so many monarch butterflies descend during their annual migration that the branches actually droop. Trust Banham to perceive such a wonderfully preposterous example of engineering principles at work in the world of nature: the live loading of these light, ethereal creatures.

We ate french fries sitting on the pier, watching the sunset. By this point, I had remembered how pointless it was to try getting a word in edgeways: much better just to sit and listen to his ceaseless stock of tales and tongue-tickling neologisms: "Picture-skew" for picturesque, "Archie" for *The Architectural Review*. "Veedub" for a VW car, "R-Eleven-D" for Richard Llewelyn-Davies. That evening beside the fire, he talked of buildings and architects, of magazines and wordsmithing. "My tolerance for masterpieces is about thirty-five seconds," he confessed. "I stood in front of the *Mona Lisa* for five." He said he'd told James Stirling that he'd spent five *hours* at Stuttgart, and the architect was really flattered. "So you should be," Banham reported his own retort. He reminisced about writing his dissertation, which would become the oft-reprinted *Theory and Design in the First Machine Age*. Studying with Nikolaus Pevsner and Sigfried Giedion at the Courtauld, he said, "There was no doubt in my mind, these were my Great Masters and they'd got it wrong—they'd missed out De Stijl and Futurism and their influence on modern architecture. I was going to write the great revisionist history." A look of glee spread over his face, swathed in beard, that bathful of grey and white soap bubbles. Around his neck, the signature bolo tie, customised with his AIA gold medal; in one pocket of his trousers, a brightly coloured cowboy's handkerchief.

Ever the pioneer, the intellectual frontiersman, pushing back the borders, Banham was cheated of his reward for long years in the academic outback: he was appointed to the highest chair in architectural history, the Sheldon H. Solow Professorship at New York University's Institute of Fine Arts, only last year, following the death of Henry-Russell Hitchcock. The Banhams' bags were already packed for the move to Manhattan when his condition suddenly deteriorated in January. Philip Johnson arranged a remarkable gathering of old friends and admirers during Peter's necessary stopover in New York. They would all much rather have come to hear his inaugural lecture, on which he was working at the time of his death.

———

Banham's ambivalent relationship with the United States was that mix of fascination for mass production and industrialised popular culture, with yearnings for European culture that had previously sparked the modernists—whose own excited journeyings he recorded in *A Concrete Atlantis: U.S. Industrial Building and European Modern Architecture 1900–1925*. In many ways this book is an autobiographical elegy, in which Banham came to terms with, as he put it, "the difference between the tangible fact and the utopian vision," the *experience* of place versus the preconceptions based on mediated impressions.

His description of his own coming upon the abandoned, derelict Concrete Central grain elevator is a gem of self-discovery:

> Coming out on to the wharf, dominated by the three largest loose legs ever built in Buffalo, now semi-transparent as the winds of the winters had blown away more and more of their rusted corrugated cladding, it was difficult not to see everything through eighteenth-century picturesque visions of ancient sites or even Piranesi's view of the temples of Paestum... I was looking at one

of the great remains of a high and mighty period of constructive art in North America, a historical monument in its own inalienable right. But at a slight cultural remove, I was also…looking at a monument to a different civilization that had been as unknown to its builders as Christianity has been to the builders of most of the monuments in Rome: the culture of the European modern movement.

And reaching the rooftop racetrack at the Fiat Lingotto factory in Turin, Banham felt it was "a strangely disturbing and moving experience for me, a kind of historian's homecoming for one partially Americanized European."

So sad that his own latest homecoming should have been his last, as it was. But in his evocations of the designed environment—from "Household Godjets" and Moulton minicycles to museums and monster silos—Peter Banham lives on.

Call That a *Fish*, Frank?

Frank Gehry
Blueprint, September 1988

Frank Gehry is frankly anxious. "Very anxious." Whether it's the immediate prospect of lecturing to a sell-out-plus-closed-circuit audience at the Royal Institute of British Architects, or of building a huge skyscraper in Manhattan, is not entirely clear. But behind the pebble glasses, this gemütlich, rumpled gnome has a distant look in his eyes.

No wonder. As his lecture makes abundantly clear, Frank Gehry is at an amazingly prolific stage in his career, and suddenly faces a quantum-leap test of his strengths. The jump from small, quirky private residences—such as the Norton House on Venice Beach or the Wosk Residence in Beverly Hills, with its cluster of rooftop forms like the juicy bits in a raspberry trifle—to umpteen-storey office towers in New York and Cleveland, would make a strong man quiver. Not that you doubt his capabilities; more, you worry for the preservation of his singular touch, for the development of his idiosyncratic formal language. You wonder whether it can survive the worldwide deluge of new commissions, whether the invention can be sustained as the number and scale of his projects multiply. Two hours and four impressive slide carousels later, you're wishing the little man with the fish fetish all the best.

Frank Gehry's star has been in the ascendant for a good few years, gathering steam with the completion of Los Angeles projects like the Loyola Law School, the California Aerospace Museum with its gnat-like Lockheed F-104, and the Temporary Contemporary museum conversion. His own house in Santa Monica—chopped and changed with corrugated metal—was already an established place of pilgrimage, its notoriety confirmed by its recent appearance in a pornographic comic book. "This guy and gal are looking for a place to make out," Gehry explains, "and they find my kitchen."

This summer, his work was on show simultaneously at three venues in New York. His cardboard chairs were at the Leo Castelli gallery in SoHo; two early houses were designated as the historical origins of deconstructivist architecture at the Museum of Modern Art; and the mammoth retrospective of his work organised by the Walker Art Center arrived at the Whitney Museum of American Art in July after a two-year US tour. Meanwhile in Washington, DC, Gehry installed a chunky confection inside the National Building Museum, to mark the Sheet Metal Workers' union centennial. Rising within the cavernous neoclassicism of the Pension Building, Gehry's exhibition pavilion served as a giant object lesson in sheet-metal working skills, its crystalline massing in conspicuous contrast both to the material of its own fabrication and to the Brobdingnagian columns of its host structure.

June saw him build the HOLLYWOOD sign backwards in Barcelona, out of galvanised steel, to mark an American film festival; from this month, Milan gets the Gehry treatment with a giant boat made from gold-painted stainless steel as his contribution to the Triennale. With longtime collaborators Claes Oldenburg and Coosje van Bruggen and sculptor Daniel Buren, Gehry was invited to take part in a section sponsored by the city of Miami. *The Golden Calf* started off as a vessel to display art commissioned for the city, but now "it's a piece all by itself... it fills the space." This kind of reciprocal development seems characteristic: Gehry's buildings are increasingly organised as aggregated sculptural units, while his museum pieces—especially the giant fish sculptures—have tended to mushroom into proto-buildings that can be entered and explored. Scale and scales are now the central issues in Gehry's work; Oldenburg's influence is apparent in regard to both sizing and the rigid/flaccid play of materials.

The fish business? Ah, that apocryphal tale about the carp in his grandmother's bath...bought at the Jewish Market on a Thursday, allowed to swish about in the tub for a day...then killed and turned into gefilte fish. Gehry is rather tired of recollecting this particular boyhood memory. "Can't we think of something else?" he says, when asked for the origins of his trademark obsession. Then, as if giving away the obvious: "It's all sexual frustration."

For a while, the symbolism is safely abstract and innocent, kind of Brancusi meets Flipper. But when you see the white plaster fish maquette for the Fishdance Restaurant in Tokyo, which he had to have computer-scanned for full-scale construction (in tiles of fishnet, or Japanese chainlink, at least), you know what he means. Call that a *fish*, Frank?

The fish thing began because he was fed up with postmodern classicism: "I was so furious that people were drawing Greek temples, regurgitating the past, abandoning the present. I said to myself, since the Parthenon came from man, why not fish?" Turning to an organic source for inspiration, perhaps to an image that has had subliminal potency since childhood, Gehry has developed the fish into a personal icon—one which he'll doodle when he's blocked on a design, and which increasingly makes its presence felt in his buildings, however far removed from the representational animal form.

Gehry had already toyed with animal figures for a colonnade on a private house when he began work on a collaborative project with the sculptor Richard Serra: Frank did a fish, Serra a snake. After that came a fish/snake combo for the *Follies* exhibition in New York, and then, when Frank got angry and smashed up the ColorCore Formica whose commercial versatility he was supposed to be demonstrating, the fragments became scales in a seductive, if rather impractical, fish lamp. Since then, he's done a room-size fish in glass for his Walker show. "It sort of looks like it's been in a frying pan," he concedes, referring to a structural shortcoming which means the glass scales flatten out at the bottom. Gehry is clearly fascinated by the problems of translating slithery shapes into buildable forms at full scale, developing both the supporting framework and the imbricated skin. "I'm enamoured with the multiple curvilinear movement. As I kept drawing these curves, these 'fillets of fish' became part of my language. Then I got smart and cut off the head, cut off the tail, and explored the internal space."

This topped-and-tailed belly or upturned hull figure—"more abstract, more architectural"—appears as a kind of canopy in Gehry's Camp Good Times (an unrealised project designed with Oldenburg for a summer camp for children with cancer in the Santa Monica mountains); it reappears, clad in copper, in a massive $8 million luxury residence on Malibu Beach, currently under construction, and in the University of Iowa laser laboratories, a project which provides a succinct demonstration of Gehry's current position. Different portions of the building are set off against each other in curved, rectilinear, and cascading neocrystalline formation, their animal/vegetable/mineral distinctions expressed in contrasting materials. Steel-clad offices erupt higgledy-piggledy from one side of a sober stone-faced block ("They're meant to look like an infill"), while a copper-clad fish-ish form to its rear houses support labs. "They're not hawks," Gehry hastens to assure, regarding this project. "It's for medical laser research. It was an important consideration for me. I checked before I accepted that it was nothing to do with Star Wars."

A different kind of self-reflection is called upon for the Manhattan skyscraper project which Gehry is doing with David Childs of SOM New York. A more contrasting collaboration of talents could hardly be imagined. And Gehry is well aware of the risks he's taking, not just in doing a double act with another architect who works in a very different language—he terms Childs a "representative classicist"—but in extrapolating his own sculptural strategy from "economy" to "giant sized."

"These are developer buildings, and if you're going to play with them, you have to play by their rules. The rules for high-rise—in terms of location, rental values, construction costs, and the comparison with their neighbours—allow a very limited margin of play in terms of sculpture. It becomes a very thin veneer, a skin job. Making sculpture out of it is very difficult, especially within the budget. You can't manipulate pure form at that scale without penalties. High-rise jams you back into skin. That's the area I'm having some trouble with. It's difficult to translate the small stuff. The struggle with my kind of language, pulling it up into a higher kind of building, is the window patterns…they're like pegboard. It's a long way from successful just yet. Windows," he says with a faint note of chagrin, "you have to have them."

Claes Oldenburg, true to sculptural form, likes windows even less. He's having trouble accepting them in Gehry's Chiat/Day advertising offices, to which he contributed a pair of giant binoculars. "Now I've got him working with me on a high-rise which he *has* to put windows in. I haven't seen him for months." Oldenburg first proposed a giant C-clamp for Gehry's Cleveland tower—at fifty storeys, one million square feet, Progressive Insurance will be a bit smaller than the one in Manhattan, and completes the Daniel Burnham-et-al.–designed Group Plan of 1903. But he's changed his mind, and now has the skyscraper "reading"

a copy of the Cleveland *Plain Dealer*. And there are the three giant
tea bags he's hanging off the Massachusetts Transit Building that
Gehry just renovated in Boston.

Gehry was as surprised as anyone else when he scooped the
New York and Cleveland projects. In fact, he'd just denounced
the tall building as a type when the commissions came his way.
"About a year ago, I declared in public that since I would probably never get a high-rise building, I could safely say they were a
bad thing. I had just made that pronouncement when my life
changed! If you win a high-rise, it's like Mount Everest: you try to
climb it. The freedom I had in my smaller buildings is being trun-
cated, but I'm enjoying the struggle to deal with that idea."

When he was selected for the New York project last year, the
intention was to have three towers, one per architect, plus another
done in collaboration. Now there's just one each. Gehry takes
Childs's sixty-four-storey tower as a foil for his own, a few storeys
lower, though there's been give-and-take: "I've added stone to
mine, he's added metal to his. We made a choice of non-symmetry
in the relationship between the buildings. I have enormous
respect for classicism, but it just manifests itself differently. I
decided to profile my building against his…it's interesting playing against a moving target. Every time he takes his pineapple and
raises it higher, I have to take my fish up a few storeys."

But Gehry seems to concede that only the skyline and ground
levels are susceptible to sculptural organisation, the interven-
ing levels remaining more problematic. His tower has a kind of
gullet-to-gills fish portion forming the upper section, to be clad
in pillow-steel panels, exploiting their billowing surface, "when
everyone's spent years trying to make them flat."

"People who like his building hate mine, and people that
like mine hate his. We're varying degrees of crazy, so it's very
interesting. It's a kind of fusion and ignition; we just play off each
other. What we won the competition with and where we are now

are quite different. We're being forced to change some things that are very crucial to the design, so we're reevaluating the whole project. When you've made a commitment it's hard to let go of it, but I knew it would be like that, and that's the challenge."

His thirty-person Venice, California, office is busy making giant mock-ups—models being Gehry's preferred method of deciding on architectural form. All his projects evolve through successive stages of three-dimensional development, and it's hard to imagine how Gehry now has the time to keep the necessary close personal involvement in the schemes currently on the drawing board. But the diversity and invention seem to be maintained in a truly astonishing portfolio that also includes a 350,000-square-foot furniture factory for Herman Miller in Sacramento, a factory-cum-museum for Vitra in Weil am Rhein ("You can see where all the fish and snakes stuff went"), a psychiatric clinic at Yale University, and the American Center in Paris, near the Gare de Lyon.

Gehry beat Richard Meier to this relatively small but prestigious commission in the late spring. A small complex housing a theatre, museum, dance studios, and language laboratories, it is an exercise in "putting dissimilar objects together," or what Gehry, in a revealing phrase, speaks of as the "lazily but actually *carefully* set" arrangement of pieces. "It looks like a bunch of lettuce leaves right now," he says, self-deprecating as usual.

Gehry is also in the running to do an entertainment center at the new Euro Disney outside Paris. Michael Eisner, head of the Disney Corporation, has been interviewing leading American architects for different parts of the new leisure kingdom, including Michael Graves, Robert A. M. Stern, and Stanley Tigerman, as well as Europeans Jean Nouvel and Rem Koolhaas. "The imagery of Disneyland comes from Europe—castles and so on—it's a bit like coals to Newcastle," Gehry explains. "So they're looking for a more American architectural expression."

In case this workload isn't enough, Gehry's name has also been mentioned in connection with the Mass MoCA museum conversion of the Sprague Electric complex in Williamstown, Massachusetts (as has Robert Venturi's). He was also recently invited to do a new biological sciences building at Princeton, just down campus from Venturi's Lewis Thomas Laboratory.

All this seems like fair consolation for having lost a chance at King's Cross. Gehry is diplomatic when it comes to discussing that huge project, declining to air his opinions about the backstage politics that led to Norman Foster's secession from the SOM master planning team, and his eventual success as nominated architect for the London Regeneration development consortium. "I'm saving my hurt feelings," says Gehry, who was instrumental in getting Foster involved in the first place. Elsewhere in London, he has done "a little study" for housing in Docklands. "If you're standing in the middle of the Isle of Dogs, you see a slip of river and a lot of dark, dank buildings. It looks like Tribeca. I'd love to do something like the Temple—as it would be without the road: all that grass and green sloping to the river."

But Gehry seems sceptical about building here, much as he'd like to. "We might get something down the line. I think London wants British architects. I don't want to get heart failure, and I wouldn't want to give Prince Charles apoplexy." Or, more likely, have His Royal Highness choke on a fishbone. Still, Norm could afford to toss Frank a sprat.

When the Sky Falls In

Coop Himmelb(l)au

Blueprint, December 1988–January 1989

Vienna, where they sell gift packs of Mozart Kuchen in the *Konditorei*, and Freud glares interrogatively from the fifty schilling note. On Seilerstätte, two yellow eyes blink on the billboard declaring *Cats—6 Jahr!* Opposite the Ronacher theatre is the Coop Himmelb(l)au office, a capacious studio arrived at from a typically gloomy staircase twining round an exposed elevator. Two faces glower from a fading poster on one wall, captioned, in German, "Architecture Must Burn." Side-by-side mug shots, they have the sullen ferocity of the Baader-Meinhof. Folie à deux.

Helmut Swiczinsky and Wolf Prix are the principals of Coop Himmelb(l)au, and they've been partners in crime, as it were, since the 1960s. Lately they've been garnering notoriety well beyond the Ringstrasse: the Museum of Modern Art's *Deconstructivist Architecture* exhibition featured their work among its Magnificent Seven, and now the Architectural Association in London is giving them the full exhibition-plus-publication package tour. A one-to-one chunk of a house they're doing in Malibu, California, has taken up residence in a corner of Bedford Square to coincide with the London show.

Who are they, and what is Coop Himmelb(l)au?

A perusal of their out-of-print treatise *Architecture Is Now*— that fat black book which did the rounds at the AA and was similarly sought after at Jaap Rietman's in New York a few years back—reveals the two gentlemen to be of a poetic persuasion, keen on enigmatic slogans, generally following the formula "Architecture plus verb plus noun." They also manufacture a fair quantity of mystical manifestos. And they have built a few small interludes of...well, is it architecture, or has that word already been, so to speak, co-opted? Should it perhaps be reserved for rather larger chunks of built form?

Let us say that Coop Himmelb(l)au is on the experimental end of the profession, teetering toward performance art and happenings. And the work—at least the drawings of the buildings they might become—looks a lot like the kind of creatures that crunch when you tread on them: arthropods with articulated carapaces of metal and glass and quivering proboscis-like tubes of stainless steel. Messrs. Prix and Swiczinsky are architecture's Beastie Boys. But don't mention the reptilian resemblances—it's been said too many times before. What they're really about is... SPACE!

"We want to build architecture like clouds," Wolf Prix tells me. "Architecture which reacts to people, not the other way round." Himmelb(l)au, he explains, means "sky blue." "It was the time of very poetic names: Archizoom, Ant Farm, Archigram, the Beatles, the Rolling Stones," Prix continues, describing the climate in which the practice was founded in 1968. "We were trying to expand this boring thing, architecture, to make it more complex than it is now."

No modest enterprise, this Coop Himmelb(l)au. What it has done to date are a lot of projects with evocative titles (try Hot Flat) and some built interventions, mostly in Vienna: the Studio Baumann (1985), a glorified mezzanine structure inside a small art gallery whose neoclassical facade is ruptured by a lava of aluminum, now dusty like a sloughed-off carcass from *Alien*; the Red Angel, a small theatre/wine bar (1980–81); the offices for

ISO-Holding (1986), featuring an arrow-like tube of stainless steel charging through from the executive suites to the reception area; and the Passage Wahliss, which could be described as a corridor between display windows for a china store on Kärntner Strasse.

Most ambitious of all is the rooftop remodelling currently under construction on Falkestrasse, around the corner from Otto Wagner's Post Office Savings Bank, which Coop Himmelb(l)au is doing for its lawyers. Deconstructive midwife Mark Wigley reached for the parasitical metaphor in acclaiming this project in his Sermon at the Tate (the "Deconstuction and Architecture" conference, previewing the MoMA exhibition) last March. It symbolised, so Wigley would have us believe, the repressed forces of architecture bursting out of their constrictive envelopes.

"We wanted to make a very attractive corner solution, so that if you're standing in that space you have the feeling of being protected and free at the same time, like flying," says Prix.

Well, the light was fading when *Blueprint* paid a call, but it struck me that this adulterated attic was rather like an exotic piece of jewellery attached to a double-breasted suit. From the street all you see, if you look carefully, is a couple of steel tubes dangling like molten chopsticks over the cornice of a regular Viennese block. Inside, a formidable medley of steel sections disport themselves beneath—at present—a flapping red tarpaulin which, when glazed, will be the world's most complicated rooflight. Hope it doesn't leak.

Right now, Coop Himmelb(l)au is breaking into the big time, with a factory for a wood and paper processing company nearing completion in Carinthia, Austria (a box with gizmos festooning one end), and work proceeding on the Open House in Malibu, California (Prix teaches at SCI-Arc in Los Angeles). Then there are two major projects in Vienna: a hotel and the wholesale transformation of the Ronacher theatre.

Prix shows me two foam-block models, fastened together with dressmaking pins, approximately three inches cubed. These demonstrate a radical change in the orientation of the structure (more floors, more performance space); they're also adding to the theatre roof—another case of The Locusts Have Landed. Seems the planners weren't too keen on this disturbance to the skyline, so Coop Himmelb(l)au obliged by shifting the offending bar in a bit, so as to avoid it looming visibly over the street. Attention turns from foam collage A to foam collage B. Such a big alteration, so swiftly, economically achieved.

Now, you may be wondering where the inspiration for this "architecture" comes from. Believe me, I have tried to probe its secret heart. And what it comes down to is a sort of spatial ecstasy experienced jointly by a pair of adult men and captured at the moment of epiphany in runic squiggles on paper. Or, as the critic Brian Hatton calls them, "vomited doodles." At the origin of every Coop Himmelb(l)au project is an angry, twitching scrawl of pencil lines which only its makers can truly understand.

"The ground plan, the section, how high, where the light is coming from, the view—all these things are in the drawing. No one can read it but us." Dense, intense scratchings, these are the concentrated hieroglyphs from which the buildings will hatch, almost fully fledged, with only a few miles of working drawings (and the services of a dedicated engineer, Oskar Graf) between the mesmeric moment of conception and the final, full-scale realisation. Building, for Coop Himmelb(l)au, is a matter of proving whether they can retain the quality of the initial sketch.

"We call it the *psychogram* of the design: it contains all the feelings and emotions the building will awaken."

What kind of feelings?

"There's a good answer to that," says Prix, smiling earnestly through his tinted spectacles. "It's like asking a movie director to describe his film. If he could describe his film, there would be no necessity to make the film."

A certain rapport has developed between him and Swiczinsky over the years. At times it sounds like a form of religious rapture, though Prix prefers a musical analogy. "Sometimes it's like working in a band. Some of the ideas come from playing the guitar. The more you play, the more you hear." By now, they communicate not only in words but...well, you could call it telepathically. "We've developed not only verbal communication, but also a body language, so a third person is excluded. We're very fast. Sometimes I can describe the city just by doing this [*points hands and fingers out*] or this [*crooks fingers*] or this [*embraces a yard of thin air*]."

Looks like Milton Keynes to you? No: must be Melun-Sénart, satellite new town southeast of Paris, first fruit of the new calisthenic school of planning. Coop Himmelb(l)au won first place in the recent competition for a master plan for the city that will take well into the twenty-first century to come about. A series of (computer-aided?) drawings shows the major elements of the development. One can say with certainty that this is not the kind of thing Camillo Sitte would have recognised as town planning.

Prix offers an interpretation. There are some "circumstantial pressures," such as the TGV (high-speed train) line running almost north–south past one edge of the site, and the existence of three other settlements. Aside from this, "We just thought of how a city should be, containing all the variety and discrepancy of cities: not only silent but noisy, not only high-density but low, not just cold but also hot. Otherwise it gets monofunctional." His favourite cities are Vienna, New York, and LA, the latter "maybe because it's nonphysical. The power of the city comes from travelling on the freeways and hearing twenty-one music stations."

I venture a question of scale, since the Melun-Sénart plans appear to be conceived with minimal regard to the matter of eventual human occupation; the constituent parts have a logic on the page, as plan diagrams, but there is no guarantee that the "excitement" of their angles and curves will be borne out when blown up across the greenbelt of suburban Paris. "I don't know what human scale is," says Prix. "That's an architectural term. I think the scale of a city is not a size, it's an anticipation of human desires."

Canonised in the MoMA show, and now popular travelling preachers (Prix gives a hundred-odd lectures a year, his American assistant tells me), Coop Himmelb(l)au has gained a cult following among students eager to escape the conventional limits of architecture. "For two thousand years we did architecture like this," says Prix, scrawling a column-and-beam structure on a piece of trace. "Palladio, Vitruvius, additive things—this kind of architecture is dead. Architects are in a bad position against politicians and clients, so they've built up a certain philosophy. But we exclude all these clichés. In the 1970s, when we did the projects that were in the *Deconstructivist Architecture* show, we felt isolated. We thought it just couldn't be true that the pomo stuff was in the brain of every architect. So we were glad to see people like Zaha Hadid and Danny Libeskind were around. There's a kind of invention in all our projects. Otherwise it gets boring."

"Open Architecture," as practised by Coop Himmelb(l)au, is not the sort of thing destined to endear itself to civic building authorities, but it's an uphill struggle which perhaps is beginning to be won: the practice was awarded the City of Vienna's annual award for architecture in October, and its accomplishments are marked on the tourist board's map of "Architektur vom Fin de siècle bis Heute," alongside those of great uncles Otto, Adolf, Joseph, and Josef.

The pigeons swirl in Michaelerplatz, the limpid autumn sun gleams off the arbored globe of the Secession building, and against the great glory of Jugendstil Vienna, Coop Himmelb(l)au is just pie in the blue sky.

A Tale of the Riverbank

Sir Christopher Wren

The Independent, January 5, 1989

(The scene: a gondola upon the River Thames, heading downriver just above Richmond. Handel's Water Music, *or something similar, fades on the soundtrack as the camera closes in upon the two passengers in conversation. One of them is wearing a spectacularly large wig.)*

———

Sir Christopher Wren, as Surveyor-General of the Royal Buildings, and more particularly as the architect of St. Paul's Cathedral, you have been much in the media recently. Your plan for London has also been the focus of discussion among urban designers who are concerned about the development of the capital. A number of schemes along the banks of Thames, both actual and proposed, raise difficult questions concerning architects' attitudes toward history. This riverside office development for Haslemere Estates, for example. How does it strike you?

At first glance, ma'am, I find it a devilish Conceit. Are these Buildings of a singular Vintage, hastily concocted as if to dissimulate many of different Pedigrees, or an accretion of dissimilar Specimens, grown up over Time? I cannot tell, and 'tis worriesome if the Whole be an instantaneous Sum of Parts.

In fact the buildings have all been completed recently to the design of one man, Mr. Quinlan Terry, although the composition is arranged to suggest a historic accumulation. It represents an extreme position in the current debate over "Post Modernism." Some theorists have derided it as mere pastiche, but clearly the general public—whom we see here strolling in the riverfront gardens—obviously appreciates certain aspects, irrespective of academic opinion.

Well, I can only repeat what I wrote in my family memoirs. **Modern Authors who have treated of Architecture, seem generally to have little more in view, but to set down the Proportions of Columns, Architraves & Cornices, in the several Orders, as they are distinguished into Dorick, Ionick, Corinthian, and Composite; & in these Proportions, finding them in the ancient Fabricks of the Greeks and Romans (though more arbitrarily used then they care to acknowledge), they have reduced them into Rules, too strict and pedantick, and so as not to be transgressed, without the Crime of Barbarity; though, in their own Nature, they are but the Modes and Fashions of those Ages wherein they were used; but because they were found in the great Structures, we think ourselves strictly obliged still to follow the Fashion, though we can never attain to the Grandeur of those Works.***

---

*All quotations in bold taken from "Of Architecture; and observations on Antique Temples, &c," the appendix to *Parentalia: or Memoirs of the Family of the Wrens, viz Mathew, Bishop of Ely, Christopher, Dean of Windsor, &c. but most chiefly of Sir Christopher Wren, late Surveyor-General of the royal buildings, president of the Royal Society &c, &c, in which is Contained, Besides his Works, a Great Number of Original Papers and Records on Religion, Politicks, Anatomy, Mathematicks, Architecture, Antiquities and Most Branches of Polite Literature,* a collection of the writings of Sir Christopher Wren, published in 1750.

I take it, Sir Christopher, that you are not a great believer in slavish copying of the Ancients.

Mr. Terry, though clearly learned in the great Treatises, illustrates the Pitfalls of which I have spoken, adhering to Historick precedent for the sake of Cosmeticks. If this be a Manifestation of your Poste-Modernism, I tremble at the prospect of more of its whoreson Off-spring.

(They proceed along the Thames, navigated by their gondolier, Canaletto. Sir Christopher looks with wonder at the profusion of new bridges and construction. Just beyond his own Royal Hospital at Chelsea, the great chimneys of Battersea Power Station soar aloft, but no smoke issues from any one of them.)

What is this ruined Monument? I see its Columns are intact, but they support Nothing. What has happened to its Roof?

It never had one, Sir Christopher. It used to be a power-station, that is, a large edifice designed for the generation of electricity. It has been gutted, apparently with some liberties taken in order to comply with the Fire Regulations pertaining to Places of Recreation.

A Place of Recreation? A Power Station?

Yes, under the auspices of Mr. John Broome, Proprietor of Alton Towers, it is being transformed into a Theme Park for the diversion of the masses. In fact, by a paradoxical interchange, Sir Christopher, this actual Power Station is to become a Palace of Entertainment, while the National Theatre downriver has recently been designated a Nuclear Power Station.

What Wit performed this Trick of Rhetorick? Some scoundrel Member of the Royal Society, I'll be bound, with Nought better to engage his Intellect.

None other than the Prince of Wales, who delivered his Theory of Aesthetics in a broadcast to the nation on television. His pronouncements caused quite a flurry among architects, especially when he called for Ten Commandments to regulate fine buildings and urban space.

But what, pray, is a Television?

It is a contraption for the extraction of revenue, Sir Christopher, based on the Laws of Electromagnetics, Optics, and the Free Market. People install them in place of the hearth, and enjoy watching the pictures which they initiate at the press of a button. These satellite dishes, which you see sprouting from the rooftops, act to trap the electronic particles sent by Mr. Rupert Murdoch and other proprietors of the Air Waves.

Manna from Heaven, indeed. And what a charming effect these Lenses have, too, like Buttercups growing Wild in the inner city.

Well, the Prince called for more curves in the Environment, in addition to Spires and Domes, but I fear that these concave dishes are not quite what he had in mind. We are in the age of Electronic Communication, Sir Christopher, when people work before computer screens and send all kinds of data across the globe in a matter of seconds by devices like the Facsimile Machine...

And yet the structures in which these transactions take place resemble Renaissance Palazzi, the gabled warehouses of Dutch merchants, or the Hanging Gardens of Babylon, or whatsoever taketh the Fancy of the Real Estate Developer at that precise moment. It would seem there is a vexing disjuncture nowadays 'twixt Appearance and Reality. **Beauty, Firmness, and Convenience are the principles as the great Vitruvius wrote, and they are equal sisters.** Some family contention seems to have occurred.

Well, you could put it that way. You can find counting houses wrapped around skating rinks at Broadgate; a grocer's store resembling an aerospace centre at Camden Town; a hardware suppliers masquerading as a cross between a fine art museum in Stuttgart and a tomb from the Valley of the Kings.

An Architect ought to be jealous of Novelties, in which Fancy blinds the Judgement; and to think his Judges, as well those that are to live Five Centuries after him, as those of his own Time. That which is commendable now for Novelty, will not be a new Invention to Posterity. Your architects seem to pay too little heed to this, if any purpose may disport itself in Vestments borrowed from any other, ransacked from the Treasure House of History. If Society has advanced from the Slide Rule to the electronic Abacus, it would be foolhardy to suppose that a modern Bank should look like a Counting House of Yore. Unless the Publick, quivering before the awefull strides of Science, prefers to retreat into the duplicitous Comforts of some nostalgick Vision of Britain.

(*As they pass the National Theatre, Sir Christopher briefly succumbs to sentiment, wiping a tear from his eye with his lace-trimmed handkerchief.*)

'Tis not the Nuclear Playhouse that distresses me but the Ravages of the Sky Line on the opposing bank, obscuring the Vista of my

Cathedral Church of St. Paul's. A pox on the Fools, they should have rebuilt the City in Correspondence with my Plan, after the Conflagration.

The controversy continues still, Sir Christopher. There has been great debate over the site adjacent to St. Paul's called Paternoster Square. John Simpson has proposed a scheme which reproduces the medieval street pattern…

By G—! Spare me the Disclosure that they actually constructed it. The Destruction of that ancient Trash and Clutter was a most fortunate Freak of the Almighty's imponderable providence—a consumption devoutly to be wished.

It seems an unlikely prospect, Sir Christopher, but now we are approaching a site where he might yet build, opposite the Tower of London, at London Bridge City. Here is a drawing of a scheme by Mr. Simpson commissioned by St. Martin's Property Corporation.

Odd's fish! But this, surely, is a reincarnation of San Marco in Venice, compleat with Campanile. Is this to be transport'd here from Italy's watery trading post? My head swims, for this Estate befuddles all sense of Authentick Place and Time. I tire of saying it but **Architecture has its political Use; publick Buildings being the Ornament of a Country; it establishes a Nation, draws People and Commerce; makes the People love their native Country.** Surely this Fabrick will only sow confusion in the breasts of the loyal Briton. I fear that your descendants may say with a mournful voice of this decade: *Si monumentum requiris, circumspice.*

Britischer Architekt

James Stirling and Michael Wilford

The Independent, June 26, 1989

Cigar in hand, wearing a pair of collapsible half-moons, James Stirling is finishing off some correspondence in the airy *piano nobile* studio which he shares with his partner of eighteen years, Michael Wilford. There is a striking Churchillian resemblance, appropriately for a man who has just reached the End of the Beginning. No Whitehall bunker this, though: the walls of the Fitzroy Square office are adorned with framed drawings in delicate coloured crayon, and canonic photographs of the Stuttgart Neue Staatsgalerie by their court photographer, Richard Bryant.

This interview has been prompted by the Environment Secretary's recent pronouncement on the No 1 Poultry development, which allows Peter Palumbo to demolish eight listed buildings at the epicentre of the Square Mile, and to build Stirling Wilford and Associates' commercial triangle in their stead. Caught in the apex between Poultry and Queen Victoria Street, opposite the Mansion House, this small patch of land has become the focus of the battle between Conservation and Modernism.

The architects are cautiously jubilant at the decision. "Delighted," says Jim Stirling. "What more can one say?"

Quite a lot, one imagines.

"If you sense a certain reticence," says Michael Wilford, "it's because the battle may not be over. The conservationists are taking advice as to whether they have legal grounds to appeal. It could take until Christmas to resolve." He admits to some chagrin at the likely loss of the listed buildings. "I think it's wrong to relish in sweeping them away, but we're not doing it with alacrity. As I understand it, the purpose of listing is not necessarily to preserve buildings for posterity. It's a recognition of relative value, according to their grading, and ensures that adequate consideration is given to their merits, before they are demolished."

Stirling is more adamant. "I regard them as second-rate Victorian buildings, and I truly believe they are not worth preserving. I think it's more appropriate to have a big set-piece building which is of its time and complementary with the monumental buildings in that context." He rejects the conservationists' argument that the listed buildings form a valuable group. "They're not a coherent ensemble. They're more like a row of dusty old bookends."

Throughout the conversation, Stirling and Wilford finish each others' sentences, like a double act. If Stirling is much the better-known partner, he claims this is just "because I've been around longer. I'm older. Antique." He refuses to enlarge on their precise division of labour. "If you look round this room, you see Michael works over there and I work here, and we both meet at this table."

"We bounce ideas off each other," says Wilford, "whether it's about a design, a new project, or a building in construction. We do have disagreements, but most of the time we reach a rapid consensus. The radio's on all day."

"Third Programme," says Stirling.

"Preferably opera," says Wilford.

"Verdi," says Stirling.

"Mozart," says Wilford.

It's a typical exchange. Wilford frequently deflects his partner's Daddy Bear gruffness, a tendency to be brusque born of a suspicion of journalists and their customary short-term view. "Journalists usually manage to get in before they're finished, and write critical articles. Then the building opens, the public loves it, and after about six months the journalists write rather more enthusiastic articles."

The Stuttgart Neue Staatsgalerie is a prime example: copies of the more vituperative German critiques are said to be lodged, along with one of Stirling's famous outsize blue shirts, in the time capsule buried beneath the museum. The Stuttgart Museum is now tied first with the Cologne Museum as the most popular in Germany, having risen from fifty-sixth position to the top in two years after the opening of Stirling's addition. The Clore Gallery has also substantially increased the Tate Gallery's attendance.

This brings us to the question of the famous "Stirling backside"—the ruthlessly utilitarian treatment of rear elevations.

"We were trying to make a distinction between public facades and service facades. There's nothing new about that, it's quite traditional in the history of architecture. If you look at Palladio's villas, their front sides are elaborate and grand, and the back sides are sometimes like broken-down farmhouses. That's the way they were designed. It's only a recent assumption that buildings should be pavilions, in the round, with similar front and back. In fact, the modern movement went even further, saying that the inside should be similar to the outside, which I don't believe. That's one of the more simplistic notions of twentieth-century architecture. We like to stress certain parts of our buildings, usually the entrances."

Stirling rejects another modern movement precept: that an architect should stick consistently to a single style throughout his career. "It's very strange the way architects are expected to go on repeating themselves. There is no set iconography in our buildings. Each is a particular design for a set of circumstances, though recently we have shown a preference for stone."

The change in material vocabulary parallels the practice's major career shift since Stuttgart, leaving behind Stirling's controversial ventures into public housing and university facilities such as the notorious Southgate Estate at Runcorn and the Cambridge History Faculty. Large public buildings now dominate the portfolio, most of them, significantly, abroad. Germany and the United States have proved most welcoming: the Wissenschaftszentrum (Science Centre) was recently completed in Berlin, where Stirling and Wilford maintain a twenty-person branch office; Cornell University's performing arts centre, in Ithaca, New York, opened late last year. Current projects include a vast science library for the University of California at Irvine, a corporate campus for the B. Braun medical and pharmaceutical products company near Kassel in West Germany, and the Music and Theatre Academies at Stuttgart. Many of their projects were won in limited competitions, and a notable proportion have involved extension to or modification of existing buildings, such as the London and Liverpool Tate galleries, or the Brera Museum in Milan, where they are converting the eighteenth-century Palazzo Citterio. "We're actually very much preservationist. In fact, I think it's more the norm that we're involved with existing buildings than greenfield sites," says Stirling.

Nevertheless, he doesn't subscribe to the "bygone-ism" which he discerns in Britain. "One does feel that this country is obsessed with nostalgia." Both partners note that architects are held in higher esteem in Germany, where the construction industry is more sophisticated, and the quality of workmanship is much higher. Stirling points admiringly to the way the Staatsgalerie drum is made of stone blocks hewn on a curve. No 1 Poultry or not, he will go down in history here as the *Britischer Architekt*, the unseen hero of the Rover 800 car commercial, which makes an ironic nod toward his exported eminence. Even this accolade doesn't satisfy him.

"They never asked us. They didn't even bother to go to the building and photograph it. The car is driving up to some other building, *not* the Staatsgalerie. The one image you see of the building is a postcard they sell at the museum."

Whereas one would expect Stirling to enjoy this indication that his work has passed into popular mythology, he seems obsessed with the visual subterfuge, returning repeatedly to the "el cheapo" studio production technique.

"I think it's bloody great," says Michael Wilford. "It's just a pity they didn't put our name at the end."

Phyllis's Choice

Phyllis Lambert
Blueprint, April 1990

"My father had a piece of land on Park Avenue, and he was intent on building a building there." The father, in this case, was Samuel Bronfman, paterfamilias of the Seagram whisky dynasty. It is Phyllis Lambert (née Bronfman) speaking, in London, where she has recently lectured at the RIBA on her own creation, the Canadian Centre for Architecture in Montreal.

The conversation may ostensibly be about architecture and her decisive role in directing its course during the latter twentieth century, but it is the relationship between Phyllis and her father that forms the insistent subtext. Perhaps, if things had been different between them, the world would never have got the Seagram Building, Mies van der Rohe's crowning glory and a lasting monument to both public (that is, commercial) success and private... well, failure of communication.

———

Talking to Phyllis Lambert is a reminder that the story of modern architecture (and that of most other eras) is on the one hand a catalogue of great men and great buildings, and on the other, an expression of complex and highly specific personal motivations, not all of which necessarily reach the light of day. She would, rightly, object that architecture is also a catalogue of great *women*, though there are fewer of them in the authorised version. Phyllis Lambert will have earned herself a place in it, doubly, for having insisted that her father hire no less an architect than Mies van der Rohe for his Manhattan flagship, and now for having set up an institution dedicated to the exhibition and study of architecture that already ranks as the third most significant archive of architectural texts and images in the world (following the RIBA and the Avery Library at Columbia University).

"I guess my three-minute life story starts off with the fact that my father wanted a boy when I was born." Phyllis, the second daughter, was followed by two sons, Edgar and Charles, who were "slated for the family firm" and duly took it over. What was her involvement with the Seagram business? "Zero." It's one of those clipped responses that reveals as much as it conceals.

As a young girl, Phyllis realised that she was unwilling to conform to her family's expectations: "I was meant to marry, a rich man, a man of substance, and have a nice family and do good works. I hated it. Hated it all. Being Lady Bountiful's not me." But in fact, marriage—albeit short-lived—proved an effective means of escape. A graduate of Vassar, the all-women's college where she had majored in American Culture, Phyllis married the Frenchman Jean Lambert in 1949 aged twenty-two. "I just found the whole thing appalling," she says of her three years as a society hostess based in New York and Paris. She wanted only to go to Paris to paint and sculpt (a passion since childhood) but "my parents wouldn't hear of it." When the marriage broke up, her father's rebuke was severe. "He said, 'You're not just divorcing your husband; you're divorcing the whole family.' I said, 'That's quite right.' But I was a married woman, and no one could tell me what to do anymore."

The following few years in Europe were a period of great emancipation. But the arrival of a letter from her father containing a clipping from *Time* magazine about the plot he was proposing to build on in Park Avenue changed all that. Suddenly her energies were focused.

"I wrote my father a massive letter. The basic message was that when a person makes a decision to build a building, they are making a decision that affects everyone in the city, not just the people who work in that building. You have a great responsibility, and if you don't want that responsibility you should go into somebody else's building and just rent it."

Her father, no doubt impressed by her zeal, but also— as she sees it—sensing a way of luring her back to North America, gave her the task of selecting the architect. She asked for six weeks to choose, consulted Lewis Mumford and Philip Johnson at the Museum of Modern Art, and rapidly came down to two serious contenders: Mies and Le Corbusier. How did she make her decision? "I couldn't see a Le Corbusier building on Park Avenue. He was much too personal. But when I went to Chicago and saw Mies's Lake Shore Drive apartments—*black*," she stresses with relish, "*ugly*, powerful, and clear, I just thought they were marvellous!"

————

Phyllis Lambert herself later qualified as an architect, setting up a practice in Toronto—"I didn't go back to Montreal till my father died," she adds pointedly. She declined to have anything to do with the family's development firm, Cadillac Fairview, beyond an advisory role on a few projects, ensuring, for example, that Mies was the architect for the Toronto Dominion Center. Becoming disillusioned with her own attempts to design periphery shopping centres, she moved to Montreal and began photographing greystone buildings there. It was the beginning of a passionate involvement with her native city, spanning from the championing of a six-block area called Milton Park against redevelopment to her founding of the CCA in 1979. It is hard not to see these activities—especially the latter—as the Return of the Prodigal Son. Or, in this case, Daughter.

Phyllis Lambert describes herself as "mostly interested in the city, and how buildings relate to the city. I'm concerned with how you make whole sections of the city work, not with how to invent a new skin or a new form. What matters is whether a building works well in its environment—whether it cuts corners or reinforces the street line, how it relates to the buildings beside it, what kind and height of entry it has, where the cornice line and floor lines are."

She sees her role since the 1970s as having been a kind of urban conscience, drawing attention to the calamitous consequences of overdevelopment. "The basic problem is that by raising land values, you start making land so expensive that small shops and low-income housing are squeezed out. You start a cycle of deterioration, and you lose the diversity of use in the city." Is that something architects can have any bearing on? "No, they're too busy. If you're an architect, the thing you want to do is build. There have to be people outside the process of trying to get commissions, able to affect much larger areas."

This is part of the CCA's broader mission: to make evident the influences at work in the city on intellectual, social, and cultural levels. She takes obvious pleasure in developing the CCA's collection, selecting documents that help to trace the genealogy of ideas. She refers to the plan for Milton Park as "Corbusier mixed with Clarence Stein: you have a pedestrian roadway next to a vehicular roadway. I find Corbusier's Voisin Plan one of the most horrific documents: those huge towers and the street given away to motor vehicles…" Her voice rises to a pitch of indignation, tempered by the collector's rationality: "I love following these perversions of an idea…these undigested theoretical thoughts. It's the same as what's happening with Prince Charles."

"One is not operating under the same conditions as in the 1920s and 1930s, when it was assumed you were going to start all over again. The people I admire are people dealing with the fabric of the city. Léon Krier is certainly very interesting because of his absolute volte-face. John Hejduk is raising fascinating issues and narratives." Rem Koolhaas surfaces more than once in the conversation.

Phyllis Lambert's concern for active street life, for congenial public spaces, for new buildings that enter a neighbourhood and re-establish its strengths, sounds laudable. Against this fervour, however, is set a picture of a rather solitary, younger Phyllis, the one "dreaming of my future and pretending I had no siblings," looking forward impatiently to "getting out from under my family"—perhaps the tightest-knit community she could ever have been a part of.

———

It is telling that for her undergraduate thesis she wrote on Henry James, and why he went abroad. "I guess what interested me was the problem of an American in exile, relating to his or her own culture. That fascinated me because I was an exile in the United States and was deeply attracted to European culture myself."

And what were her conclusions? "The major conclusion was James's deep need for tradition, for the physical touching of stones, for being able to say: 'When I touch Oxford, I feel the hundreds of years of tradition behind them.' He needed that contrast of the innocent American and the complexity of older cultures, of the European society which he adored."

The World According to Mickey

Michael Eisner

Blueprint, February 1991

Michael Eisner, Chairman and CEO of the Walt Disney Company, is the Second Most Powerful Person in Hollywood. So said *US* magazine in its November 1990 special issue on the entertainment industry's "Heavy 100." (The numero uno, in case you're wondering, is Barry Diller, chairman of Fox and Eisner's old boss at Paramount.) Eisner, forty-eight, took the helm at Disney in 1984, joining the company after the failure of a hostile takeover bid by some of Wall Street's most infamous raiders, including Saul Steinberg and Michael Milken. Since then he has presided over a remarkable revival of Disney's fortunes, earning legendary status in "the industry" for his turnaround of Walt's limping legacy, as well as legendary personal remuneration: $40 million in 1988.

Eisner has also turned into one of the largest, and most unlikely, patrons of celebrity architecture in the world. And it is this interest, the fact that he has invited them all—from Michael Graves to Frank Gehry—to participate in the Disney dream, that summoned me to Burbank, in the smog-wreathed valley north of the Hollywood Hills, where the Disney lot is set. Street signs of elegant freestanding metal lettering indicate the various departments on the leafy production campus. Past the topiary Mickey Mouse and the Mickey Mouse mailbox on Dopey Drive, you find the Animation building, built in Walt's time to a double H plan which maximised north light for the studio's principal artistic talent. Just beyond it, a long reflecting pool and double pergola lead the eye through ninety degrees to the front facade of the new headquarters building by Michael Graves, complete with giant-size Seven Dwarf caryatids.

"The Real Michael," as Graves calls his client, arrived from his 8:30 a.m. meeting with the air of someone whose day had long since got underway, sporting a pale blue shirt and maroon tie with Mickey motifs. Well over six feet tall, he has the lanky build of a basketball player and a deceptively cherubic face, at odds with his Daddy Bear voice.

He slapped the desk and asked bluntly what it was I had come to ask. Why, I wondered, was Disney patronising many of the world's leading architects for its headquarters and its theme park developments in California, Florida, and outside Paris?

"First of all, we are NOT 'patronising' architects," Eisner retorted, demonstrating a strategy of sharp rebuttal which would become familiar during the interview. "We are not a royal family, or a government," he continued, at pains to distinguish corporate necessity from monarchic or civic indulgence. "If you build a building, you have to have an architect." Disney's buildings, in his eyes, should be "functional, efficient, and at the same time aesthetically pleasing structures which hopefully are consistent with our business aims."

This emphasis on the functional rather than the symbolic aspects of architecture seemed significant coming from the man who had persuaded Michael Graves to add cartoon characters to his sober neoclassical facade, arguing that without them it looked too much like a bank. I asked him to expand. Functional, he explained, means "that you can find the front door and, in the case of a hotel, that the walks from the elevator to the rooms are not so far that you have cardiac arrest when you get there, and the food is still hot, and the corridors are wide enough for the linen carts."

The hazards of health, a preoccupation of the gut-busting businessman, provide a metaphor worth pursuing. "You can be an absolutely perfect specimen—Jane Fonda'd to death—but if you have high cholesterol and clogged arteries and you drop dead at the fiftieth press-up, the fact that you were a beautiful body is irrelevant. What's on the inside is as important or *more* important than what's on the outside. If it isn't functional and efficient, it's an architectural failure." Struck by his own extemporisation, he gets out a notebook to record the preceding remarks for adaptation in his Annual Report.

We turn to the problem of superficiality, or the art of illusion, whichever you prefer. Eisner recently explained to *Metropolitan Home* how the company achieves desired effects using real materials, like wood, where people can see them, and cheaper imitations where they can't. What is the relationship between architectural depth and surface treatment? "If you're a royal family with an unlimited amount of money, then it's better to use the depth of stone. But if you're building under economic restraints you can shuck and jive, and if you're creative enough you can achieve things in a less costly way. It's often harder, but it brings out more originality." Graves's Team Disney headquarters uses the same rich red schisty stone that Arata Isozaki employed on the LA Museum of Contemporary Art, but only on the first three floors. "People now assume that was intentional, but it was a way of bringing the cost down."

Disney's expansion is taking place on several distinct fronts, reflecting its three-pronged leisure interests. The theme parks and resorts in Anaheim, Orlando, and Tokyo are the company's chief source of revenue: $3,019.5 million in the year ended September 1990, compared with $2,250.3 million for films and television, and $573.7 million from consumer products. The revival of the company's film studio, under Eisner's former Paramount protégé Jeffrey Katzenberg, and the spawning of its adult label, Touchstone Pictures, has also contributed in large measure to the company's growth and consequent need for more corporate accommodation.

Hence the development of the Burbank production campus—the factory at the heart of the empire. Here, Graves's building is just the first of a projected series by star architects, according to a master plan under the supervision of Alexander Cooper, urban planner of Battery Park City and of Donald Trump's once-vaunted Television City in Manhattan. A site is reserved adjacent to Graves's building for an Employee Center designed by Arata Isozaki, and, meanwhile, Isozaki's Team Disney administration building is nearing completion at Walt Disney World in Florida. There also was talk of Aldo Rossi designing a new animation building for another portion of the Burbank campus—as Robert Venturi, Charles Moore, and Stanley Tigerman learned, to their considerable surprise, from Eisner's aforementioned *Metropolitan Home* interview. The three of them had just competed for the same site.

"I read that *Metropolitan Home* article, and I was stunned," says Tigerman. "Bob Venturi likes to give the impression of being an absent-minded professor, but he used language that made me look like Grandma Moses, and I'm more like a Chicago cab driver. Charles Moore sounded causally embittered."

Right now, Eisner says that he is deliberating over whether to hold another competition for six new projects, three in France and three more at Walt Disney World, likely to include further hotels, offices, and convention centres. There are plans to develop Port Disney, a new theme park and resort in Southern California, where the Queen Mary Hotel at Long Beach has been a Disney property since 1988. And rumours have circulated for some time about a fourth "gate" (i.e., paid-entry park attraction) at Walt

Disney World, themed around either live animals or work, in the sense of old-fashioned manufacturing industry—the kind that bit the dust with the rise of the service economy. Still more nebulous at present, but under consideration, is the idea of a Disney residential development, a reworked attempt to create what EPCOT (the Experimental Prototype Community of Tomorrow) was meant to be.

Eisner is obviously very enamoured of architects, and architecture, although his enthusiasm seems to be that of the recent convert: exuberant, omnivorous, and perhaps a trifle indiscriminate. He knows he wants the best and, with a notable exception, the international celebrity architects who have gotten the call have all jumped to attention. So how does Eisner seek out the talent? "We stay aware of what's going on, talk to architects, read magazines like yours. We're in the business of managing creative enterprises. I personally have been managing live entertainment for many years, and I've dealt with directors, writers, movie stars. This group is similar, but they are more polite. Architects are the most polite, gracious and attractive people I've met.

"Euro Disneyland expanded our horizons and we've had to overcome certain preconceptions of what Disney is, which the American architects didn't have any problems with. We're finally getting into a good dialogue with European architects— although we ended up using only one French architect, Antoine Grumbach—and we've spoken to everyone."

James Stirling is the one architect who declined even to participate in the competition for Euro Disneyland. "He was very polite, but probably didn't understand what we're doing," says Eisner. "We'd love to do something with him one day. He's a terrific architect."

Stirling himself remembers "about three phone calls in the space of about two weeks. We're very admiring of Walt Disney's film work, but not the commercial offshoot, Disneyland. It's the theme park thing. The whole of England is a theme park, from Prince Charles to the Changing of the Guard. It was not specifically said, but I imagine there would have been some sort of historical theme: Joan of Arc, the guillotine, or the Revolution. I find it a very demeaning role somehow. Themes which are to do with aesthetics are not usually prescribed. I think *kitsch* is a word I used in the conversation."

Has he ever been to Disneyland? "I must confess I haven't."

———

"Disneyland," it's true, has entered the vernacular as a term denoting pastiche, simulation and (in Europe) all that is superficial and artificial about America. Even there, a certain intellectual snobbery prevails, though perhaps less so among the fellow-travelers of Umberto Eco and Jean Baudrillard. I can remember architecture school juries at Princeton where schemes were shot down for being "Disneyland," no longer a specific place, but a state of mind, a synonym for kitsch. Would Eisner accept that this derogatory image still lingers?

"No," he fairly booms. "Just the opposite," hastening to cite Charles Moore's encomium on Disneyland, "You Have to Pay for the Public Life," published in *Perspecta* in 1965, by way of evidence. "Most architecture critics, city planners, and landscape planners have no sense of the pejorative about Disneyland. It is an extremely intelligent and well-designed model, a kind of definitive urban planning. It's a people place." What exactly does that mean? "A place for people to interrelate, have a sense of closeness, pleasantness, like the great European cities. I feel similar walking through Siena as I do through Disneyland." He is completely in earnest, and goes on to describe the radial plan (not exactly a brand-new idea in 1955), with its central hub focused on Cinderella's Castle, which acts as an icon drawing visitors up Main Street.

With Euro Disneyland based at Marne-la-Vallée, close to one of Ricardo Bofill's new-town schemes, does he see any underlying similarity between the two developments? "No, they're hundreds of kilometres apart," he laughs, stretching his arms wide, and sinking back into his executive chair. Again his critique is based on practicalities, like transport access, rather than stylistic or urbanistic qualities.

"I believe Euro Disney is a certain kind of new town, but we think about what it's like when you get there, and how you get to it from the RER [the Parisian metropolitan railway, which is being extended to Euro Disney's front step]. You have to start with how people feel against these architectural 'scapes. What is the arrival sequence? How far is the walk from the parking structure to the main gate? What will it be like to see Frank Gehry's Entertainment Center and the buildings next to it? I think of that same journey when I go back to my own house." This perception of space as a linear sequence of events—like frames in a three-dimensional movie—is telling.

Evidently the idea of the journey preoccupies him, for he suddenly switches tack. "If you go by fifty homeless people in the gutter and don't see them and react to them, then you're ignoring your own environment." To what extent is Disneyland a model of urbanism, then, if it so patently excludes the real traumas of the modern city? "Architecture and city planning has to be aware of these problems, but we are not a government, we're not building middle-income housing, and hospitals, and schools. There's too much outside our control. Obviously there's no homelessness in Disneyland. We don't deal with social problems. Maybe Disneyland *is* an idealised version of the city," he concedes.

With its quaint "futuristic" conveyances, happy pedestrians, orderly queueing, and Autopia miniature car rides instead of clogged, smoggy freeways, the original Disneyland now functions as the perfect antidote to the dystopia of greater Los Angeles in which it is embedded. So does it engender a false sense of security? "No, it's a *real* sense of security. You have to remember that when Disneyland was built, LA was not what it is today." Eisner points out that, thirty-five years ago, the Anaheim site was surrounded by strawberry fields and orange groves. But, pressed further, he admits that Disneyland really refers to a halcyon past more imagined than real. "I'm not sure the world was ever like that. I have to assume that the idyllic towns from [Henry] Fielding's novels or American remembrances of New England never really existed. Perhaps there never was and maybe never will be a Disneyland. But we like to think we can walk down Main Street and not have to hold onto our purses, and that if gun control came in, crime would no longer exist."

The issue of history becomes far more heightened as Disney ventures into the Old World. The Paris project will put to the test many of the European preconceptions about Disney and, by extension, America. Eisner takes the issue of cultural imperialism by the horns, and even begins to sound as if he's been consulting Kenneth Frampton's writings on critical regionalism. "American exported culture is suspect. Most countries have their indigenous motion pictures and their American motion pictures, and they're pretty equal. They have their indigenous music and their American music. They no longer have their indigenous cars and their American cars—they have their indigenous cars and their Japanese cars. Times have changed. America has been educating a pretty good group of architects for the last twenty years, or even longer, and they're getting along with Japanese and European architects. It's becoming one community now, more than ever before, but that's both good and bad. It's good in that architects from anywhere can work anywhere, but it's bad in that there seems to be no indigenous style any more. Every city you go to seems so much the same. There is no regionalism."

This seems a curious lament from the chairman of a company which is in the very process of furthering the confusion about local identity by transplanting a series of American regional vernaculars, in the form of themed hotels, to the outskirts of Paris. "We're certainly not transplanting them exactly, but in a modern, or a more...emotional way." It might be argued that part of the reason for the perceived loss of regional identity is the very ease with which specific places can be replicated and experienced secondhand, through images, films, and physical reenactments, such as the World Showcase at the EPCOT Center.

Consider three New Yorks in the life of Michael Eisner: the one he actually grew up in, living on the Upper East Side; the New York backlot at the Disney-MGM Studios theme park in Orlando, Florida, which he describes as "a Hollywood environment, if anything, a Mexican-Spanish sunbelt and stucco glitz simulation of New York where it doesn't rain"; and the forthcoming Hotel New York, Marne-la-Vallée, France, which he says is "Michael Graves's quasi-expressionistic view of the New York cityspace." What is the difference between the real thing and the replicas, especially for those visitors to Euro Disneyland who have never crossed the Atlantic? "They're just not related," he says, a touch gruffly. "Everyone will have seen an image of New York. There will be people who look at this hotel and immediately get that it's New York." But how does the deliberate physical re-creation of a city based only on a received impression affect people's perception of the original? "I don't know," he says, refusing to take the bait. "It just seemed like a fun thing to do at the time. We're going to deliver to people coming to Euro Disneyland an expressionistic view of New York, and one of the Northwest, and one of the Southwest, and one of Newport Bay, and a bit of Frank Gehry on top, and then mix a lot of Walt Disney into it, and hopefully we'll end up with a whole that is diverse, and complicated, and interesting."

Perhaps it is too early to judge whether Euro Disneyland will be a rich mix or just a mishmash. Does Eisner think that the range of different architects he is employing on neighbouring sites, both at Burbank and Marne-la-Vallée, are stylistically compatible, or do they strike differences which he is actively trying to achieve? "Well, we believe in the melting-pot theory. Being a New Yorker, having lived in German town next to Hungarian town and across the street from Spanish town, I do think there's strength in putting them together. We put them all in the same room, as many as we can get, and make them all help us with our land planning." Meetings of the Disney architectural team have been held in Florida, Paris, and at Eisner's log cabin retreat in Aspen, Colorado (designed by Robert Stern). "We're interested in having them all tell us how stupid we are, not how smart. They always tell us if we're building in the wrong place, if we're not thinking about people, if you can't find the front door, or it's ugly, or it doesn't work. I like to hear it before we build. It's a lot cheaper when you hear it at the plans stage than when you're halfway up the building."

One word permeates all discussion of things Disney, even the new architecture. The old term *parti* now seems to have given way to the *theme*. What exactly does it mean? "It's just a euphemism for what is a design. A cinder block wall is themed to a cinder block wall. A cinder block wall with stucco over it is a different theme. It's a word which has become attributed to us. We never called it a theme park or an amusement park. We called it Disneyland. It's become part of the lexicon. Theming is synonymous with design. The design of this building right here," he says, swinging in his chair to the window, and gesturing to the Graves-designed headquarters, "does have a Southern Californian, Spanish, Mexican, Latin-derivative feeling, in a contemporary sense. With Seven Dwarfs holding up the roof."

Are these two types of iconography not entirely at odds? "No." Couldn't they have used female caryatids, in the classical style? "Yes. But that wouldn't have been as much fun, or as appropriate for Disney." Is there anything he *wouldn't* do, architecturally? "We probably would not do a…er…," he slows, temporarily stumped for an answer. Finally: "We probably would not do a cheap box."

And is he going to use Robert Venturi? Not at the moment, despite the fact that he competed recently for a site at Burbank, where Eisner says neither Venturi's, nor Moore's, nor Tigerman's, nor Rossi's designs will now be built. "What we are now putting in that place are sound stages, because we need them to stay in our business. So I gotta call all of them."

Who will design the sound stages? "They're just boxes." But he just said he doesn't like boxes. "Those are different kinds of boxes. Those are soundstage boxes. Those are not offices." I mention that Venturi was the person who pointed out that boxes have a place in the environment. "Well, if you've been in Walt Disney World, you'll have seen our stages down there, and they are boxes, so I take that back. We may build boxes."

"This Must Be Progress"— The Master of Modernism on God, Graphics, and Other Devotions

Paul Rand

I.D. Magazine, September–October 1993

A living monument of American graphics, Paul Rand turned seventy-nine last month. Age has hardly withered him, nor lessened his legendary feistiness. Built like a bullet with short white hair and a tanned face, there is something about him that reminds one of a sun-ripened coffee bean: a hard nut, seasoned with time, but capable of yielding pungent flavor, even—with sufficient loving care—an addictive mellowness.

———

Talking to Paul Rand over two days in May, shortly after the publication of his third book, *Design, Form, and Chaos*, I could appreciate why one of his clients, Steve Jobs of NeXT Computer, would describe him (in a forthcoming film profile) as having "the exterior of a curmudgeon but a heart of gold." And how he could inspire such contradictory feelings among those who have encountered him during an exceptionally long career as a designer and educator: on the one hand, undying devotion from many former students and colleagues, on the other, a kind of weary resignation—invariably "not for quotation"—on the part of those who regard him as an unreconstructed modernist, rigid in his views and dismissive of new approaches to graphic design.

Now professor emeritus at Yale University, Rand continues to work solo, as he has done for some thirty years, from a studio at his home in Weston, Connecticut. Here, under a bright-red Le Corbusier–inspired skylight, illuminating a long wooden desk, the dialogue begins.

If I had been looking forward to a friendly chat about some of the ideas in Rand's new book, I was in for a surprise. After only a few minutes it becomes clear that his conversational style and writing style are two entirely different things. Face-to-face conversation is like a boxing match, with swift jabs back and forth. Rand doesn't suffer fools gladly, and those who try to engage him in debate had better be prepared for tough combat. Slight deafness tends to exacerbate a characteristic gruffness, and his tone becomes thoroughly stentorian when you cross him, with firm thumps to the table supplied for emphasis. Rand bluntly repeats the terms of enquiry when he prefers not to answer, frequently asserts that "it's obvious" until pressed to offer elucidation of a given point, and, when push comes to shove, throws back: "So, what's the question?" by way of response.

On certain topics, however, his voice abruptly softens, his right hand settles on his right cheek, and you can tell that the curmudgeonly exterior is just defensive armor plating to a vulnerable, even endearing, core. Often, he'll finish sentences with a sort of schoolboy chuckle, a mischievous wheeze of amusement—sometimes denoting self-deprecation, sometimes egging on the questioner to take up a particularly egregious challenge. Ten minutes into the interview, he decides to call it off; an hour and a half later, he's suggesting we meet again the following day to carry on the conversation, which we duly do, this time on the beach a few miles from his home.

Readers must use their imagination to identify his bêtes noires, since Rand follows up his more unbuttoned flourishes with instructions that the foregoing remarks are not for publication. Suffice it to say that Armin Hofmann, and London-based designers Abram Games, Derek Birdsall, and the late Hans Schleger figure highly in his pantheon of admired associates; former students Lorraine Wild (now teaching at CalArts) and Sheila Levrant de Bretteville (current head of graphics at Yale) do not. Though he was on the Yale faculty from 1961 to 1992, Rand resigned shortly after de Bretteville took up her appointment and professes disdain for academia and its denizens. (He still teaches the first week at Brissago, Yale's summer school in Switzerland.)

But he reserves his greatest scorn for design critics and theorists, because they take things "literally" and lack hands-on experience of the process of design; on the scale of things, they are scarcely higher than the marketing executives who come in for a drubbing in his essay "Good Design is Goodwill," the first in his new book. "People who write about art and are not artists are very suspect in my library," he remarks.

In contrast to his pugnacious spoken persona, Rand's own essays are lucid and eloquent, larded with references from Vasari to Bacardi by way of the Brothers James and Alfred North Whitehead. On closer examination, they are also studded with arbitrary value judgments passing for objective analysis, and statements that might be considered merely sententious if they did not happen to issue from one of the *grands seigneurs* of graphic design.

Nevertheless, the carefully hewn prose is obviously the fruit of long cogitation. On the dashboard of Rand's gray BMW a small notepad is fixed at the ready for any passing pensée: its front sheet currently declares "Depends on the context" in slightly jerky, on-the-move pencil script, an insight he mentions is destined for his next book.

In consistently reflecting on his own work, starting with *Thoughts on Design* of 1947, Rand is one of the few practitioners to have seriously attempted to codify a theoretical position, and his writings have served to consolidate his reputation. Yet he is not necessarily willing to discuss his ideas, once committed to print, still less to acknowledge differences of opinion. "This is very serious stuff," he tells me later. "I don't write for your benefit. I'm writing for myself, to understand. The by-product is a book for other people."

Over the years, Rand has worked in magazines and advertising, as well as on corporate identity programs, producing benchmark logos for IBM, ABC television, and UPS (United Parcel Service). At the precocious age of twenty-three he was art director of *Esquire* magazine, which he left in 1940 to join Elkan Kaufman and William Weintraub in a new advertising agency, launched with funds from Weintraub's sale of his 50 percent interest in *Esquire*. Rand clearly relished the variety and hectic pace at the agency, where jobs often had to be executed in a matter of hours for the following day's publication. "It's good experience to work fast and efficiently. That's the thing about design—or art: you have to have your hand in it, or you lose the immediacy of good work, which is what makes the job pleasant."

During the next fourteen years, Rand produced some of his most memorable advertising designs, for El Producto cigars, Dubonnet, Ancient Age, and Disney (the other Disney) hatmakers. He also turned out a prolific assortment of book jackets and magazine covers, perhaps the most celebrated being those for *Direction*, from 1938 to 1945. Identities for Cummins, The Limited, IDEO, and NeXT are all documented in Rand's new book, and he continues to design posters for various institutions.

The later, pared-down Rand typically deploys figurative and geometric forms in a bright paintbox palette on a simple white plane, or plays photographic and typographic elements against each other to produce a visual pun. To an eye acclimated to the work of younger designers, whose experiments he finds so dismaying, Rand's recent work is tempered, but in its restrained formal clarity, sometimes leaves one wishing for more.

On the Sunday just prior to our meeting, the *New York Times* had carried not only design historian Victor Margolin's review of *Design, Form, and Chaos*, but also an op-ed piece by Rand on why, as he so delicately puts it to me, "corporate design stinks." In it, he basically bemoans the absence of great corporate design programs in contemporary America—the kind in which he had been involved at IBM and Westinghouse—and argues that this is due to a lack of great business leaders as well as of good designers. The brief duration of such programs "is no evidence that design is impotent. What is evident is that somebody is not minding the store, and that management does not really appreciate the contribution that design (art) can make, socially, aesthetically, and economically."

Rand's article inadvertently invites us to consider the role played by the all-powerful paternalistic company chairman—an oft-celebrated, if rare, species—whose obsessive passion for order and identity tends to have been a prerequisite for noteworthy corporate design. But which comes first: the design program that makes a company look organized, coherent, and impressive (when it may be a managerial shambles), or the corporate culture that merits such representation? Lamenting the lack of good design programs seems a bit like looking through the wrong end of the telescope. I put it to Rand that surely what's actually at stake has less to do with design per se than with the transformation of American culture in the years since companies like IBM rose to become unassailable benchmarks of white-collar capitalism. Rand is quiet for a few moments. Then, having sized me up, he begins an oration. "The questions you are asking me are unanswerable. It's like asking 'what is art?'"

That was going to be my next question.

"Oh, I know what it is. Art is an idea that has found its perfect visual expression. And design is the vehicle by which this expression is made possible. Art is a noun, and design is a noun and also a verb. Art is a product and design is a process. Design is the foundation of all the arts."

A splenetic outburst about Victor Margolin follows.

"The review of my book was written by an academe character, not a practicing artist. He makes absolutely irresponsible statements about me at the end of the essay: that I'm not interested in social things and that it's too bad I'm not interested in the latest stuff. He's dead wrong. I could flunk this guy in two minutes on a design history test."

What would you ask him?

"I would ask him things that he doesn't know. Listen, I've lectured to Germans in Berlin about German design. Things they knew nothing about."

Fortunately, the tirade is interrupted by a phone call.

Rand returns, and resumes: "See, my life is what I do. When people start picking on me I get very angry. And to be accused publicly of not being interested in social issues is an outrage."

I discern that I have, unwittingly, aroused his wrath.

"The very fact that this guy gave me a good review then starts criticizing me means that he doesn't know what he's talking about. It's completely untrue what he's saying, because he doesn't read things properly."

I read out loud the offending section of the review, in which, in fact, Margolin has taken exemplary care to present Rand's position accurately. Far from misrepresenting him, Margolin has merely stepped on his Achilles' heel. "Part of the problem, he believes," writes Margolin, "is that design classrooms have been turned into forums for social and political issues."

"Absolutely," Rand confirms. "And it's the reason I left Yale. I resigned."

———

Turning to what I hope will be a less inflammatory topic, I ask Rand what he thought of Thomas Watson Jr., whom he credits in his op-ed piece with having "almost single-handedly put the IBM design program to work." The tactic proves effective. Rand immediately softens. "This guy was the reverse of Jefferson's definition that 'All men are created equal,'" he chuckles. "This guy was not created equal: Thomas Watson was handsome, rich, tall, and bright. Still is. He's my age, maybe a couple of months older."

Presumably he worked quite closely with Watson?

"No...I don't know much about him. I would see him, you know, in the hallway. I had dinner once at his house on the occasion of his giving Eliot Noyes and Charles Eames and me a trophy."

Convinced of the importance of access to the company chairman, Rand has actually forfeited work rather than deal with underlings—or rather Marion Swannie, who runs his business, has done so. (Rand's second wife, known affectionately as Swan, was manager of design at IBM for thirty years, relinquishing the post when they got married. "Her department would pay us but the work came from the different divisions. She never used her influence for me. In fact, I got ten times as much work after she left the company.")

During the late 1980s, in one of the country's most fascinating outbreaks of mass superstition, rumors began to circulate that Procter & Gamble's century-old logo, comprising a Man in the Moon and thirteen stars, was a coded sign for the devil. "Two people from Procter & Gamble came to me because they were having problems with their logo. My wife wrote these guys and said, 'We don't deal with anybody unless he's the CEO.' She just gave up the job. We know that in order to get anything done, you have to deal with the top guy."

Rand has a simple template for what makes a good client: they don't interfere, don't tell you what to do, and appreciate whatever the designer proposes without questioning it. So much for the ideal situation, with a hotline to the top. "Most clients are nice clients. It's the people in between who give you the problems: the account executives, the marketing people. They destroy people's work: 'This should be bigger, this should be up here, there should be a sun here with a price.' What else have they got to show for their accomplishments? If they don't change your work, all they can say is you've done a good job. It's much more convincing to show something graphic!"

Another noteworthy aspect of Rand's relationship with his clients is his fee structure. His compensation has entered graphic-design mythology; he is said to have commanded more than $100,000 for doing the NeXT logo. While he insists that he has no interest in the financial side of life ("My wife is the money girl in this family; if I need money I have to ask her"), Rand is nevertheless attuned to his own market value. "When somebody pays me a lot of money, he's not doing so because he likes to. He pays me because this is what I deserve."

How much would he have charged for doing a new logo for P&G? I wondered.

"One or two hundred thousand."

And what do you actually buy with that?

"You buy a logo. I write a brochure, go through the steps, like in the book. That's the market value: what studios get, though some get $300,000."

What's the fee measured on?

"It's measured on nothing. If it takes me an hour, I do it in an hour. If it takes me a year, it takes me a year. I don't work on time. You give me the problem, I let the idea come. Most of the time, it's immediate. I don't start making sketches—that throws you."

No second thoughts?

"Very rarely."

On occasion, however, Rand has looked back and seen fit to revise a design, as with the logo for UPS, originally created in just one week in 1961. "I offered to make some modest changes," he explains, "to make it right. I changed the bow and the drawing of the P. It wasn't right before. If there's something wrong with the drawing, then you change it." But UPS stood firm, and declined. "They didn't give any reasons. They just said no."

It would be quite far-reaching and costly to implement such a change, given the extensive applications—surely something of an indulgence unless the company had undergone managerial changes that it wished to express visually.

"It's not far-reaching to change the shape of a bow. Nobody would notice it."

Then why bother doing it?

"Because it bothers me. Just as much as it bothered my mother not to clean above a molding that you didn't see. It's just not right."

———

One of the more intriguing aspects of Rand's life is how this son of a Viennese immigrant fabric cutter, brought up in a very poor, strictly orthodox Jewish household, turned out to be the graven-image maker to *echt*-WASP America in its most institutional form: the great corporations of the '50s and '60s. Born and bred in Brownsville, Brooklyn, Rand had an older sister and a twin brother who became a professional jazz musician, playing sax and clarinet. "Guy Lombardo!" Rand chuckles, recalling the kind of music he played. Then, in an undertone, "He's gone…killed in an accident. She died years ago. My family's gone. Everybody's… dead." A few more sentences pass between us, and the mood has grown suddenly so poignant I can hardly hold back tears. "It's sad," he concedes, and at such moments one cannot but forgive this man his usual hectoring manner.

Though he is at pains to keep his observances a private matter, he is clearly a devoutly religious man. On each of our two days of conversation, he thrusts his left arm toward me, proud to show the impression of his *tefillin*, the ritual leather straps (which hold a box containing verses from the Torah) bound around a man's arm for daily morning prayers. It is hard to resist making a connection between his deeply held religious tenets and the strength of his commitment to orthodox modernism: both rigorous systems of belief, each in their way strivings toward a kind of mortal perfection. When I asked him how he chose to become a designer, his answer was unequivocal: "I didn't choose, God chose." There is no trace of guile when he explains that he performs these rituals "because I want to. Because I think God is more important than I am. It's important to be modest in the world. To think there's somebody who is better than we are, and more significant. Right?"

A major portion of our first meeting is taken up with discussing the importance of doing pro bono work and donating to charity. He relates at some length, and in his customarily pugnacious storytelling mode, the occasion when he was moved to give his copier-machine repair man several thousand dollars to help bring the latter's family out of the Soviet Union. "And I didn't even know this guy." I remark that his gesture seems very generous. But he's off again.

"This is a social issue, right? Or is it not? It has nothing whatsoever to do with design. Design issues are form and content and proportion. And color. And texture. And scale. You can't say any of these things about social issues. Design can help elucidate or explain social issues. Social issues are not design issues, though the visual arts have done a hell of a lot for social issues. They're two separate things, as different as milk and corn beef." (And as we know from the scriptures, "Thou shalt not seethe a kid in its mother's milk.")

It's not that Rand isn't interested in social issues. Rather, he has made his own decisions about which ones matter to him, and attends to them in his own, sometimes narrowly focused, idiosyncratic way. And he vehemently rejects what he sees as the corruption of design education—that is, as he conceives it and practiced it at Yale. "They don't teach design because they don't understand what design is. They'll give you a poster to do, let's say, for some social issue and they consider that teaching design."

OK. So if we accept that design issues are only form and content…

"That's all they are. They're never anything else."

…then, what if the *content* of the poster is a social issue?

"Then…then…Then the designer deals with it. He uses the power of design to express the social issue."

———

Hoping to steer back to safer ground, I ask which pieces of work he's most pleased with, meaning, of course, his own work. The answer, needless to say, is indirect.

"I don't know. If I'd done this"—he points toward a lively abstract print by Henryk Tomaszewski on the wall behind me—"I'd probably be most pleased. I'm going to use it in my next book as an example. I think it's terrific."

Why?

"Here, I have this little note and I was going to print it." He rummages on the desk for a scrap of paper, then reads aloud: "Better to be silent and have folks think you are a fool than to speak and remove all doubt."

He looks up. "If I start talking about it, then maybe I'd better not. I think it's obvious."

But what's obvious? *Why* is it terrific?

"The colors. They happen to be the colors I always use, red and green. The way it's done. The idea, which is very expressive of circus activities…calisthenics, twirling and twisting. This child-like quality that it has. Not child*ish*. The distinction is tremendous. It has all the good qualities that children have: honesty, spontaneity. Most people who try to imitate that kind of stuff do lousy drawings, rather than understanding the spirit of childlike drawings, I mean, as in [Paul] Klee, [Pablo] Picasso, [Joan] Miró. Picasso said about Miró that he ought to stop playing with his hoop. In other words, grow up. But I think Miró was a genius, as was Picasso."

For Rand, as for his heroes, childhood creativity is still vivid. "I always drew. Since I was a little kid—three or four years old. During the First World War. I used to use a chair as a drawing table. I'd sit on a little tiny stool or on my knees, and draw soldiers and trenches and photographs. My education was mostly from books and magazines, not from teachers. I used to be so admiring of people, I would stand in the rain, I would just stand there *looking*, for hours, in the drugstore, for example, or the gasoline station." Rand studied with George Grosz for a while when the German artist first came here, at the Art Students League. "He didn't even speak English. He would say a few simple words. But design I just picked up. From libraries, bookshops. From magazines. German magazines."

In "A Mentor" (on the typographer Jan Tschichold), Rand mentions the initial "indifference or outright hostility" that greeted painters, architects, and designers of the modern period, before their work became recognized and subsequently acclaimed. Yet, in "Cassandre to Chaos"—the most indignant and bare-knuckled of the essays in his new book—he fulminates against (unspecified) designers who are experimenting with formal vocabularies and production technology. This "bevy of depressing images… collage of chaos and confusion…art deco rip-offs…sleazy textures…indecipherable, zany typography" is mostly "confined to pro-bono work, small boutiques, fledgling studios, trendy publishers, misguided educational institutions, anxious graphic arts associations and a few innocent paper manufacturers comforted by the illusion that this must be progress." But such rhetoric puts him at risk of proving as blind to innovation as were the critics of his early twentieth-century heroes. Isn't he being a bit harsh toward today's young innovators?

"I don't consider these 'young innovators' innovators. I consider them a pack of undisciplined gibberish. I'm not going to mention any names…mostly posters for the AIGA and crap like that. The difference is a difference of talent. These people are untalented people."

How does he measure talent?

"By looking."

That, I find, is a rather haughty position.

"Well, I'm haughty."

It's potentially a very unpleasant attitude.

"I know it is, but that's the way it is. I've been doing it sixty, seventy years. I am the judge of a good designer. I don't consider myself an old fuddy-duddy. I haven't changed my mind about things and I don't consider it a weakness. I'll debate with people that I respect and do good work, and if I think their work is lousy I want nothing to do with it because we don't talk the same language. I have my track record. If you like it, fine. If you don't like it, that's too bad. I expect a certain kind of respect from people. Not only because I'm a great designer—which is not my opinion, this is the *world's* opinion. But because I'm older than you are. You question me in a way which elicits a doubt. What did you major in—psychology?"

I smile. We sit across from each other in silence, enjoying a temporary ceasefire. Despite his vexatious and, by his own declaration, "impatient" mien, I have to admit I'm warming to this guy.

I can imagine why his students—especially the one who, according to Yale lore, once punched Rand on the nose after a particularly fractious crit—would never forget him. From time to time it's crossed my mind that perhaps Paul Rand has no sense of humor. But actually he does; it just takes patience. Just then, he pipes up.

"See, I know what your problem is. You lack humor. That's your problem. You take things too seriously. Le Corbusier—you know who he was? He said that to me. He said, 'Young man, you're much too serious.' So I can say it you."

We're made for each other…

———

Returning to Manhattan after our second meeting, I catch a serendipitous image through the train window: a huge parking lot in which dozens of UPS delivery vans stand in serried ranks, like mechanical cows in a paddock, presumably a distribution hub. There is Rand's logo, multiplied dozens of times, receding into the distance—a cattle brand on each van's haunch. I'm forced to think afresh about the design, to *notice* rather than merely perceive it out of the corner of my eye, a reliable motif for a ubiquitous service. The dark brown livery, the spindly lower-case letter forms, the grace note of the bow: altogether the identity looks dated, a vestige of another era, that age of men in hats and men in charge. Yet strangely timeless, by now a piece of the visual landscape, a bearing-mark against which America goes about its business. To have been the creator of that symbol must be a very satisfying feeling, a bit like naming a species.

I think about Rand's wish to perfect what has already served quite well for a long while. If it were suddenly changed, even only slightly, the entire edifice of trust that inheres in that arrangement of lines on a surface might suffer a seismic jolt.

Rand would surely enjoy the scene, having extolled (in *A Designer's Art*) the "exciting spectacle of marching soldiers…

neatly arranged flower beds...crowds at football games...rows of methodically placed packages on the grocer's shelf." I think about his appreciation of repetition, with respect both to the arrangement of items in space (that is, as a formal device), and in terms of regular activity—as much in the ritual of daily prayer as in creative practice.

As the train rushes past, I realize what's missing from the UPS logo, and yet scarcely needs adding: that looping signature, like the vapor trail from an aerial acrobatics display, whose free-hand strokes—child*like* but not child*ish*—appear on much of his earlier work. An unmistakable trademark: the artist's guarantee of authenticity.

Woman and Her Symbols

April Greiman
it'snotwhatyouthinkitis
cen'estpascequevouscroyez
arc en rêve centre d'architecture, 1994

The first thing you think about when it comes to April Greiman is technology. A woman in command of all the digital tools of the moment, inventively putting information through the electronic sieve: filtering, distorting, layering, manipulating, until she arrives at a sufficiently dense mesh of imagery to let it stand.

What's less obvious—though it makes perfect sense once the surprise has worn off—is the other side of this pilot-ess of the multimedia mission control: her earthiness, and strong sense of connection to nature and the more mystical aspects of science. "How Californian," I hear you say to yourself. Well, yes. But Los Angeles does that to a person. It's a dreamy kind of place, sultry as well as a touch sinister, and being right out there at the edge of the continent between the ocean and the desert gives it a special charge. (Dreams, we'll come back to dreams...) It's hard to imagine her work blossoming quite the way it has if she was based, say, in New York, where the sky comes presliced into streetwide strips.

Greiman isn't a native Californian but by now has effectively earned that status. Asked where else she might live, she responds with genuine incredulity: "I have no idea." Having worked at the Museum of Modern Art, on the *Taxi Project*, curated by Emilio Ambasz in 1976, she found herself "fed up with New York and pretty sick of MoMA and the politics." Looking around the city for other work, nothing grabbed her interest. "It was all packaging, corporate identity, signage, and I didn't want to specialise."

Her move to LA in 1976 was "accidental"—she came out to visit friends and got hooked on the Southern California landscape. The relocation enabled her to develop her own blend of work outside of the categories by which US graphic design was then recognised; desktop computer technologies were just about to enter the market, and Greiman was among the first to recognize their potential for the integration of different media.

"When I came here in the late seventies it was really a cow town, unexplored territory. The bad thing about LA was that it had no tradition. The good thing about LA was also that it had no tradition." She acknowledges the presence of the hi-tech and entertainment industries as important background influences, although she is scathing about the latter. "It's a sleazy industry. They steal your ideas, work you to death, don't keep agreements, and don't return your calls," she says with the tone of someone once bitten, twice shy; thus far, she hasn't done so much as an album cover. But there were definite advantages to being in Tinsel Town.

Everyone who comes to LA notices the curious quality of the light: often smog-filtered and restive, but sometimes (especially after rainfall) possessed of a hallucinogenic clarity. The vibrancy of LA's visual spectrum had an immediate impact on Greiman's early New Wave work. "There were three color palettes that really bowled me over when I got to LA: the Asian, that is, the look of Little Tokyo; the Latino/Hispanic, with its pink, turquoise, and intense yellow; and the desert, with its very subtle colors. The desert palette really turned me around."

LA's proximity to the desert—Joshua Tree only two and a half hours' drive east, the great expanses of Death Valley and Arizona a day's drive away—has been a very significant influence on her work, in terms of tonality, the use of texture gradients to suggest depth on a two-dimensional surface, and the wide vista.

"The desert is so mind-blowing in terms of scale," Greiman declares. "It's just you and your electrons, you being part of the universe again. When you're at your workstation, you *are* the world. You're tied to your box in your corner, in three square feet. Whereas in Death Valley, or Monument Valley, you're like...a speck." Then there's the silence, in contrast to the necessary hubbub of the office, "where there's lots of energy and lots of other bodies around. The desert is one of the few places I've found I'm comfortable being by myself, simply reading, drawing, sleeping, or driving around." Nonetheless, since meeting architect Michael Rotondi—her Significant Other for the last few years—Greiman has gone on many such forays *à deux*. "It seems we've spent a lot of our creative juices being out there shooting things."

An early adopter of new technologies, Greiman was quick to recognise the potential of the Kodak stretch camera (as its disposable panoramic was originally known) to capture what she calls "the big view," and use its elongated proportions to harness the grandeur of natural landscape. The menus for Nicola restaurant in downtown LA (a recent project in collaboration with Rotondi) feature gorgeous panoramic shots of a garden, the ocean, and Death Valley's luminous ochre soil.

Vastness versus the confined four corners of the screen: the issue of mutable scale runs through the body of Greiman's work. Her portfolio runs from business cards to billboard-size images. In the giant-size posters for the Southern California Institute of Architecture (SCI-Arc), the promotional poster for Pike's Peak large-sheet printers (measuring 44" by 65", but bearing its gleeful promise: *soon to be 54 ½" by 77"!*), the 80-foot-long billboard for the *Graphic Design in America* exhibition, and the life-size, not-quite-centerfold nude self-portrait for the Walker Art Center's *Design Quarterly* (treated as a single concertina sheet, 6 feet in length, instead of the usual stitched magazine), we see her reaching for the physicality of actual dimension, perhaps in response to the infinite choice of scale offered by the Macintosh computer.

Using the Mac's thumbnail command, a whole design layout can be shown in miniature for appraisal (a scale at which text is reduced to illegible shaded blocks), and yet the same image can be progressively enlarged until not just the individual letters, but even the bitmapped fragments of which they are composed can be blown up to display their own discrete essence. Greiman's interest in fractal geometry is not surprising, given her daily exposure to such exponential shifts. "In fractal theory, the more deeply you go into a subject, the more the part indicates the whole, and likewise, from the most finite element, you can project out the whole. The pixel is like the DNA of the electronic world."

————

Surveying her work, one can't help observing a likeness between the graphic pixel and the individual stitch of a Navajo rug, that unit of measure which builds in ziggurat formation to create larger patterns, wholes out of integers. It is strange to look at an electronically reproduced image, and see in it the vestiges of something so handmade, so textile, but the parallel is unmistakable. And not inappropriate. Greiman has had a long-standing interest in the arts and culture of the Native Americans. "[Carl] Jung's *Memories, Dreams, Reflections* is what first got me into indigenous culture, and to understanding the American Indian approach of thinking with your heart." In her most recently completed work, collaborating with architect Barton Myers on the Cerritos Center for the Performing Arts, in California, the patterns she has devised for the roof tiles and various interior surfaces are like escapees from the screen, dancing under the changing light, shimmering warp and weft.

Asked what have been the principal developments in her work since the publication of *Hybrid Imagery* in 1990, she points to the changes that have occurred with graphics technology. "Six years ago, we used to go out and rent the equipment to complete the process at the level I was used to"—Quantel Paintboxes and other exorbitant gadgets, running $500 to $700 per hour for rental. "Now it's here on my desk. Traditionally, the way you proceed in graphic design is very linear: you make your sketches, take your photos, set out your type. With video, sound, and motion, the whole process is much more fluid. It has its own architecture. You watch it build in front of you. Very often I'll see an image that implies space, three dimensionally, and I'll just take a 'snapshot,'" using the command of that name on the Mac. "This process really breaks down categories. It really allows us to shift paradigms. The creative process isn't controlled from the top down like television."

Greiman's aptitude for technology is probably something that runs in the family: it turns out that her father, John, has been in the computer sciences for forty years, and she describes her only sibling, fondly, as "a genius." Trained as an accountant, her father was an early computer programmer who set up the first mini-computers for Technicolor and Warner Brothers. Meanwhile, her brother, Paul, is a leading meteorologist, working for the government "diagramming out the universe," as she puts it. A child prodigy, he had already published learned papers at the age of ten. "As a child, I remember we had every kind of weather forecasting equipment on the roof."

The last few years have been marked not just by technological but also personal change. Greiman's relationship with Rotondi has been a catalyst for new areas of work, providing an opportunity to expand into literal (as opposed to illusory) three dimensions. Formerly one of the partners in the celebrated LA architecture practice Morphosis, Rotondi went solo and set up under his own name around the time he and Greiman met. As Director of SCI-Arc, he is ringmaster of LA's most vivacious and helter-skelter architecture school. Greiman's designs for SCI-Arc literature, including bulletins and program announcements, have given the school a graphic identity congruent with its radical reputation. Her latest project, a school brochure, features a hole punched right through its thirty-two pages, a graphic confirmation of the center-spread statement that "Architecture can punch a hole in your sky."

———

Lately, she has found herself reading a lot about the overlap between science and spirituality; hitherto, growing up in a science-oriented household had made her "stay away from all that." She and Rotondi share an interest in Taoism and Zen Buddhism, and they're more apt to launch into a conversation about chaos theory, psychology, or neurobiology than about the latest activities of fellow designers. Operating from adjacent buildings in downtown LA, connected by a catwalk, they feed each other ideas, and increasingly work together in a way that's reminiscent of that earlier LA partnership of Charles and Ray Eames.

"Once a day, one of us goes back and forth between the buildings. It's more of a spiritual collaboration. We have a conceptual compatibility. It's not like we sit down in a meeting. On Nicola, I was in from the beginning, picking the color palette and materials" she says, describing her role in designing the new restaurant for Larry Nicola in the Sanwa Bank Building in downtown LA, for which Rotondi is the architect. "It was obvious that one day I'd get involved in three dimensions, because I've always treated the page as a three-dimensional space."

So it's appropriate that Greiman is now getting commissioned to undertake multimedia projects. She's just beginning work on designing the interface for interactive CD-ROMs being produced by a Honolulu-based company for NASA and the Smithsonian Institution. Though the project is at an early stage, she reveals that one of the titles will be created by the digital artist Tom Van Sant, and is "a bit like the Eames's *Powers of Ten*," allowing the user to zoom in to different aerial views of the earth.

Greiman is unimpressed by the majority of current multimedia titles. "The people who are putting them together tend to be from engineering. They're mostly coming out from nerds who know nothing about typography. People are treating the multimedia interface like *pages*," she says, exasperatedly, "instead of trying to get 3D and motion, more like a movie."

———

Commissioned to produce five- or ten-second station-identification spots for *Lifetime*, the New York cable television station, Greiman demonstrated her commitment to using low-end equipment so as to extract the maximum creative potential from minimum funds. "We took the pitiful budget and instead of spending it on postproduction, we used an 8 mm handicam, shot on my shoulder, and Kodak disposable cameras." The cheap color prints were scanned into the computer, and manipulated via various Mac programs. One of the most beautiful spots, entitled *Yucca* after the native plant, dances before your eyes: a pan of the landscape, slightly out of focus, shot from a moving car, swirls before the viewer, in the blazing greens and blues of desert foliage and mountains. Meanwhile, in the center of the screen, within a separate box (containing the channel's initial L), a sequence of rock formations glides counterclockwise, in bright orange, at a stately pace. The whirling blue of the main picture— objects etched against the sky, yet as if seen through a petroleum jelly haze—has exactly that combination of chromatic lucidity and inspired narrative lunacy that normally occurs in the private screening room of one's subconscious.

——

Greiman's inner life may be even more fecund than the images she brings into tangible existence. For fifteen years she has been recording her dream diary in notebooks. "I've got a closetful of books, notations of dreams, epic dreams. I've been a Jungian since art school," she confesses, hesitating a little to talk in detail about dreams and spirituality because "it's too spooky. People confuse it with religion." Yet she takes them seriously. For many years she met once a week to narrate her dreams to a woman who had trained at the Jung Institute, who helped her to interpret their symbolism and the mythic significance of colors.

When Greiman reveals this, you begin to understand the fluid assembly of image types that characterise her posters, the runic presences that people her compositions, the virtual depth of the graphic plane, and the aleatory drift of texture and typography that typify her best work.

Think, then, of her posters as photographs of a slow-moving cloud formation, momentary snapshots of the shifting contents of her mind. Often in her work (especially in the SCI-Arc material), it's as if the words are streaming by, written in evanescent script like the vapor trail of an aircraft, briefly depositing their message before deliquescing into a solid background of the same color or evaporating altogether. Then again, maybe they're smoke rising in the wilderness above a desert campfire (a Coleman stove at Zabriskie Point, Death Valley—one of her annual rituals), concentrated and legible in origin, then magically dissipating into the vastness of the atmosphere.

Gesamtkunstwerk: Coming Home to Rome

Michael Graves

Michael Graves: Designer Monographs 3, 1994

When I first met Michael Graves he was working from an office on Witherspoon Street in Princeton, in a kind of attic above a Chinese restaurant. It was 1982, and I'd flown to the States to interview the "New York Five," find out where they'd each got to, ten years on. Eisenman/Graves/Gwathmey/Hejduk/Meier: their names were like a mantra. Everybody knew about the "white" architects; the lucky ones even owned a copy of *Five Architects*, the bible of their becoming. I've forgotten exactly what we talked about, though I distinctly recall spilling tea down my suit out of sheer nervousness five minutes before Graves entered the conference room. There was a long, possibly staged, interlude during the interview when he took a phone call from fellow-Fiver Peter Eisenman; they are still close buddies even if, by now, aesthetically, further apart than ever. I also recall the atmosphere of the office, the little painted collages that seemed to lurk on the tops of plan chests, the *homely* quality of the space, which was a true atelier, and quite unlike most architects' offices I'd visited thus far.

Graves was in the ascendant. Already known for a number of neo-Corbusian domestic projects in the Princeton vicinity, and "paper projects" like the Fargo-Moorhead Cultural Bridge, he had leapt to attention with the Portland Building, completed in 1982. Its defiantly decorative elevations fired the opening shot in the Great Facade Wars, and the building (which played a cameo role in the movie *Body of Evidence*, 1992) was claimed as the harbinger of postmodernism in architecture. Eleven years later, he is a household name—a rare achievement for an architect anywhere—and the Graves portfolio encompasses buildings in America, Europe, and Japan, plus a wide array of designs from interior furnishings to items of personal adornment. Today, the entire operation (the architecture studio and the affiliated Graves Design) occupies an atmospheric building at 341 Nassau Street, Princeton's leafy main artery, some fifteen minutes' walk east of the Ivy League university campus where Graves has taught for over thirty years.

A designer's own living and working spaces are usually indicative of their personality and design persuasion; in Graves's case, his home and studio are open books of an intense aesthetic sensibility. Where Witherspoon Street was a cozy warren, 341 Nassau Street is a maze, with scuffed flights of wooden stairs and narrow passageways leading up, down, around, and through the many levels of this distinctly uncorporate headquarters. Cased models of recent architecture projects line the walls, prototypes are stacked in the bustling product-design studio, and—adding to the atmosphere of a creative menagerie—Graves's dog is usually to be found padding the hallways. A small building across the street has recently been annexed as a "studio store" (taking cues from one of Graves's best-known clients, the Walt Disney Company), and a branch office is maintained in New York.

Though separate domains, Graves's office and his own home, just around the corner, form a kind of workplace/residence continuum which reminds one of a Palladian agricultural estate. Over the years, he has used his house as a practical laboratory for his own architectural development, much as Frank Lloyd Wright did in his studio-home in Oak Park, or as Frank Gehry has done in

Santa Monica. Documented in Graves's first Rizzoli monograph
as the anonymous "Warehouse, Princeton," but identified in the
subsequent volume as the architect's own residence, the house
and its grounds have undergone gradual transformation from a
simple L-shaped warehouse (built by Italian stonemasons who
were imported to work on the university buildings) to what is by
now a veritable stately home.

A demonstration not only of Graves's taste in architecture
and landscape, it is also a setting for his own domestic artifacts:
light fittings, clocks, picture frames, bowls, chairs are resplen-
dently arrayed in this ultimate show home, a walk-through catalogue of his aesthetic. One is reminded of the Ralph Lauren Polo
store on Madison Avenue—a palazzo of consumption, decorated
and trimmed with all sorts of authentic knickknacks—except
that in this case, it really is a *home*—the dog hair on a rumpled
white-covered armchair in one guest bedroom a rare lapse in perfection, testifying to actual use.

If a detective came to the Graves residence and wanted to
know what kind of a man had lived there, I would point to just
two sets of things. Not the neoclassical paintings, nor the piles
of illustrated books on landscape and architecture, nor the fine
library with tall shelves reaching toward a skylight, nor the Etruscan pots secreted in high niches like the cherished trophies of
some latter-day Sir John Soane. No, I would choose the following
clues: the collection of souvenir Tempiettos and the set of antique
magnifying glasses. Here, condensed as if dream motifs, are
architecture and optical illusion, the miniature and the magni-
fied, the distortions of history and the play of scale. Graves's chief
preoccupations, in talismanic form.

The house, as it has gradually matured, is like a slow-evolving
Polaroid of one man's passion for classicism. It is the coming into
focus of an Italy of the imagination—the place which Graves continues to paint in his "Archaic Landscapes," whence he derives

the crisscrossed tunics of his costume designs, the chiseled letterforms of his graphics, the heavy, medallion-like shapes of his recent jewelry.

It is obvious that the formative experience of Graves's career was the time spent in Rome, from 1960 to 1962, as a Fellow of the American Academy. For a young man from the Midwest, who had never previously traveled to Europe, landing in Rome was an utter revelation. Until then he had had very little exposure to the history of architecture. "I had one history course in six years at Cincinnati, the last term of my senior year: the Greeks, the Romans to the Byzantines." A course with Sigfried Giedion at Harvard on Swedish Town Planning sticks in his mind—"buildings that looked like keyholes." But overall, "it was an anti-intellectual time, a *doing* time. We talked about architecture in terms of keeping the rain out. We had a very curious idea of what architecture was." Arriving in Rome was bound to make a deep impression, and Graves spent his time drawing buildings by Francesco Borromini, selling his drawings to fund travel around the country. "I went everywhere. We'd get up and decide on an itinerary for the day, like, 'Today we will see round churches with wall paintings.' I can hardly believe how much time we had."

While Rome was pivotal to his subsequent career, Graves also acknowledges some influences back home in America. He jokes that "I'm the one architect that didn't work for anybody important, but I worked for wonderful people." A short stint at the office of Walter Gropius ("about one and a half minutes, actually working for somebody third in command doing Baghdad University") counted for less than the year he spent at the office of the multifaceted designer George Nelson, after taking his master's degree at Harvard. Trained as an architect and a Rome Prize Fellow himself, Nelson was also a writer, photographer, graphic designer, furniture designer, and editor of *Architectural Forum*, then the most important design magazine in America.

The diversity of Nelson's activities (which included film titles and product packaging alongside his better-known seating) seems to have been a lasting inspiration. It was during this period, just prior to his departure for Rome, that Graves became familiar with the work of Charles Eames and textile designer Alexander Girard, who were also working as design consultants for Herman Miller. Girard's palette, influenced by the Native American culture of the Southwest, remained a powerful source for Graves's own use of color.

The General Motors Tech Center, designed by the Saarinens, *père et fils*, was also an "extremely important" influence. Completed in 1956, in the heyday of pink Cadillacs and tail fins, the Detroit research campus of the giant auto manufacturer was a dramatic example of corporate modernism: an arrangement of spartan Miesian pavilions, enlivened by vibrant color on certain elevations which gave them what Graves calls "already an adjectival, decorative look." He likens their simple colorful exuberance to the work of the Mexican architect Luis Barragán. "I remember going to the GM Tech Center when I was seventeen, when it had just opened—it was hard to see modern buildings growing up in a backwater like Cincinnati. I walked into the Information Center, and there was a blonde in a white dress sitting at a round white desk, and behind her, a staircase going up with no visible means of support except some very thin metal struts." The totality of the mise-en-scène—what one might call the designed artifice—made a deep impression. "We did aspire to put ourselves into our buildings in that way."

Graves has always cared deeply about his own surroundings, and talks with equally fond recollection of arranging his home in Cincinnati, his studio at the American Academy, or his apartment on Bank Street in New York. When he was a young married student in the six-year architecture program at Cincinnati in the 1950s —"In those days," he recalls with a wry smile, "you had to get married to get laid"—many of his classmates were setting up households, and confronting the shortage of well-designed domestic artifacts. So they improvised, making their own furniture such as tables and TV cabinets (the device was then new). They went window-shopping at the local Good Design Store, which carried items approved by the Museum of Modern Art, and even drove up to the Herman Miller headquarters in Zeeland, Michigan, to buy Charles Eames furniture.

Consciously emulating Eames, whose artful photographs certainly contributed to the mystique of his designs, Graves made his own photographic compositions: Eames's House of Cards placed on a table, plants hanging, the light falling just so. Early in his career, Graves was asked to show examples of interiors he had done, having been recommended for a commission to design a house. Lacking a portfolio of interior design work, he swiftly put together some forty still life photographs of his own house. He arranged flatware, plants, furniture, and the one Etruscan vase he then owned (bought in a flea market in Rome during his Fellowship years), shooting them "all very close-up because if you showed any more you'd see the background. It was all stage-setting." He got the job.

If the range of choices was limited when Graves was a student, he finds the anonymity of much contemporary product design just as dismaying. "Whether you go to Pottery Barn, Conran's, or Tiffany's, it seems to me the level of personality is missing. The design has been watered down." His admiration for Eames, Nelson, or earlier heroes, such as Josef Hoffmann of the Wiener Werkstätte, is based on a sense that "there's somebody home. There's talent, there's some *body* in the work." But the ideological distance between Graves's design and the mainstream of contemporary product designers is striking. (He claims to have "no relation whatsoever" to the product design community. "It's really just like architecture … it has its own little club.")

His design ideas spring from an intensely personal vision, rather than seeking form through investigation of specific functional problems and resolving them by pushing the envelope of modern materials technology. Graves's repertoire of materials is emphatically deluxe, often employing choice timbers or precious metals; even if mass-produced, his designs refer to crafts traditions rather than to mechanized production. One could say that his work is actually *antimodernist* in this respect, since it is not primarily concerned with designing good-quality generic items for everyman (the implicit goal of modern design), but with reclaiming the notion of the handmade object, the elegant appurtenance.

While other architects of his generation have also turned their hand to design—one thinks particularly of Richard Meier, Charles Gwathmey, Robert Venturi, and Frank Gehry, all of whom have designed for Swid Powell, for example—few have developed as comprehensive a range of artifacts and furnishings. For Graves, architecture and interiors are a continuum. "I never thought of buildings as being distinct from their interiors," he says. "That's part of the Rome influence. A room is set up around furniture the way buildings are set up around landscape." He cites a mentor, the veteran architectural theorist Colin Rowe, who asserts that it is easier to rearrange the furniture in a classical house than a modernist home, because the latter tends to require more set pieces to sustain a sense of intimacy.

Following the success of the Portland Building and the Humana Building in Louisville, Kentucky, Graves's architectural work made a quantum leap. Suddenly his practice was commissioned to design skyscrapers, hotels, and multiuse developments on urban tracts, and projects poured in from Japan.

As the scale of his architectural projects has grown, his enthusiasm for designing small-scale artifacts seems only to have increased. Old hands at the office joke about having to stand around, waiting patiently for approval on modifications to some multimillion dollar skyscraper, while Graves is immersed in detailing a new vase or clock.

Looking at the vast array of Graves's projects over the last decade, one can identify elements of a formal vocabulary that tend to crop up irrespective of the scale of the artifact. For example, the Lucca and Urbino wall sconces, manufactured by Baldinger, bear a strong family resemblance, in their cylindrical form girded by metal, to the Alessi press-filter coffee pot, a glass vessel held in a metal portcullis. This basic drum form appears again, at much vaster scale, in several building projects, be it the original design for the Whitney Museum (where a perforated cylinder was to have served as a columnar seam between the Marcel Breuer building and Graves's addition, never realized) or the rotunda terminating the west end of the proposed 2121 Pennsylvania Avenue development.

Indeed, his product designs often have the look of miniaturized architecture: the birdhouse of 1987, explicitly, and the Alessi mantel clock of 1986 in bird's-eye maple with ebonised wood columns. There's a distinctly architectural presence even to the infamous Alessi kettle, the *conehead* for which Graves will remain known, long after the controversies over the Portland Building, the Whitney Extension, and the Disney Headquarters—with its giant Seven Dwarfs—have been forgotten.

Some of the most attractive designs are those to be worn or held, attuned to the proportions of the human hand, the pleasure of touch, the sensuousness of materials used close to the skin. When asked how he tackles the shift in scale from designing buildings to designing portable artifacts, Graves replies that "it's more a question of tactility than a scale issue. When I was first thinking about the leather objects, I thought that the ones on the market felt awful, made of stuff one didn't care about." The series of desk books and personal documents in supple suede (by

Spinneybeck) beg to be stroked, their gold embossed squares a
finger-luring Braille. The watch for Cleto Munari and the flatware
are dainty and almost feminine in their detailing; neither of them
bear much kinship with trends in contemporary watch or cutlery
design, and therein lies their charm, a willful antiquity.

High-rise commercial architecture in the 1980s essentially
boiled down to designing the hat, boots, and overcoat—in other
words, the penthouse suites, lobby (plus elevator cabs), and glaz-
ing/curtain walling. The floorplates of new skyscrapers were
machines for maximizing rentable square feet, undifferentiated
shelves (around a service core) on which to stack contract furniture and tenants, in arrangements devised by their own interior
design consultants.

Declining to submit to this traditional division of labor,
Graves has reclaimed these orphan spaces as legitimately within
the architect's sphere of attention. His diversification into
architectural lighting and furnishings is a spin-off of his large
commercial projects: the light fittings designed for the Humana
Building appear, for example, in the Disney projects, customized
with appropriate motifs, and elsewhere. Indeed, in the Disney
hotels in Orlando, every surface comes under scrutiny, from
the giant swans and dolphins on the roof to the oversize flower
murals in the entrance lobby and the wallpaper along guestroom
corridors, to the bedside lamps and cabinets. "It's an enormous
accomplishment to get your furniture, rugs, and lighting
into a hotel room," says Graves, explaining the economics of
the lodging business, which make it hard to compete with
manufacturers who can produce knockoffs of original designs.
"If someone, say in South Carolina or Toronto, can find the way
to make a cut-price version, you can't beat them." But with his
hotel track record—he's since completed the Hyatt Regency in
Fukuoka, Japan, and is nearing completion of the RadissonBlu
on the Astridplein in Antwerp—the Graves name has become a

strategic marketing tool, a brand in its own right. "They want to use our furniture, to sell a Michael Graves room, not a Michael Graves-selected room."

With the end of the Design Decade—the Reagan/Bush era of conspicuous consumption—a more contemplative mood has hit America. Architecture, as handmaiden to the real estate industry, has suffered severely in the global recession. With the downturn in construction, there has been a discernible shift in design consciousness toward neglected issues of infrastructure, the environment, and provision for the disadvantaged. In the thickets of theory, the debate has moved on even beyond deconstructivism, while that buzzword *postmodernism* is little heard and, as a movement, appears to have passed into history. For Graves, whose work was so closely identified with the aesthetic upheavals of the 1980s—indeed, whose buildings became the very beacons of debate in architecture—the cultural pendulum swing poses dilemmas in terms of critical assessment.

For a significant period in the early to mid-1980s, the Princeton School of Architecture was definitively Gravesian. (Many of his students spend time in his office after graduation, hence its affectionate nickname, "the finishing school.") With the arrival of younger faculty in the past few years, the school's ideological direction has changed, toward critical theory and gender issues. Graves's once-dominant position on the faculty has therefore waned; one senses that this shift is disconcerting for him— the erstwhile Young Turk now finding himself a member of the Old Guard. But success as a built architect and accomplished product designer is perhaps inevitably at odds with a reputation as a radical.

To some, his focus on the formal and the visual—informed by his very particular synthesis of historical precedents— represents a reluctance to engage with issues currently high on the social agenda, and a retreat into a world of his own invention.

To others, the consistency of Graves's aesthetic investigations and his prolific output are what mark him, indisputably, as an artist. Even if the media searchlight has, for now, moved on, that imaginary world is no less fecund, the Graves Warehouse a place of continuing development, those "Archaic Landscapes" as fertile as ever.

Richard Saul Wurman Gets What He Deserves

I.D. Magazine, March–April 1994

One day, the Preservation Society of Newport County, Rhode Island, may add The Orchard to its tour roster of celebrity mansions. Outside the wrought-iron gates, an interactive touch screen will explain that one of the early Cyber-Barons of the Information Age made it his headquarters from the last decade of the twentieth century.

A beaming portrait of Richard Saul Wurman as TEDzilla—part human, part monster conference organizer, striding the globe from Monterey, California, to Kobe, Japan—dissolves to a menu bewildering for its variety of alternative biographies. Press One for Richard Saul Wurman architect, Two for professor, Three for city government appointee, Four for mapmaker, Five for author, Six for corporate consultant, Seven for conference maven. Whichever choice is selected, the text quotes Wurman's favorite self-explanation: "I was just trying to make things that I didn't understand understandable to myself." Sidebars list books published, awards garnered, and articles enumerating these career highlights.

Next, a United States map will chart the stations of the cross in Wurman's peripatetic career: Philadelphia, Los Angeles, San Francisco, New York, and Newport. Beside each city, tongue-in-cheek captions grade quality of life, color coded (with appropriate visual icons) under work, love, personal finance, dining, and domestic architecture. As the visitor cruises this ocean of data, mini-windows pop open, replaying testimonials by sundry CEOs and best-selling authors. "I really don't know what he did," they all say, in so many words, "but whatever it was, he was damn good at organizing information. Plus, he cut his own hair."

Press Star Now to Speak to an Operator.

———

The real Richard Saul Wurman is a rotund Santa Claus figure, given to roars of laughter and sentences loaded with subordinate clauses. And a studied line in self-deprecation. "I usually say I've failed sidewise throughout my life, had a bunch of different careers," he opines, sitting at a table of his own design in his Newport study. An overachiever's showcase, the room is designed to dispel any lingering doubts about Wurman's productivity. Display shelves against two walls are loaded with his publishing output in several editions and translations. Were it not for the fax, computer, and TV/VCR, one might be in the library of a nineteenth-century English country squire.

Certainly, his new address puts him on the map socially, albeit a century too late. Once the Firestone family guest house, Wurman's thirty-room new base is a short stroll around the cliff-walk from The Breakers, summer cottage of Cornelius Vanderbilt—the Barry Diller of the Railway Age. But if Newport was the watering hole of the late nineteenth-century industrial elite, Monterey now serves a similar role for their postindustrial counterparts—thanks to Wurman's TED conferences, the latest of which was held there last month.

First held in 1984, these tribal gatherings have become the Yaltas of Data, where the statesmen of Technology, Entertainment, and Design (TED) get together to discuss hot issues, show off new gizmos—and cut multimillion-dollar deals in the corridors.

TED regulars include such Digital Age luminaries as former Big Apple chairman John Sculley (now of Spectrum Information Technologies), Microsoft chief Bill Gates, and MIT Media Lab founder Nicholas Negroponte. But Wurman's trick has been to mix CEOs, rocket scientists, and designers with specialists in other fields, from music to medicine to movies. The audience profile is just as eclectic, and just as carefully composed.

"It's easy to talk about convergence today," says Negroponte, "but in 1984 it was considered lunatic. TED was a force in changing this. The most salient characteristic is the degree to which the participants are his friends. Ricky *is* TED."

In much the same way that Wurman's Access series revolutionized guidebooks by slicing cities up geographically (thereby reuniting topics—such as food and lodging—usually treated in separate chapters), so the TED conferences have reconceived the professional shindigs, bringing together people from diverse disciplines that have become highly segregated.

The TED timetable is designed to maximize just such no-holds-barred schmoozing, recognizing that this, for most delegates, is the main point of being there. "What you really go to TED for is the stuff going on in the audience," says Paul Saffo of the Institute for the Future. "There's intense conversations, everybody's doing breakfast and dinner. We're all wrung out by the end. It creates a community of interests for people who would otherwise pass like ships in the night. *Wired* magazine was more or less launched at TED3; they got a lot of their people and ideas there."

Negroponte confirms this. "I've been to every TED conference, and in each case something important happened in my life as a result, the first being the Brand book (Stewart Brand's *The Media Lab: Inventing the Future at M.I.T.*)."

A simple flyer announces each conference, but as time has passed, word of mouth has become sufficient. Wurman keeps the audience to around five hundred despite an applicant pool that would easily allow him to double that, carefully sifting prospective participants for diversity.

"I'd make a lot of money if I did it for a thousand, but it would completely undermine the conference. The hall holds about five hundred people, so in three or four days you can meet everybody. I still think of it as giving a great party."

Trip Hawkins cites TED2 as the place where he got the idea for his multimedia company, 3DO. He credits Wurman with creating "the only real conference in the industry. By that, I mean the only one where people really sit and listen to the presentations, and talk about real issues. They go for meaningful exchange of ideas." But Hawkins notes the downside of such *embarras de richesses*. "You always feel like there's lost potential, because the possibilities are so great with the terrific people he's able to bring together."

With an individual registration fee of $1,450, it's perhaps not surprising that some 60 percent of last month's TED5 audience were CEOs, a statistic Wurman is fond of reciting. Less impressive is the number of women speakers over the years: a mere handful. Wurman admits that he has "a really difficult time finding women speakers equal to the men in the field. They haven't been in the profession as long, haven't caught up in certain executive and power positions. There's been a glass ceiling." While acknowledging these shortcomings, and the restrictive admission price, he is unapologetic. "This isn't a scholarship group. I run a private business and I'm not ashamed of saying things that are not PC. My life and this conference are indulgent."

No press passes are granted—"I'm not looking for publicity," he claims. And no special places are reserved for speakers, so aristocrats and hoi polloi mingle equally. "I don't want a 'Them and Us,'" says Wurman. "This isn't a conference about bells and whistles, it's about 'Why are we doing this?'"

Although he has had enormous success in attracting technologists and entertainers to the conference, Wurman strongly believes that designers should also heed the message of TED. "The raison d'être of the design professions is communication," he says, "and TED is about responsible communication and learning." Wurman thinks designers need to keep up with innovation: "Just because they're using computers doesn't make them modern."

TED4, held in Kobe, Japan, in 1993, was "a good experiment," according to Saffo, but apparently less successful than its predecessors. At this version of TED, Wurman invited key companies and designers to submit five-minute video "Idea Bytes." Americans who went to Kobe reported that while many of these productions made the trip worthwhile (a videoconference jam session between musicians Herbie Hancock in Kobe and Makoto Ozone in Tokyo, for example), others came off as inept self-promotions. "The people with the good ideas didn't have access to the technology and vice versa," recalls Saffo. "Richard takes risks, and there's always something that fails. The good news is that when things fail, they fail in interesting ways." As Wurman sees it, "If you're willing to fail, you can't lose—you just try again. A huge lesson we learned at Kobe was how poorly Japanese and American companies describe themselves."

While declaring TED4 "socially a triumph," he nonetheless swears he'll never try holding another conference in Japan after the problems with translation (which reduced the number of speakers) and other cultural differences, nor is he interested in running them anywhere else outside the US. "The conference is not my life. For sure by the year 2000, if it hasn't really peaked already I'll stop it then."

Wurman goes to considerable lengths to foster the convivial atmosphere so central to TED's success, for example, by wrangling party favors from certain sponsors. One of the freebies at TED5 was a sampler from the forthcoming "Best of TED" CD-ROM anthology, to be released by Voyager. At TED3, the going-home gift was a Sharp Wizard personal digital assistant, loaded with the names and addresses of all the delegates.

Wurman's cultivated knack for knowing the right people works toward getting what he wants as well. "You see," he continues, schooling me in the social graces, "in this office, we work on the following model: if you don't ask, you don't get. For instance: there is a best room in a hotel that somebody's going to sleep in. If you don't ask for it, you can never get it. I have to assume it's always gonna be me."

One does, or *you* do, you in particular?

"*I* do. *I* do."

Why should *you* get the best room?

"Well, I really think I deserve it. If I go to a restaurant, I always want the best table. I don't always get it, but I want it."

What does it do for you, to get it?

"It fulfills the fact that I deserve it—although I don't necessarily expect to get it."

——

By now a veritable one-man brand (the middle name is included as a way of "grabbing some dignity"), Richard Saul Wurman first made his reputation as creator of the Access guidebooks series. But there are other, earlier publications he's equally proud of, principal among them the "technocratic snow job of an atlas" he did for MIT Press in 1966—the first comparative statistical atlas of major American cities; and the Spanish-and-English newsletter he produced while deputy director of Housing and Community Development for the City of Philadelphia in the early '70s.

Wurman's training as an architect seeps through all his work, and he insists that that's how he envisages himself, despite the plethora of professional incarnations. "I'll be an architect till the day I die. I'm very interested in the structure of information as the way in. And I do see it as architecture."

At one point in our conversation, I hand Wurman my copy of an early *LA Access*, bought in a secondhand bookstore in Santa Monica last year; I definitely prefer the design of the earlier editions: their longer format, quieter graphics, and radiused black covers. "That's a hand job, too expensive," he explains of the rounded corners, taking hold of the copy and going suddenly quiet. "Oh my God, this is an early one. First edition. I don't think I have one of these..." He turns the pages with genuine tenderness, as if greeting a forgotten child.

"This brings back memories. Of a little office where I couldn't pay the electricity bill, of taking all the money I had in the world and really inventing something, pasting everything up by hand because we didn't have a computer. Nobody would distribute it. Nobody would publish it, so I went around and sold it myself at bookstores, gas stations, car washes. It was a very difficult time of my life. I was going down the tubes—bankrupt."

Stretched to the limit financially, in 1981 Wurman sought advice from a colleague on the board of the International Design Conference in Aspen, Frank Stanton, ex-president of CBS. "By the time we finished talking, he said 'I'll buy half the company.' It saved my ass." Stanton's support funded the next edition of *LA Access*, and new guides to San Francisco and Hawaii over the next few years. In 1991, several years after Wurman bought Stanton out, he sold the venture to HarperCollins publishers.

The Access concept has proved applicable not just to major world cities, but also to cultural events and institutions such as baseball, the Olympics, medicine, and the *Wall Street Journal*. The format takes an architectural approach to a subject, using

abstracted diagrams and color to unpack privileged knowledge—
be it the rules and folklore of a national pastime, or the codes and
rituals of the financial markets—and explain it to the intelligent
layman. The recent city guides deploy more garish graphics and
have lost the purist charm of the originals; the nonurban guides
also sacrifice aesthetic subtlety in favor of sheer density of factual
information.

"Every page is a word-map," Wurman explains, drawing the
basic distinction between his books and their illustrious Baede-
ker forebears, a pile of which lies on the far shelves of his office.

"Richard's taken modes of information that have been
hidebound for a hundred years and thought out ways of digest-
ing them," says natural-sciences author Stephen Jay Gould, a
TED speaker. "Nobody thought of maps as anything other than
spatially coordinated. What Richard has done is try and convert spatial information into time. One of the things you want to
know when you're driving is 'What is an hour?' An hour in Arizona is very different from an hour in New York." For a scholar,
however, Gould finds the Access guides don't carry enough information. "They're an entrée. The *Guide Bleu* is so dense with scholarly detail that you're going to lose other things. The answer is to
carry both."

The increasing recreational and cultural use of city
centers—which the Access guides facilitate—coincides with the
transformation of the urban economy, the exodus of traditional
downtown employment to the suburbs. "Cities are too expensive
for work. Work has gone out to Stamford, Connecticut, or New Jersey," Wurman observes, adding that when he travels, he no longer
visits cities. "They're more hostile, harder to get around. When
it snows, it's slush, you don't see the change of seasons, and you
can't leave anything in your car." Perhaps induced by his new rus-
tic perspective, Wurman professes an enhanced appreciation of
the extra-urban. A new series, called the *In Between Guides*, will

cover "the wonderful idiosyncratic hotels and indigenous restaurants" of regional America.

Like a work of architecture, each Access guide proclaims
Richard Saul Wurman as its author (even now, his name appears
on the cover, as mandated in the terms of the sale to HarperCollins), but their inside-back covers reveal a team of assistants, writers, designers, and translators whose compendious efforts yield
the singular vision.

"Richard is very much a person who has an idea and goes
out and finds someone else to realize it," says Loring Leifer, who
worked with Wurman on his two "theory" books, *Information
Anxiety* and *Follow the Yellow Brick Road* (she's credited in them
with "turning Wurmanspeak into English"). "He used to say, 'My
books aren't written, they're assembled.' I put his ideas into sentences, from the vast amounts of interviews he had done. He put
in lots of sidebars, so people would be able to read at different levels, to leap from one idea to another. It's in his nature to make
those leaps. He's very impulsive."

Yellow Brick Road was much less successful than *Information Anxiety*. Wurman argues that it fell victim to managerial
upheavals at the publishing house Bantam Press and, hence,
to inadequate marketing. "I'm waiting for it to go out of print
so I can do a paperback and sell it myself." Two-thirds of a projected trilogy, these books attempt to emulate the flavor of face-
to-face communication by incorporating snippets of data in the
margins, and diverse "voices" within the body text, including
extended first-person testimonials by friends of the author. "The
act of transferring information from one human being to another
is extraordinary, really sublime," says Wurman. "I try to capture
small parts of that complexity and, to the extent that I can, make
my books like frozen conversation."

The trouble with anything frozen is that it needs thawing
before you can enjoy it again in its original condition. Both of

Wurman's books are stuffed full of insights, anecdotes, and raw nuggets of information, but the net results are cacophonous ensembles from which one struggles to extract any sense of a memorable governing thesis. In their frenetic hopscotching from one topic to the next (or backward, at random, as advised in the introduction), these books seem to suggest the mode of attention of a TV viewer, distractedly flipping the remote control, rather than the sustained concentration of a conventional reader. "I fall asleep reading narratives," Wurman admits. "If I pick up [Allan Bloom's] *The Closing of the American Mind*, I close it after three pages."

Among Wurman's numerous upcoming projects are a book on "The Information Architects," featuring some twenty designers: people like New York graphic designer Peter Bradford ("the most thoughtful person in graphic design in terms of thinking about the structure of information"), Nancye Green of Donovan/Green, Joel Katz of Paradigm:design, and Nathan Shedroff, the point man behind *Danny Goodman's Macintosh Handbook*—with *Richard Saul Wurman*.

Then there's a guide to Newport, *Twelve Issues That Face America* made easy-to-understand, and a new book on the Media Lab, where Wurman is currently a visiting scholar—a duty-free position bestowed by Negroponte, who predicts the book will be "a window into the Lab for a wide mix of eyeballs and minds. I have no idea how it will turn out, which is why I asked Ricky to do it."

"King Philip Chose Ohio for Going Skiing," Wurman suddenly announces. Then, noticing my bafflement, proceeds to translate: "Kingdom, Phylum, Class, Order, Genus, Species." He reaches into his briefcase and cheerfully unloads fat wads of Xeroxes from *The Life That Lives on Man*, *Our Skin as an Eco System*, and the *Atlas of Medical Parasitology*—background reading for a new book he's coauthoring with illustrator David Macaulay and Stephen Jay Gould. "We're structuring a story about the animal kingdom starting from man. If we incinerated our bodies and everything died except for the things that are living on it, you'd still see a human body. There's that many mites and bugs and worms all over us," he says, enraptured. Then Wurman vouchsafes his real ambition. "One of my fantasies is to be head of a big company, like president of IBM. There's no way I'd ever be offered one of those jobs, but I really think I'd rise to the occasion." He stops for a moment. "Maybe I'd be a fuckin' disaster."

Many people in Wurman's extended network of contacts remark on his gregarious and fearless ability to ask questions, especially the simple ones others are too shy to ask. And how he has managed to retain a childlike curiosity, "a willingness to be the kid in front of the emperor," as Macaulay puts it. Wurman has certainly hit upon a very beguiling strategy: proclaim your ignorance and people will grant you a psychological advantage, floored by your gutsiness in admitting such a shortcoming. He has taken his own, average, sense of insecurity and turned it into a lifelong crusade, a business. Sometimes it's hard to know whether he's having you on.

"There's a real dichotomy in my personality. I really, genuinely believe I'm stupid. I'm always feeling this insecurity of being dumb, not being able to read hard books. Everybody seems smarter than me. On the other hand I know I'm pretty fucking clever. I can see patterns. I can go into some pretty demanding meetings with a fundamental question, maybe as the Last of the Great Innocents, and come off smelling of roses."

In his recent profile of Bill Gates in the *New Yorker*, John Seabrook noted that "one of the lessons you learn in becoming an adult is that it doesn't always pay to be curious. Some people learn to avoid curiosity altogether. My impression is that [Gates] still has the fantasy of the giant, all-knowing brain, and that this is what the information highway means to him. It's a place where curiosity is rewarded." Reading this, I was struck by its aptness as a description of Richard Saul Wurman: the fantasy of the limitless capacity to absorb vast quantities of data, the guzzling voracity of his appetite to digest information on whatever subject.

Wurman talks admiringly of "single-agenda personalities"—Yasser Arafat, Mahatma Gandhi, and the architect Louis I. Kahn are his favorite examples—as if yearning to see himself (or be seen) as having that kind of unwavering vocation. But he is pulled by an equal and opposite drive. "I have this feeling that I have to keep on starting over, having these other lives. It's a way of cheating the grim reaper."

Even now, Kahn is his hero. Wurman studied with him at the University of Pennsylvania and later compiled an anthology of his writings (*What Will Be Has Always Been: The Words of Louis I. Kahn*). "His agenda was architecture with a capital *A*, and nothing else really mattered. I get teary-eyed talking about him," he says, suddenly pensive. "I was really angry at him for dying. How could he dare die on us when we still needed him? He allowed that it was OK to have simple thoughts, simple not being pejorative. He was a permission giver, that was his magic."

Shortly before Kahn's death, Wurman confessed his "interest anxiety" to his mentor on a long transcontinental flight. Already immersed in a smorgasbord of activities, while running an architectural practice with two partners in Philadelphia, he was beginning to doubt his true path. "Kahn was quiet for a moment. Then he said 'Even when I get a haircut, I'm an architect. You'll always be an architect.'" It was a kind of benediction. But lest the prophecy should turn out not to be correct, Wurman takes precautions. He cuts his own hair. "At high school I wanted to be a painter. At my father's doing I took all these tests to see what I had an aptitude for. They revealed three possible careers: as an architect, an archaeologist, or a hairdresser. Two out of three ain't bad. I haven't been to a barber since I was twenty-two."

———

Outside The Orchard, the touch screen has almost run through its menu. Among the snippets of bio-infotainment that the visitor has downloaded, there's the occasion when the Cyber Baron passed up an invitation to become office manager for Charles Eames; the nadir in the late 1970s when he lived in a Venice flophouse on a borrowed mattress; the Eames lecture where he met his wife. A closing sequence replays a segment from Gloria Nagy Wurman's introductory speech at TED3, in which she revealed how the First Couple of Access really get around. "Richard and I have driven hundreds and thousands of miles together across the world, and the way we navigate is by SCREAMING at one another for fifty miles at a time about whose fault it was that we missed the exit to the New Jersey Turnpike."

———

Press Zero Now for More Options.

Muriel Cooper's Visible Wisdom

I.D. Magazine, September–October 1994

When new land is sighted, the Corps of Engineers is sent out to survey its hills, vales, caves, and treacherous rocky shallows. They take theodolites and plumb lines, the tools of their trade, and hike the terrain—one step at a time, with plenty of loose footings and clumsy backward tumbles—then stand in the baking sun measuring its features. Later they translate their notations into maps on which snaking contours and numerals will tell future travelers where to climb for pleasant views, where not to steer a boat, where fresh water may be drunk. When the map is made, few who use it think of the exertions of those who trod the slopes the first time, how they read the land before a path of symbols had been laid for us to follow. Their names are scarcely known; dedication to the tasks at hand diverts them from the limelight they might otherwise enjoy.

One such pioneer was Muriel Cooper, a designer and educator who will be recognized as having charted new territory for design in the changing landscape of electronic communication.

I had the great privilege of meeting Cooper in late April and early May for this profile of her work as director of the Visible Language Workshop at MIT's world-renowned Media Lab. Those two occasions turned out to be her last major interview. Three weeks later, Cooper died suddenly of a heart attack, just as *I.D. Magazine* was arranging to send a photographer to take her portrait. Four hours' worth of tapes now seemed both wretchedly meager—given how much more we could have discussed—but also, under the circumstances, an exceptionally valuable bequest.

The official history of the Media Lab by Stewart Brand (*The Media Lab: Inventing the Future at M.I.T.*, 1989) makes scant reference to this remarkable woman who was, at the time of her death, the only female tenured professor at the Lab. Three entries in the index lead to passing mentions but, despite chapter-length discussions of other departments at this latter-day Bauhaus, not one is devoted to the VLW.

And yet, when Cooper showed the latest work of the VLW at the TED5 conference in Monterey last February, no less than Bill Gates of Microsoft personally asked for a copy of the presentation. As Nicholas Negroponte, director of the Media Lab, comments, "The impact of Muriel's work can be summed up in two words: Beyond Windows. It will be seen as the turning point in interface design. She has broken the flatland of overlapping opaque rectangles with the idea of a galactic universe."

"Muriel was a real pioneer of a new design domain," says Bill Mitchell, dean of MIT's School of Architecture and Planning. "I think she was the first graphic designer to carry out really profound explorations of the new possibilities of electronic media—things like 3D text. She didn't just see computer-graphics technology as a new tool for handling graphic design work. She understood from the beginning that the digital world opened up a whole domain of issues and problems, and she wanted to understand these problems in a deep and rigorous way."

And in her last few months, with the triumphant presentation at TED5, she had the sweet victory of knowing that she had proved her case. "Her peers had really pooh-poohed her," says Ron MacNeil, cofounder of the VLW and Cooper's closest colleague for over twenty years, alluding to the skepticism among graphic designers about the "Brave New Dynamics" she had for so long talked about but, until this year, not shown. "Conventional 2D graphic designers use all kinds of tricks to create a sense of dynamics. We've *got* the dynamics. All those stuffed shirts were just brought to their knees. She really felt she had begun to slay the dragons."

"She sat there on stage, looking like everybody's aunt," says TED organizer Richard Saul Wurman, "and took the audience on a trip—stumbling, not particularly articulate—through the projects she and her students have been working on. So many of us know that in this next stage, the answer isn't going to be found by putting a book on the screen. Her presentation captured the dream we all have of flying through information."

Listening to the tapes after Cooper's death, I found myself laughing out loud again at the impish humor of this gentle, gray-haired lady in baggy black sweater and pants, paisley blouse, and blue-rimmed spectacles—a wardrobe that had changed in pattern but not palette when we met again the following week. And I could easily picture her—black-and-white ankle-socked feet up on her desk—giving long, meditative responses to my questions between bites on a handheld chicken bone (her take-out version of that day's Sponsors' Lunch), while Suki, her omnipresent black poodle, nosed around the book-lined office and eventually went to settle in the kennel under another literature-encrusted desk.

"I have a profound disdain for answers," she told me, early on, winning my instant empathy. This would be no express ride via predigested sound bites along that gleaming mirage known as the Information Highway. Instead it would be a many-branched meander through the perplexities of design in largely uncharted electronic terrain. "We do a lot of groping here," she said. "I don't think there are answers. I think there are thoughts."

We first met at the end of the week in which SIGCHI (Special Interest Group on Computer Human Interaction of the

Association for Computing Machinery) had just held its annual
conference in Boston. The Media Lab, being tech Mecca, still
resembled Grand Central Station on Thanksgiving Eve, awash in
international visitors from corporations and academe. No shy,
retiring R&D shed this: the Media Lab leads a double life as a scientific research center and its own intellectual cogs-a-whirring
self-advertisement: visitor tours and Sponsors' Lunches are as
much a part of the daily routine as all-nighters, plastic-boxed
meals, and eye strain behind permanently drawn venetian blinds.

Meanwhile in the VLW, knots of lingering conference delegates crowded around the computers, watching student-run
demonstrations under a clock whose quarter positions inscribe
the local credos: CRASH/BURN, DEMO/DIE. Scarcely five minutes went by in front of any given screen before Cooper was interrupted by some or other high-powered telecom exec passing
through.

Things were, thankfully, a little calmer when we met again
the following week to talk further about the goals of the VLW, its
evolution, the delicate but obviously rewarding relationships
with sponsors, and the excitement of current research. "This year
has been a good one," she said. "I think we're on the threshold of
some very, very interesting ideas."

———

Part of the challenge of writing about the VLW (and about the
Media Lab in general, as Stewart Brand also found) is that the pioneers of this new technological frontier speak fluently in a coded
language replete with terms like *anti-aliased*, *bandwidth*, *territory*, *assertion rules*, and *double precision floating point numbers*,
to name but a few. The uninitiated visitor sits before the screens in
the penumbral Workshop, watching hypnotized as words stretch,
yawn, and flex, simultaneously emitting a baby's nursery yowl or
some other perfectly synchronized sound; as interpenetrating

planes of financial data revolve and zoom in *Star Trek*–style deep space; as freestanding lines of type hover in this velvety-black computer universe, then come closer, revealing behind them a fuzzy colored mass that proves (on further zooming) to be another chunk of text…scarcely in focus when yet another typographic nebula looms into view in the infinite beyond.

The elegance and apparent effortlessness of these demonstrations are easy to take for granted. But the more one learns, the more complicated it gets. Only when one catches a VLW grad student switching back and forth on-screen between the demo and its underlying code—those hieroglyphic knitting patterns that make things actually happen on a $250,000 Silicon Graphics Inc. Onyx computer with two SGI Reality Engines attached, or a 16,000 microprocessor Connection Machine II—does one begin to appreciate the effort that goes into producing these visual feats.

That process—making lucid what has hitherto been conceptually and visually opaque—is very much at the heart of the VLW's mission. Transparency itself is one of the core themes running through the work. "When you've made something transparent, you've hurdled the wall," says MacNeil. "Someone caused it to be conceptually opaque, which means you can't get the information you need. The act of seeing through creates new artifacts."

———

It would be easy to see Muriel Cooper's career as having been divided into two parts: the conventional print-based graphic designer, followed by the computer graphics cartographer. Certainly, by the time she took up the computer at age fifty-two, Cooper had established a distinguished reputation as a print designer. Among many awards, she received the second AIGA Design Leadership Award for design excellence at MIT, where she worked from 1952 through 1958 and then from 1966 through 1994. There she founded the MIT Office of Publications (now

Design Services), and was the first Design and Media Director of the MIT Press, for which she designed over five hundred books. She also created the classic MIT Press logo—an abstract play on the vertical strokes of the initial letters—in 1963, while running her own design studio.

But rather than a change of course, Cooper's shift toward computers can be seen as the continuing pursuit, via new technology, of an abiding interest: the relationship of dynamic to static media. She was, she recalled, "always trying to push some more spatial and dynamic issues into a recalcitrant medium," namely, print. Having designed the epic *Bauhaus* book for the MIT Press (published in 1969), she later made a film version that attempted a visual speed-reading of the material to escape the sluggishness of the printed page. And in recent work at the VLW, she was beginning to grapple with the converse: how to translate an interactive experience with a computer onto paper, "without just dumping"—an area known technically as "transcoding." In other words: how to turn time into space.

"Electronic is malleable. Print is rigid," she told me, then backtracked in characteristic fashion. "I guess I'm never sure that print is truly linear: it's more a simultaneous medium. What designers know a lot about is how to control perception and attention, how to present information in some way that helps you find what you need, or what it is *they* think you need. Information is only useful when it can be understood."

————

Design skills have been honed over centuries for the organization of information in the static territory of the printed page. Two dimensions are tough enough, as the history of graphic design amply demonstrates. Now designers must contend with information arriving continuously from sources beyond their immediate or ultimate control. That is, they must find ways of creating

intelligible hierarchies to manage material that can no longer
be relied on to stand still, fixed in location—and hence, to some
extent, in meaning—according to where it is placed on a flat
surface.

Torrents of information already flow through electronic
communication channels. Like the swollen Mississippi and its
tributaries last summer, these streams are destined to multiply, merge, and become ever more inundating. The challenge
for designers is no longer just a matter of how you present data
once you've fished it from the rapids. Rather, the task is to make
it possible to pluck the data you want as it rushes by and eddies
into something else; indeed, it is to make discernible the information you might need (before you even know it) amid this real-
time maelstrom.

The primary mission of the VLW is to develop devices and
design strategies to filter this potential deluge and siphon it into
assimilable gulps. Cooper and her cohorts have so far come up
with a vocabulary of graphical principles for manipulating information under constantly changing conditions.

Underlying many of these "computationally expressive
tools" (to quote the somewhat cumbersome VLW-speak) are the
concepts of *transparency*, *adaptability*, and *blur*. Translated into
everyday language, these terms imply, respectively, that 1) you can
see right through the data, as if it were printed on glass, to sequential layers behind; 2) that if there's a change in background color
in a dynamic environment, the type knows to adjust its own hue
so as to remain legible against it; and 3) that fuzzy fields of information come into focus, and therefore become readable, as you
approach them.

The nursery sound I "saw" is just one prototype of another
typographical tool that opens up a whole new area of design:
the conjunction of image and sound. Using this tool, the shape,
size, color, and translucency of type can be made to change in

correspondence with a given sound and its temporal duration. Simple enough to describe. But behind these acrobatics, it takes a very fast set of algorithms to create the number of sizes required for the type to expand and contract, or what Cooper termed "on-the-fly scaling."

"In animation, there are soundtracks that give you emotional and expressive backgrounds. But it really takes a creative designer who knows both sound and type to begin to design some new form of 'poster' where the sound is as integral as the visualization," said Cooper. At a basic level, this tool could be used to give an added dimension of personality as people communicate in chat rooms on the Net. What happens when this typographical sound tool is used in relation to a complex piece of information—involving text and video—remains to be determined.

Meanwhile, under the rubric of "behavioral graphics," the VLW has developed a species of "intelligent" type, endowed with its own inherent, but adjustable, physical attributes, such as gravity and bounce, for animation purposes; and "paper" whose "fibers" have differential rates of pigment absorption, allowing variable diffusion of color across its surface—physical characteristics that the computer can model, but that cannot actually be physically produced in the real world.

A lifelong animation enthusiast, Cooper regarded this technique as a "key component to an overall set of communication vocabularies. Not as in video, not as in scientific visualization or computer animation. Just animation." Asked what is so compelling about it, she began by stating the obvious. "It moves, it tells you much more. I'm more interested in motion than character animation, though that is important as well. Did I love Disney, you mean? Was I turned on by Pinocchio as a child?"

Grinning, she paused for a moment, then revealed a rather different inspiration.

"One of the most important animators in my view was Norman McLaren. In the early years of the Canadian film board, McLaren made images that moved by doing this linear scratching on the cel, among other things. He also did soundtracks. They were quite marvelous."

Whatever the underlying source, Cooper always tried to have a student on the VLW team with expertise in animation. Until recently, one of its sponsors was Paws, Inc., the company behind Garfield the Cat, whose creator, Jim Davis, wanted to find a more efficient way of generating character animations for all the Garfield licensees, which range from Saturday morning television cartoons to cat food. The small size of the company made for an intimate and highly productive sponsor relationship that lasted about three years; among other animation issues, the VLW looked at how to build characterizations for diverse applications while maintaining quality control.

When Paws, Inc. withdrew from sponsorship for its own financial reasons, Cooper was determined to find ways of sustaining the animation research. Her strategy under such circumstances was to modify the work just enough so that it had relevance to another unit of the Lab, such as the News in the Future group, and thus became eligible for alternative resources. "If we think the work is important and we have a good person but the funding goes away, then we continue to support it. To some extent we rob Peter to pay Paul, and vice versa."

The work shown at TED5 represented a leap in computer typography, a way of superseding the long-standing cliché of interface design with a compelling new metaphor. Instead of having opaque panels of information layered one on top of the other like a deck of cards (the accepted, but crude, convention of windows-based software), now, with three-dimensional graphics capable of changing size and orientation in real time, the screen turns into a cockpit windshield, admitting onto a landscape of data one navigates with the press of a button.

According to VLW research specialist David Small, the idea for the TED5 demonstration was conceived on a flight back from Japan in the fall of 1993, with Cooper and Suguru Ishizaki, another of her collaborators, and the second person to earn a PhD from the VLW. "When we got back," Small recalls, "Silicon Graphics had dropped off a Reality Engine for a week for us to play with." The arrival of this machine, with its high-powered computational ability, was what propelled Cooper and her team into a new phase of typographic investigation.

"Nobody had really done high-quality three-dimensional type," Small explains. "I had always had this idea of using fast texture-mapping to do anti-aliased type. To get smooth edges on the type in any arbitrary position and size, you need a machine that can do some of that computation in the hardware."

This is where the Reality Engine comes into its own, capable of making calculations fast enough to give a believable impression of three-dimensional motion.

"Not only can you take a letter and manipulate it in three dimensions," Small explains, "but on this quarter-of-a-million-dollar computer, you can have a few hundred words on the screen—a few thousand letters—and still do thirty frames per second. If it's that fast, it physically feels three-dimensional. Below that, and you lose the whole visceral feeling."

That feeling, as the TED5 delegates recognized, is just like flying. "Not literal flying," says Small, "but the kind of flying you do in your dreams." Looser, less controlled. And physically impossible. A corporeal yet out-of-body experience.

"When Muriel got her hands on an SGI Reality Engine, that really was a turnaround," says professor Stephen Benton, head of the Media Lab's Information and Entertainment division, which incorporates the VLW. "She started using it for

three-dimensional graphics, and the infinity zoom idea just blew
her away. She was absolutely fascinated by being able to zoom
in and out by factors of thousands, like some kind of hovercraft.
Once somebody showed her what it could do, she didn't stop
playing with it."

———

Here was a woman, hooked on computers and what they could do,
yet she herself could not write code. "I've tried to learn to program
many, many times, and it frustrates the living hell out of me," she
confessed. I asked several people whether it was significant that
she was not a code writer.

"No. Nor is Marvin Minsky, nor is Seymour Papert, nor am
I," came the emphatic reply from *nicholas@hq.media.mit.edu*,
aka Nicholas Negroponte, referring to two Media Lab colleagues.
"Muriel's difference was as a person, not that she was not a computer scientist. She saw things differently. That perspective is
worth the world."

"Not only was she not a coder," says Benton, "she was not
mathematical. All she knew was what she wanted to see, and she
couldn't know that until she saw it." He regards Cooper as the last
in a line of "pioneer artists" on MIT's faculty, including Minor
White, Richard Leacock, and György Kepes.

"She was a klutz!" says MacNeil, affectionately, when asked
to define their division of labor. "She was the design brilliance
and administrative muscle. I was the guy that built the tools, the
technical underpinning. She had learned how to think visually, to
create multilayered schemes of possibilities in her head, which is
what writing software is. Because she was a completely original
thinker, she just refused to learn somebody else's symbology. It
was just anathema to her."

Cooper's first encounter with computer programming was a
summer course run by Negroponte around 1967, while she was a

conventional print designer at the MIT Office of Publications. It was not a promising start.

"Nicholas invited me and Ralph Coburn [another MIT designer] to be design shills, basically. I nearly died. We were in this big room with these teletype machines doing Fortran and there was nothing visual about anything. You had to translate any idea you had into this highly codified symbolic language that didn't make any goddam sense to me, and I was crazy."

So how did she get over the trauma of Fortran in a room full of nothing visual?

"We cheated! *Ha ha ha!*" She let out an uproarious chuckle. Negroponte recalls that the pair of them "clowned around with a simple time-sharing system, and got it to draw simple pictures with letters, overprinting for graytone."

However frustrating and bewildering that course, Cooper came out of it with "a conviction, naive as it could be, that there lay in computers the possibility of a huge amount of flexibility that the publishing procedure did not have. At that time, twenty years ago," she recalled, "you sent out for type and paid $2,000 or $3,000 a pop for a book. You could never change your mind at that price. Every time you made a design decision, you narrowed down, because the production process was closing you in. It seemed to me that something as trivial, in retrospect, as computer composition would begin to allow you some flexibility of design thinking. Remember, this is long before Apple."

Later on, Negroponte (then at the Architecture Machine Group, one of the precursors of the Media Lab) sent over a couple of Imlac machines (one of the first graphics computers) and a pair of students to work in Muriel's department at the MIT Press, which she had now labeled the Media Department, "in the hopes that I would get into media, not just publishing." They spent nights experimenting and scoping out the idea of desktop publishing using the Imlac, which combined an eight-bit computer with a high-resolution stroke font display—an early antecedent of the personal computer. "The machine could lay stuff out: it could flow a manuscript into columns, and the kids created a few little tools that allowed you to make it wider, shorter, maybe fool with the leading. But it had no real graphical capability. Still, it was very clear to me, without really understanding computers, that there was a huge potential."

The next significant turning point was the arrival of a 3M color copier, the first of its kind. The experimental printmaker Tom Norton made a deal with 3M to loan the new machine to Cooper's department, using the MIT Press as a showcase to try selling it. "That really started off my own little Media Lab," said Cooper. Through Norton, she met Ron MacNeil, a physicist and photographer who had helped Minor White set up his photographic studio at MIT, and together, in 1978, they founded the Visible Language Workshop.

———

What Cooper brought to the Media Lab was a background not only as a practicing designer, but also as an art school teacher. The atmosphere of an atelier permeates the VLW; its physical layout (and hence, social organization) has influenced other sections of the Media Lab, where personal office cubicles have gradually come to be replaced by its more open arrangement of workstations. The physical environment was related to Cooper's idiosyncratic teaching style, as Small recounts.

"She was a different kind of teacher: very reluctant to tell you what to do. Once you've started with the assumption that there's no right or wrong way of doing anything, what becomes more important is getting students to think on their own. Muriel set up the right kind of environment for that: the space encourages interaction. Even naming it a workshop, not a lab, was important."

Cooper appreciated the skills of designers and programmers in equal measure, and at the VLW nurtured a cadre of people who possess both—graduate students, pursuing either a master's or PhD degree in Media Arts and Sciences, and research associates. Only ten or so students are enrolled at any given time, and they are recruited from all over the world, from diverse backgrounds that may include some design, though this is not a prerequisite. Those not already fluent in computer science are expected to acquire sufficient software skills before they arrive.

"My model is very much more an art school, or a design school, where you don't give recipes for things. But it's not purely a studio, because there's a lot of rigor in making a machine do something you want it to do."

—

As is the case throughout the Media Lab, VLW projects are supported by sponsorship from government departments and an array of international media conglomerates and hardware and software companies. The work shown at TED5, for example, was funded by NYNEX, the Joint National Intelligence Development Staff, the Department of Transportation, Alenia (part of an Italian aerospace and electronics company), ARPA (the Advanced Research Projects Agency of the US Department of Defense), and the News in the Future Consortium (a cluster of some twenty sponsors that runs the gamut from Advance Publications to Ziff Davis).

Sponsors generally fund experimental research that would be too expensive to support in-house; in return, they get the rights to advanced concepts from which they can then develop commercial applications. "It's cheaper for them to sponsor us than to set up a laboratory to explore ideas that may or may not work," said Cooper. "We make mistakes, and it's less costly for them to see our mistakes. So in fact this place is more of a crucible than a crystal ball. They can take code away, but they understand it's a group of concepts."

The Joint National Intelligence Development Staff approached the VLW to find more efficient ways of sifting through vast amounts of information, and turning it into reports of various lengths, from long-term research to short-term executive briefings. "One of the things we made very clear with these people in the beginning is that we would not take on secret information. This is an open shop. So we're working with news. You know what one of their major news sources is?"

The answer is about as far from the realm of spy thrillers as could be imagined.

"CNN! If all we did was find a new way to browse and gather and generate new information out of CNN material, the intelligence agents would be happy."

With spooks as sponsors, issues of command and control implicit in *all* VLW work—who gets access to information, how fast, and to what end?—become more apparent than in projects sponsored by entertainment or publishing enterprises. This is clearly sensitive terrain, but Cooper endeavored to clarify her ethical position by drawing a careful distinction between the graphical representation of data and its semantic content.

"The electronic environment seems to me to have significantly different characteristics than any medium we've communicated in before. There are problems that come out of that. Information to me, on one level, is information. A table to do with tanks and a table to do with poverty in New York City are both statistics, and to some extent they're both content-free. That is not to say the real subjects are content-free. Content makes a *huge* difference. But the visualization of numerical statistics is a formal design problem that can be dealt with no matter what the subject. As far as the Command and Control stuff goes, I try to make

generic information environments that we can study, and they
can use for whatever they damn please."

Ron MacNeil recalls a visit to the VLW by General Maxwell R.
Thurman, who had led the Panama Invasion, during one of the
Media Lab's ARPA open days, which are among its more elaborate full-dress demonstrations. "We were very sensitive about
not having aspects of standard military language in the demo,
so we modeled moose migrations. We were trying to show ways
of interacting with this graphical environment using objects on
the screen that had some intelligence: you could tell them to do
something by pointing, drawing, and using hand gestures. So
we had these wonderful creatures—an endangered species—
roaming the screen. After a while watching the demo, General
Thurman said, 'Enough of the mooses. Show me the Ruskies!'"

———

Driving to her house, to fetch tapes she had forgotten to
bring in for a colleague, Cooper talked about several epipha-
nies that changed the direction of her career. There was the
spring-cleaning when she went through a closetful of carefully
saved pieces of graphics, and realized that she didn't care about
any one of them "because they didn't have much content." That
propelled her move from graphic design into editorial design but,
in time, she grew frustrated by book design as well.

"Too often the role of the designer is to clothe a set of messages they've had no participation in. Here is a book. You didn't
write it. You don't change it except insofar as you present the
information somebody else has generated. You're not really collaborating either, because the stuff is there, an accomplished
fact. I decided I had to wash that out of my head and impose my
own problems."

After several years gestating a text, authors tend to have their
own view of what their book should look like, which can lead to

some interesting battles of wits. "I had that experience in spades with Denise Scott Brown and Robert Venturi," Cooper recalled, speaking of the original edition of *Learning from Las Vegas*, published by MIT Press in 1972. Cooper even proposed a bubble-wrap cover, in homage to Las Vegas's glitz—a suggestion the authors firmly rejected.

"What they wanted most was a Duck, not a Decorated Shed. I gave them a Duck," Cooper went on, referring to the dichotomy between two types of symbolic architecture posited in the book, the former being a literal representation of its function. "I thought: 'God, this is wonderful material. I'm not gonna let them screw it.' Hah! You should have seen it! Well, they hated it! I loved it."

Denise Scott Brown, for her part, remembers "a plain disagreement of philosophy between us about the design, and a strong diversion between its content and its cover. We had a tug of war all along. She was still into Bauhaus design, when that was the very thing we were criticizing in the book. In the end it's a Bauhaus book on the inside, and a protopostmodernist book on the outside."

I wondered whether Cooper had writing ambitions of her own.

"Yes, I would like to write a book. I always use György Kepes's *Language of Vision* as a model."

What would it take for her to write the book? Without missing a beat, she answered with another question.

"A brain transplant?"

———

On the way back to the Lab, Cooper reminisced about early teaching at the Massachusetts College of Art, where the students froze when faced with unfamiliar technology but sprang to life in a class doing interactive printmaking—rotating the plates, changing the fonts and the inks as it moved through. That experience clearly catalyzed her belief in using technology as "a partner in the creative process."

She also talked, hesitantly, about what it was like to be a woman in what is still predominantly a man's world. "I think that's been something of a problem in the Media Lab, though it's changed a lot. You start a meeting and—unless you're much stronger than I am—the conversation almost inevitably dissipates into equipment discussion. And they couldn't be happier. But I'm a terrible toy freak, too. I love little computers, lots of audio-visual equipment, you name it. As one of my old friends used to say, 'Remember, there's no depression so deep that it cannot be solved by a new piece of equipment.'"

———

At one point I asked if she minded telling me her age.

"No. Sixty-eight. Much to my surprise."

How old did she feel?

"About thirteen. I don't know. I'll walk down the street and look at myself off chance in a reflection in a mirror or someplace, and I'll think, 'Oh, my Jesus, who is that person?' It has very little relation to how I feel. Most of the time."

She suddenly drew pensive. "Does it matter? I don't know." She paused. "Do I have to have this in the article?"

I said it was up to her.

"Well, I'm a little superstitious. In the sense that there is an awful lot I'd like to do. The worst thing about age, never mind the small indignities of wrinkles and bone loss and possible glaucoma, is that"—and here she raised her voice to a clarion call, addressed to herself—"you damn well better get going. Because you don't know what's going to happen."

Did she consider herself a success?

"On occasion. Has it made a difference? Some days I think it might have. Other days, I think not at all. There's a lot to be accomplished."

A Man for All Media

Bob Stein

I.D. Magazine, March–April 1995

Bob Stein is sitting in his office at the Voyager Company's New York headquarters, giving the dog-and-pony show to yet another party curious for an inside look at this fabled multimedia publishing house. The tourists this time are a dozen or so graphic design students from the School of Visual Arts' class in Culture Jamming and Media Activism: quintessential urban twentysomethings in leather and denim, construction boots, and baseball hats on backwards.

Apparently past-masters in Media Passivism, they take in Stein's demonstration of *A Silly Noisy House*, Voyager's CD-ROM title aimed at two-to-three-year-olds, with inscrutable blank faces, sitting motionless at a safe distance from the focal Macintosh Quadra 650.

Stein meanwhile has a child's smile and look of rapt attention as he manipulates the mouse to make toast fly out of a toaster and erase the shading in a "dream bubble" to reveal the content of a teddy bear's unconscious. He remarks that children in Los Angeles, where Voyager was based until 1993, take particular pleasure in allowing the bath to overflow and flushing the toilet repeatedly, thereby defying (in CD-ROM simulation) real world orders to conserve water.

Voyager's creative director now loads the palm-size silver disk in which the first volume of the history survey *Who Built*

America? is committed to memory. He is about to demonstrate how you can do all the kinds of things you can do with a real book using this electronic doppelgänger—such as writing notes in the margins, folding down page corners, even (in that particularly American form of text-abuse) highlighting with one of four fluorescent "markers"…when the cursor jams. Stein prods the keyboard, which emits an odd bleating sound with each strike, but to no avail. Soon, minions are at hand to assist their exasperated leader, unplugging the recalcitrant genie and replacing it with a better-behaved Centris.

"There are two basic hits on Voyager," Stein explains to the SVA students. "There are the people who say, 'Wow, this is fabulous,' and the others who say, 'Excuse me, that looks very tired: the design looks like an easy extension of a book. Computers can do so much more than that, why don't you do it?' Someday, the way that people interact with computers will be completely different from anything we know of today. But I'm not especially interested in trying to invent the paradigm of the future. I'm interested in using the technology that's available right now to express ideas that are important."

Stein now hopscotches to an audio segment that brings to life a vaudeville sketch that lampooned people's initial difficulty adapting to telephone communication. "It wasn't until I heard this piece on CD-ROM that I intuitively understood how hard it was for humans to talk to each other on the phone when it was first invented," Stein rhapsodizes. "They had no history of talking to each other without seeing each other."

The parallel with multimedia today is striking. In its efforts to make a new and unfamiliar form of communication comprehensible, the Voyager Company faces an equivalent struggle. Without underestimating its many accomplishments, it must be said that Voyager's products often betray the same kind of quaint archaism that bedeviled early telephonic conversation.

Although Voyager seems, from a public-relations perspective, synonymous with Stein, he is in fact one of four partners who founded the company in 1984 in Santa Monica, as a joint venture between Voyager Press and Janus Films, the US distributor of modern classic films. Voyager now employs some one hundred people; approximately two-thirds of them work at the company's Manhattan office, directly opposite the SoHo Guggenheim. A certain sophomore scruffiness pervades the fourth floor, which houses sales, marketing, technical support, and the art department, as well as Stein's quarters; the couch in the reception area is as likely to be occupied by a Voyager employee, taking a nap, as by a visitor. The eleventh floor accommodates producers, programmers, and the Criterion Collection, in a calmer environment, with white fabric masking-taped to the windows to combat glare. "It's almost a religion," says Stein of his staff's devotion to their work. Voyagerites are often in the office till the early hours, but employee burnout seemingly poses no problem: résumés arrive in a steady stream each week, and wannabes are said to camp out in the hallway.

Its new media publishing efforts have so far been in four primary areas: CD-ROMs, with 45 titles now available for Macintosh and Windows; Expanded Books, which put more than 60 unabridged books on floppy disk; the Criterion Collection, developed from the Janus Films archive and now numbering some 150 films; and multimedia authoring tools such as the Expanded Book Toolkit and CD-Audio Toolkit. In January, Voyager ventured into the online world, with a website geared primarily toward promoting the company's list, but enhanced by extracts from a select cadre of magazines, including the *Paris Review* and *Aperture*. In the fall of 1994, Voyager launched *3Sixty*, a lively variation on the conventional publisher's catalogue that gives the impression of almost being a freestanding quarterly magazine, designed by Alexander Isley, one-time art director of *Spy*.

Stein, tall and lanky, sports oversize glasses that give him a sort of friendly bug appearance and, when outdoors, dons a trilby that makes him look like a cross between a raffish rabbinical student and an extra from *The Untouchables*. Once he has made your acquaintance, or has otherwise ascertained that you are "smart" or "hip" and therefore worthy of attention, Stein is tremendously engaging and humorous. But he also has a low boredom threshold, and can be aloof and downright dismissive toward those he does not recognize. When people fail to sustain his interest, or he disagrees with their position, a characteristic gesture makes it plain: arms stretched out above his head, leaning back in a total-body yawn.

There are also idiosyncratic turns of phrase: he has a disconcerting way of referring to "humans," rather than to "people" and, in an apparent gesture of kinship with Voyager's youthful staff, his favorite expressions are "Wow" and "Holy fuck!" Now forty-eight, Stein acknowledges that most of his employees regard him as "someone from their parents' generation," but he says he feels spiritually closer to those in their younger twenties. "Politically they seem much more aware and prepared to ask questions about the way society is structured. Those who came of age in the 1980s are much more cynical."

At Voyager, Stein hops from screen to screen, dispensing fleeting comments, usually trailed by two or three employees hoping to hear the end of his previous sentence, cradling their open PowerBooks like the Mosaic Two Tablets of Stone. The phones ring ceaselessly, the voice of the intercom is heard throughout the land, and Stein, summoned ubiquitously, answers by speakerphone from all extensions.

———

So how did Robert Stein come to be defender of the canon of Western Civilization in the Electronic Era—or an eclectic version thereof, which so far runs the gamut from Shakespeare (*Macbeth*) to Spiegelman (*Maus*), from Beethoven (*Symphony No. 9 CD Companion*) to the Beatles (*A Hard Day's Night*), and from *Society of Mind* (*First Person: Marvin Minsky*) to Society of the Mindless (*People: 20 Years of Pop Culture*)?

The voyage to Voyager has been long and varied: today's leader of the digital revolution was, in a previous life, an ardent proponent of political revolution. But while the doctrine and the context may have changed (not to mention the technological means of mass persuasion), Stein's current work is driven by the same fundamental zeal to change people's minds—and their lives—by putting knowledge into their hands.

A scion of New York's Upper West Side, Stein took his first degree in psychology at Columbia University, focusing on learning behavior, then went to Harvard for a master's in Education, returning to Columbia, where he spent a year in the PhD program in bio-behavior: "I wanted to understand the scientific basis of feeling and emotion and thought." But it was the first period that proved formative. At Columbia, Stein was shaken from his petit-bourgeois slumber in a course given by Richard Cloward, a professor of social work, who drew his attention to the class struggle in America—a revelation that propelled him into organizing a community center in Harlem. Arrested at Columbia during the rebellion of '68, Stein was a charter member of Students for a Democratic Society, and spent the next ten years as a political activist, becoming, by his own declaration, a Maoist.

"I was a full-time revolutionary, and I worked very closely with the Revolutionary Communist Party. A lot of my work was involved with propaganda. I started a distribution company that sold Marxist-Leninist literature all over the United States." Though the content is certainly different, Stein's earlier experiences as a distributor may serve him well in his present activities. Asked whether Voyager represents the continuation of earlier convictions, in a different guise, Stein insists that "Voyager's not part of the agenda at all. It's a publishing company. My ideological outlook is not that different from when I was a revolutionary, but I'm not out on the streets trying to make revolution on a daily basis."

Stein worked for a while as a teacher, but by 1980 had become fascinated by the work of the Architecture Machine Group (AMG) at MIT, Nicholas Negroponte's precursor to the Media Lab, which already included such landmark projects as the *Aspen Movie Map*, *Spatial Data Management System*, and *Put That There*.

"It was totally apparent to me that this was the new publishing medium because you could combine the best aspects of different media in one new medium. My work is completely derived from what was done at the AMG. Nicholas is a real visionary. All I am is a practical craftsman. I'm not trying to say that with any false modesty."

———

Pressed to outline his top ten principles of multimedia design, Stein suggests as a first rule that "the user should not be out of control for a nanosecond. If you brought me twelve CD-ROMs randomly from other companies, what would be wrong with them is insufficient respect for the users' intelligence, and for their willingness to engage with the material." The nature of this engagement is crucial, and Stein clearly believes that there is an inextricable link between serious ideas and the book form.

"Books are an exceptionally interesting medium because they seem to promote reflection. To read means to think about what's coming out of the book. It's much easier to process something out of a movie. A good [Steven] Spielberg or [George] Lucas movie is like a roller-coaster ride: it's a manipulation of my emotions. That's not the same as being in an intelligent space, with somebody presenting ideas to me and saying 'What do you think?' The real point of a book is that it's a random-access medium, that the user is in complete control, which is why it's such a powerful medium for the transmission of intellectual ideas."

For Stein, the ability to stop and think about what one has just read marks the crucial distinction between a book and a film. And the question of control seems to be of personal importance. "I'm forever wanting to refer to something I've read earlier, whether it's a mystery, or an intellectual argument, or a novel where the nuances of a character's psychology change over the course of a book. Being able to do that—being an active reader—is the essence of reading."

The result is that Voyager titles bend over backward to reinscribe the character of the printed page on the electronic screen, with results that are well-intentioned and legible but about as elegant as the original horseless carriage. Stein seems to be so focused on intellectual content, namely the authored text (with pronounced preference to date for those written by white, male academics: Marvin Minsky, Robert Winter, Donald Norman, Stephen Jay Gould, Roy Rosenzweig), that the possibility of a different kind of authorship either doesn't occur to him or is obscured by his zealous belief that significant ideas are communicated via words. Having read Jerry Mander's *Four Arguments for the Elimination of Television*, and having grown tired of the "constant negotiation" with his teenaged children over their rationed viewing hours, Stein eliminated TV from the household altogether.

And yet, was this same paragon of domestic discipline not jubilantly exclaiming half an hour earlier that two- and three-year-olds all around the country are begging their mothers to switch on the CD-ROM so they can play with *A Silly Noisy House*?

"I'm an agnostic on what this stuff is doing to children," Stein concedes. "When I was a kid, I went into the kitchen and my mother gave me pots and pans and I made noise with them, actually played with the objects. Now we're telling children, 'Here's a 2D representation of these objects and you can manipulate them on the screen.' Why are we trying to replace perfectly reasonable real-life activities with two-dimensional, much lower-bandwidth activities?"

And "actually playing with the objects" still matters to him, however much he might champion their electronic surrogates. There's clearly something very tactile and seductive for Stein about the conventional process of reading, of turning pages versus clicking a mouse, a process that comes to have distinct associations to physical locations. In an internal memo regarding the launch of Voyager online, Stein, still ruminating on the geography of electronic access, observes: "A good book is absorbed over time (days and weeks, not minutes or hours). You read in bed, then...if you're really into it, you read it on the subway to work and...take it out during your break and lunch." It is an odyssey of attachment, not unlike an obsessive love affair. Hence Voyager's extraordinary labors to reproduce "this sense of a real document, a physical thing," in transferring texts from print to screen.

Stein itemizes Voyager's victories in making an electronic book look and feel as much like a regular book as possible. In *Who Built America?*, for example, text is set just wide enough to look like proper columns, but not so wide as to strain the eye from too much horizontal scanning. Column length, per screen, has to be not too long, but not so short that it looks like a long caption. "We're terribly frustrated by the fact that the screen is horizontal, and books are largely vertical," he remarks, as if dismayed to find that a car has wheels, not hooves.

He admits that the uninspired appearance of the full-screen "plates" in *Who Built America?*—photographs with long captions in close-packed type—resulted from one person having to crank out eight hundred such pages in a month. But he also defends the relative lack of attention to graphic design on the grounds that conceptual redesign was a higher priority. "I will argue that giving people real, valid, and viable access to three thousand documents in an authored context is a completely new and radical way of presenting information, and is much more modern and important than a lot of things that *look* more modern and important."

To try doing so in an unfamiliar paradigm, he maintains, "would render it an artwork, an experiment, not a commercial product. I have to put something on the market that people are going to pay $50 for. A lot of people look at this and say 'Oh, that's a book.' But they don't understand how difficult it was to make it look like a book on the computer."

Why bother making it look like a book?

"Because it *is* a book. This is the text from a book. Remember that the glue that holds these three thousand documents together is a text that somebody wrote."

Doesn't it have to *change* to become an electronic book?

"OK," Stein begins, faintly exasperated at my pedantry. "The budget for the print version of *Who Built America?* was $2 million. If someone gave me $2 million, I would reinvent this book for this medium."

———

One of the reasons Stein became a publisher, he says, is "to engender debate" about issues that matter. "I'm frightened by a society where a substantial number of people are not reading. In 1858, the audience sat for five hours listening to the Lincoln-Douglas debates. There's a tape of Adlai Stevenson at the 1952 Democratic Convention, and the camera locks down on him for forty-five minutes. Today, people's ability simply to engage in a dialogue is vastly threatened. That's why I resent the criticism of

Voyager's stuff for not being sexy and new enough. You want to work on that problem? Great. I want to talk about the ideas in *Who Built America?*, and in Marvin Minsky's and Stephen Jay Gould's CD-ROMs."

So why publish them electronically?

"Because I believe it is a more compelling medium. The ability to hear Stephen Jay Gould speak is a more powerful entry point to his ideas than simply reading the book. There's a lot of information in the inflection and emotional tone of a voice." Less than compelling, to be frank, is the experience of sitting in front of a computer screen watching a giant-size IQ give a Lilliputian lecture; it's about as riveting as watching the radio.

Nonetheless, Stein is convinced of the importance of providing a platform for individuals to articulate their own undiluted opinions—so long as they are opinions he supports. He plans, for example, to invite Gould to issue an electronic rebuttal to *The Bell Curve*, the controversial book by Charles Murray and Richard J. Herrnstein that links intelligence to race. "Gould calls Charles Murray the retrograde racist that he really is, and he does it with the mantle of an accepted expert in his field," says Stein. How does Stein know that Gould is right? "I don't. But guess what: I'm a publisher. It's my job to guess on who's right. Do I think Stephen Jay Gould is right and Charles Murray's wrong? Absolutely."

Opinion is divided about the virtues of Stein's venture, but the one thing everyone seems to agree on is that he has "a vision." Does he regard himself as a leader? It's a mantle he declines, at least in part. "The kind of leaders I'm talking about, like Mao and Malcolm X, come forward about once every fifty years in a society and you're really lucky when you see one. Certainly the publishing industry has been willing to acknowledge some of Voyager's role, and I consider myself a leader in that context. But that has nothing to do with the bigger questions."

Conversation with Stein is studded with references to the financial constraints under which Voyager operates, and he often seems to use this as the excuse for not using more sophisticated design. "We have champagne tastes and beer budgets," he exclaims at one point. While Voyager has not made a profit in its ten years, he is quick to point out that it has not made a loss either. *A Hard Day's Night* is so far its best-selling CD-ROM, having sold fifty thousand copies—five times the average sales per title, which each costs around $125,000 to produce. According to a *New York Times* report last July, Voyager held a 5 percent market share of CD-ROM consumer publishing, ranking sixth behind Compton's NewMedia, Software Toolworks, Interplay, Microsoft, and Brøderbund.

The Macbeth and Beethoven projects were undertaken as experimental prototypes, with financial support from the Markle Foundation, a New York–based foundation that has now made program-related investments in Voyager totaling over $500,000 toward these and three other titles. "The market won't pay for these products," says Edith Bjornson, Markle's program officer, "but Voyager has the talent, and we think the whole industry will benefit from having them produced."

At Voyager, the key player is the producer, who works with an author, a programmer, and a graphic designer, the latter sometimes an outside contractor but more often in-house. The fact that the company presently has no art director—the last person in that role left six months ago—may account for the company's haphazard self-presentation. The Voyager logo is an unremarkable affair; CD-ROM package cover designs vary hectically from title to title; 12-point Palatino and Avenir seem to have been adopted as the default on-screen typefaces; technical instruction leaflets achieve clarity but are otherwise almost devoid of any graphic personality. According to Susan Griffin, Voyager's marketing director, it is hard to find designers with experience in both print and electronic design who could successfully straddle, and coordinate, both sides of the company's design persona.

In the absence of an art director, nobody at Voyager has either the eye or the authority to insist that its titles are as pathbreaking aesthetically as they strive to be technically and conceptually. Without that kind of vision, the company can in the long term only be hobbled by atavistic ambitions. If Voyager truly intends to "get there from here"—leading the quest for the new paradigm for the electronic medium—it needs to be actively on the lookout for that paradigm. (New Voices, New Visions, the international competition that Voyager cosponsored last year with Interval Research and *Wired* magazine, was a step in the right direction, yielding many entries rich with suggestive possibilities for titles less slavishly adherent to the literary model.) To retain its reputation at the forefront of new media, Voyager will have to move beyond its current primary goal—of simulating the next best on-screen approximation to a book. This, surely, will require a different attitude toward the contribution that designers have to make, and a commitment to innovation, rather than to the repurposing of existing media.

"I'm basically a dilettante," Stein remarks confessionally, when asked why, if he's so interested in ideas, he didn't pursue an academic career. "What's attractive about publishing is you get to publish a hundred different books a year. Someone else goes deeply into a subject and all you have to do is skim the top. For me, content really is more important than form. Therefore, from a design standpoint, our stuff is extremely conservative. I'm interested in using today's technology to disseminate the important, challenging ideas of individuals so those ideas can be chewed over, wrestled with, and reacted to."

When We Were Very Young

Philip Johnson

Blueprint, July–August 1996

Philip Johnson turns ninety on July 8, and the occasion is being celebrated here in New York as if it were the birthday of the Queen Mother, which in a way it is. Magazines and broadcasters have duly paid court: before we met, he appeared on the cover of *Out*, America's best-selling gay and lesbian magazine, in connection with his proposal for the world's largest gay church; the *New Yorker* carried a Talk of the Town item by Dodie Kazanjian; and Peter Blake interviewed him in *New York* magazine. At a huge fund-raising garden party held in his honour at the Museum of Modern Art, in June, guests all wore paper spectacles in the shape of his trademark circular black glasses.

Having first interviewed him nearly ten years ago for *Blueprint* ("Now We Are Eighty," March 1987, pages 81–96 in this volume), I decide not to ask Philip the obvious questions about the current state of architecture, his or anyone else's. Instead, on the principle that the older one gets, the clearer one's recollection of long-ago experiences, I ask him to recall a particularly vivid memory from each decade of his life. Still spry, if on the thin side, he looks off into the distance and answers, in a sometimes barely audible voice. "My vocal chords are shriveling," he explains.

"Fräulein Dorner, she's the key figure that stands out in that decade," he begins, launching gamely into the years 1906–16.

"A very stern Prussian: I didn't like her. She kept a portrait of Wilhelm, the Kaiser, in the closet. And she showed it to us kids. Mother didn't like newborn children," he says. So while their parents took off for Europe, he and his sisters, Jeannette and Theodate (still alive and kicking at ninety-four and eighty-nine, respectively), were left in the care of their governess, who taught them uplifting verses. In fluent and rapid German, Philip recites "*Ich bin klein, Mein Herz ist rein…*"

> *I am small,*
> *my heart is pure,*
> *no one can see in there*
> *but God himself.*

Next, Philip remembers his teens. "Ah: the discovery of sex! Falling in love, with a girl, Talita Jova, at fifteen." A classmate of his sister's, Jova was "to me a perfect beauty. Oh God, that's a nice age to be in love, isn't it? It's so much purer. Actually never went to bed. Too young. I went to Harvard and that was the end of that."

We jump to the year 1919, when the Johnson family moved to Paris. His father was working on a commission headed by Henry Morgenthau investigating Jewish pogroms in Poland. "He couldn't find any," Philip remarks chirpily. To keep himself occupied, the young Philip set himself the task of visiting every metro station, going to the end of every line. "That's how I discovered my favourite part: the Buttes-Chaumont, in the northeast, with fake mountains, towers, and bridges. It would look kind of small to me probably these days, but then it was very dramatic."

The year 1919 was also when he first visited Chartres Cathedral. "That was when I first realised I had to become an architect: it was a personal epiphany. I was emotional and teary, all the proper things. I remember the glass was gone because of the war:

they'd taken it down and put it in hiding. They had oiled paper, khaki-coloured, instead of the stained glass in the windows." He pauses for a moment. "It's sort of like sex: like any excitement when you're young, it's blown up to enormous proportions."

A second epiphany occurred in 1928 when he saw the Parthenon. "Tears, the works," he recalls. "You know, that's the best way to judge how people like a building: if their eyes glisten. If they don't, they're either not visual or they hate your building or something. The only building I've made people do that with is my new visitor centre"—the gatehouse at his estate in New Canaan, Connecticut, designed, he claims, in the manner of expressionist Hermann Finsterlin.

So it's an emotional reaction he's after?

"Is there any other?" Philip scoffs. "I always thought architecture was an art that you got excited about. That's what Mother always said."

Travelling around European museums with Mother, whose favourite painter was Duccio, Philip acquired an early penchant for Poussin ("I'm a Romantic, and all Romantics like Poussin") before developing a more abstract taste for Paul Klee and Pablo Picasso. Then there's Caspar David Friedrich, whom he discovered one summer in Berlin. "That's the only painter I go to see if I'm forced to go to that dreadful city. It was destroyed in the war, and now instead of finishing it off with a few well-placed bombs, they're talking about redoing it." He happens to be doing a "huge building" there, but nonetheless vouchsafes that "I don't think you can use capitalism to rebuild cities. The impulse has to be a passion for the city as it was for the Greeks or in the Middle Ages. You can't re-plan cities based on the idea that everybody's going to make money on them."

We skip lightly over the early years at Harvard, where he studied philosophy, found his fellow students "absolutely stupid," and preferred to fraternise with his tutors, becoming part of the coterie around Alfred North Whitehead. "I became an escort for Mrs. Whitehead. Drove her around, country driving. We talked and she smoked." More than that? "No," he says, emphatically. "She was five times my age. I was homosexual by then."

By age twenty-four, Johnson was working at the Museum of Modern Art. "Is 1930 in my third decade?" he asks, eager to keep things in chronological order. That year saw him travelling in Germany with Henry-Russell Hitchcock, "looking for modern architecture" that they would shortly canonise as the International Style. Thanks to their MoMA exhibition of 1932 and its accompanying book, we know full well which buildings they discovered. But what was the vehicle of this epic journey?

"A Cord, a front-wheel drive. Very, very long, low, and racy. Green. It was *the* car: everybody screamed and yelled as we drove through. I love to drive fast. The Cord Company: gone, long ago." Except for one gigantic silver Packard 12, it's been "nothing but Mercedes since then."

And his passenger? "Very strange. But Russell was a great architecture critic: he knew a building from a mile away. I had no eyes and had no reason to. I'd never taken a course in architecture and I still haven't any history. Hitchcock refused to take photographs. He said, 'It'll keep you from looking at the building.' So I didn't take photographs. I had the architects we stopped to see send them on."

Mies's Tugendhat House, in Brno, "was one of the great events" but he can't quite recall when he first saw it. "I can't tell, because I spent so many other trips with Mies. With him, I remember food. There were two great restaurants in Berlin. We would have these very expensive, *deee*licious meals. I had more money than him. More money? He didn't have any. He was a gourmet. He would just shut up and eat. And he had a real knowledge of wine. Whatever he drank, he drank to excess. He was no intellectual." So what was Mies's favourite dish? "*Gaense Leberpastete* *mit Zwiebel*," says Philip, savouring the memory. Goose liver pâté with onions.

We delicately reconnoitre the ugly period, documented in detail in Franz Schulze's 1994 biography, of Philip's involvement in right-wing politics in America. Then there was his time in Nazi Germany. How does he feel about that period of his life?

"Oh very much ashamed. Because I went to Nuremberg and listened to Hitler, who was a great speaker. But he weren't no Huey Long, no populist. He was a dictator. A nasty, horrid man. Ralph Barnes of the *New York Herald Tribune* said, 'Don't you know you're making an ass of yourself? Get out!' So I took the next plane."

Didn't he realise that himself?

"Not enough. It wasn't clear to me. I think Nuremberg was the most febrilely exciting day I ever had. Ten, twenty, fifty thousand people yelling in the streets. I couldn't understand the speeches, and I wasn't there because of the German boys, in spite of what people think. It was feverish, like the way Americans feel about sports. I was there for one day, and I never saw it with the lights."

———

Having suffered a major angioplasty a week before his eightieth birthday, Philip hardly expected to last another whole decade, but after a year of recovery, he gradually regained strength. "Now I'm perfect. The only thing now is I fall down, lose my balance. I was going to quit when I was a hundred, but now I realise that I can't possibly. I'm thinking of too many things. The gatehouse gave me a new kick. I'm proud of doing viscerally exciting new buildings. I'm doing sculptural building now, only," he says, as if announcing the look for the new season.

He's busy with numerous commissions, including the new gay and lesbian community church in Dallas, the nearest thing on the drawing boards right now to a cathedral, which is the kind of project he told Peter Blake he'd most like to design. "You can't get an emotional enough building unless it has an impetus that I don't happen to share," he explains, somewhat paradoxically. "I'm not religious, but it doesn't make any difference. I can work on a shape that I think is exciting. The gatehouse is very church-like." I'm reminded of the verses that Fräulein Dorner engraved upon his heart.

After an hour and a half of chatting, it is 4:00 p.m. and time for him to leave his office. We have only made it somewhere into his third decade, so we agree to reconvene in 2006. The rest, as they say, is history.

Best of All Possible Worlds

David Rockwell

I.D. Magazine, September–October 1996

Friday is Dog Day at the Rockwell Group office, so up on the eighth floor, overlooking New York's Union Square, various species of canine are wandering around underneath their owners' desks or dozing next to thick stacks of presentation boards. This real-life menagerie finds a curious echo in a rendering of the proposed extension to Caesar's Palace casino in Las Vegas, one of the many current projects on display in the architecture firm's teeming loft. The Vegas Mirage may have its volcano erupting at regular intervals, but Rockwell's Circus Maximus will go one better, with a full-scale indoor Roman hill town and an outdoor Noah's Ark of exotic animals parading several times daily on the Strip. After all, why use technology to imitate nature when you can have nature itself, albeit tamed and domesticated?

"It's all so hyper, steroidal, and blown up out there in Las Vegas," comments David Rockwell, the forty-year-old ringmaster of the Rockwell Group. So he and his team have decided to buck the trend toward more and more flashy special effects and go for "an idea so outrageously counter to technology that I think it could work": the old-fashioned thrill of wild beasts. He assures me that the project is overseen by consultant zoologists, and that the lower portion of the hill town will provide pens for the animals between sets.

Still, there's something quietly disturbing about the image itself: a colored drawing that looks more like something out of a nineteenth-century children's bedtime fable than a perspective for a casino in the late 1990s—lighthearted about using exotic animals to turn a gambling reserve into a modified game reserve, blithely innocent about the multibillion-dollar entertainment industry. Because this industry is the economic engine that has really driven the Rockwell Group's growth, from 40 people three years ago to 110-strong today. Its expansion is a measure of the massive demand for new leisure venues in the US and worldwide, a trend noted during *I.D. Magazine*'s Entertainment Design Roundtable (March–April 1996), in which Rockwell participated.

Populated predominantly by upbeat thirtysomethings and their dogs, the atmosphere at the office is that of a frenetic fun factory, an assembly plant for the combine harvesters of the late twentieth-century leisure landscape: restaurants, casinos, circuses, theme parks, theme restaurants (including Planet Hollywoods in thirty cities), movie theaters, and cruise ships, for clients including Caesar's, Disney, Sun International, Marvel, Sony Theatres, and CBS.

"I always loved the circus. I thought owning a bunch of tigers would be great," says Rockwell, patting an employee's pet while explaining the multitude of giant projects currently on the firm's drawing boards. Customarily attired in jeans and sneakers (though he sports just socks in the office), Rockwell is possessed of a charm and boyish demeanor just this side of rock stardom. It's easy to see why he has become one of the most sought-after exponents of "entertainment design"—that hybrid of narrative-driven interior design, lighting, and special effects, practiced on the same scale by only a few other American firms, such as the Jerde Partnership, Thompson & Wood, and Walt Disney Imagineering.

"The whole movement in our industry is no longer to create malls with department stores, but to do something much more theatrical," says Sheldon Gordon, client for Circus Maximus and for the conversion of London's Battersea Power Station. "That's where the mystique of the Rockwell Group lies."

———

Born in Chicago, the youngest of five boys, David Rockwell moved with his family at age ten to Guadalajara, Mexico, where he attended high school and seriously considered a career as a concert pianist. From south of the border, Rockwell remembers, American popular entertainment—TV shows like *I Love Lucy*— came to have almost mythic appeal. Another period abroad may also have served to cement this enthusiasm: while studying architecture at Syracuse, he spent a semester at London's Architectural Association, where he was exposed to the lingering influence of the 1960s Archigram group, whose heady visions of architecture and technology (such as *Plug-in City*) were peculiarly British interpretations of American pop iconography.

But Rockwell freely admits "architecture was certainly not my first love." That passion was reserved for the theater, which still evokes strong emotions for Rockwell, especially given its family associations. As a boy, he took part in amateur dramatics organized by his mother, a former vaudeville dancer who died when he was fifteen; one of his closest brothers, who died of AIDS just a couple of years ago, also worked in theater. While in college, he worked as a summer assistant to the Broadway lighting designer Roger Morgan, and his conversation is peppered with references to specific theatrical productions and their set designers, from Bob Crowley to Ralph Koltai to Boris Aronson.

"Theater, when it works, has the ability to create a lasting memory," he explains. "It's a participatory experience, something that's being done in real time, much more of a living, breathing experience. It's hotter, more involving. What's so fun is looking at the audience."

The Rockwell portfolio runs the gamut from the pumped-up high tech of the Planet Hollywood at Florida's Walt Disney World to the repro Art Deco of the forthcoming Sony multiplex in Detroit to the neo-neoclassicism of Circus Maximus. This liberal borrowing from history, and the firm's chameleon tendency to render each project in a different graphic style, lead one to wonder what exactly constitutes the Rockwell Group's own architectural signature. "It's very safe to go into a design process knowing what the result is going to be, based on a preconceived style," Rockwell says, arguing that, by contrast, his firm takes a more collaborative approach than most architects. "We are very experientially driven. We try to find out what's unique about each project, and draw that out with the client."

Gradually one realizes that this flamboyant eclecticism *is* the house style, albeit underpinned by a consistent emphasis on lighting and materials, as well as a penchant for figurative puns, like the giant popcorn-container concession stand at the Sony Loews Eighty-Fourth Street cinema, or the barstools in the form of cocktail olives at the Monkey Bar restaurant, both in Manhattan. The more populist a place is meant to be, the greater the density of eye-catching material on display, as if there were some direct relationship between profusion of detail and richness of narrative content. Or to put it another way: the shorter the time scheduled for customers to have a good time (as in theme restaurants like Planet Hollywood and the Official All Star Sports Cafe, where turnover of tables is tightly choreographed), the higher the necessary dosage of visual stimuli.

At the first All Star Cafe, which opened in February in New York's Times Square, the cornice line is taken up with a ring of giant TV monitors, offering a Las Vegas–style sports book blitz to compete with one's burger and fries. A new hybrid experience is in the making here: a kind of public TV dinner. "In All Star, the mission was to try and create a stadium-type experience, through video," says Rockwell, though in a real stadium the crowd is usually focused on a single point of action, whereas here, the diners' attention is centrifugally dispersed along multiple sightlines. "It works best when all of those screens are used together," Rockwell concedes, explaining that his team doesn't have a lot of control over what gets broadcast. "We try to have input on the content, on what's actually happening there. If not, the system is designed to do one thing, and it ends up doing another." As architecture becomes more intertwined with moving-image media, their programming becomes integral to the overall spatial effect.

———

At the June press conference unveiling the Mohegan Sun casino, scheduled to open in October in Connecticut, I listen as the Wolf People's cultural attaché explains the project's allusions to tribal customs and rituals. Developed by Sol Kerzner's Sun International in partnership with the Mohegan Indians, this new out-of-stately pleasure dome is being built on the reused foundations of the former United Nuclear Corporation, and is clearly intended to rival Foxwoods Resort Casino ten miles east. Rockwell explains that "the language of the Mohegan tribe is practically gone," and that "to take its two or three basic building types, all very small, and blow them up to mammoth proportions was an obvious no-no." Adopting a strategy that historians have termed the Invention of Tradition, his team developed "a mythic landscape that is not a literal re-creation of anything that existed before," and "an 'order' of architecture that relates to this tribe, incorporating the two key Mohegan symbols, the Path of Life and the Medallion." Each quadrant of its circular plan is associated with a season, a theme that extends from the canopied entrances at the cardinal points to those places where the demands of food-court nationalism require a sudden shift in decor from Mohegan to some other culture.

While Rockwell is eloquently outlining the scheme, my attention strays to the presentation boards arrayed all around the assembled press. Color interior perspectives, mostly by night, their palette and rendering style are reminiscent of storyboards by movie art directors, concept sketches that convey the look of a film, its atmosphere and emotional cadences. It crosses my mind that the Rockwell Group designs not so much real places as scenarios. These images are meant to conjure an *impression* of a place that does not yet exist, and moreover, never will: the environment that you enter, when construction is completed, is only the 3D realization of a fictional elsewhere. The original existed only as a fantasy in a comic book or movie or TV program. Entering a Rockwell Group project is tantamount to entering the film itself, the story come to life. How this tallies with real life, and what impact that has on our perception thereof, remains to be determined.

––––

At the end of the nineteenth century, a whole spate of utopian novels appeared—including Edward Bellamy's famous *Looking Backward* of 1888—that offered detailed accounts of fantastic future cities. Such technological visions fed the imaginations of civic architects and world's fair dreamers; theme park attractions are the everyday successors to those spectacular expositions, theme restaurants their downtown spores.

The Rockwell Group is continuing in this time-honored tradition: designing fantasy environments that satisfy a fin de siècle appetite for escape. But by now, the technologies (like elevators and telephones) that were so radical a century ago have become standard infrastructure. So the firm's projects speak not to the excitement of a future yet to be realized, but of a past that seems in collective memory to have been more magical. If a dream represents a wish, then these entertainment complexes represent the desire to return to simple childhood wonderment at the marvels of Science and Technology, to a culture in touch with nature and the turning seasons, rather than distanced from it by communication technology and media-based spectacles such as sporting tournaments.

Talking with Rockwell and his senior associates—all equally effervescent in their enthusiasm for their work—one sometimes marvels at how they can be so relentlessly upbeat, so unvexed by the implications of creating environments for high-octane spectatorship and consumption. Not for them the agonized inquiries of "culture industry" critics or academic theorists. One must look elsewhere for discussion of the ethics of gambling as a tool of economic regeneration, or the curious trade-off between authenticity and artifice whereby a Native American tribe willingly permits its symbolism to be recast as the ersatz architectural vernacular of a giant casino. The politics of mass leisure are not easily broached with those daily immersed in its manufacture.

———

In an attempt to root out some—any—intimations of inner disquiet, I send Rockwell a recent interview with Benjamin Barber, author of the 1995 book *Jihad vs. McWorld*, in which he argues that global media and service corporations are reducing diverse communities to one homogeneous world culture. Referring to what he calls "Disney colonization," Barber likens the almost imperceptibly gradual process of cultural domination to "a very shallow but extensive flood tide that seeps into everything. It doesn't seem deep or disastrous at the time, but then we find that mud is…everywhere."

When we meet for lunch at Nobu, the Japanese restaurant in Tribeca that is one of Rockwell's most celebrated designs, he has carefully read and highlighted the article, but rejects most of its key contentions. "I disagree with the implication in the essay you sent that technology is flattening and homogenizing time and culture," he tells me. "So does travel, and so does old age. You could pick out the same things Barber says are terrible, and find the wonderful, magical things about them. To say Disney is bad as a thing is so simplistic. I'd say Disney's done some wonderful stuff and some that's not so wonderful. And if you don't want to watch Disney, don't turn them on."

He turns and asks me a question: "You find Disney interferes with the way you proceed with your life?"

I suggest that what Barber is referring to is much more systemic, having to do with ownership and control of technology. "I understand the point, though I think it's overstated," Rockwell says. "I just have a much more optimistic view of technology. The combination of craftsmanship and technology is very exciting."

While he's talking, Rockwell's positive outlook succeeds in making one suspend one's deep-seated qualms about the kinds of places his firm produces, their saccharine appeal to a common denominator culture.

"I think playfulness and a sense of humor are survival skills," he says. "It's no mystery that people want to be in places that encourage that. I certainly believe that optimism, humor, magic, and wit are the flip opposites of tragedy." Asked if he could conceive of doing something as sober as the Holocaust Museum, he replies, "It would be a real challenge, but sure." (Actually, what he'd *really* like to do next is a Caribbean resort or an airport.)

"My own experiences are sort of wonderful and horrible all at the same time," he reflects. "I think optimism is just the smarter choice."

Information Overlord

Michael Bloomberg

Rethinking Design 4: Medium, 1997

At the turn of the twentieth century, the "daylight factory" was all the rage. Its steel frame, supporting broad expanses of glazing, allowed workers ample light and views of their proto-Edge City greenfield surroundings, and was vaunted as promoting healthful working conditions. Manufacturers proudly gave tours of their innovative premises to impress visiting dignitaries. Today, perhaps, the New York headquarters of Bloomberg L.P. play an equivalent role as a prototype factory of the information era.

Unless you're in financial services, you probably had not heard of this sixteen-year-old "information service, news and media company," or its eponymous founder, until recently. With his knack for public relations, a recent autobiography, and an expanding share of the financial information market (Bloomberg's two closest rivals being Reuters Holdings PLC and Dow Jones Markets, formerly known as Telerate), Michael Bloomberg is rapidly implementing the vision of cross-media integration that has become the holy grail of much longer-established publishing and broadcasting enterprises.

At the heart of this enterprise is the Bloomberg terminal, an online system delivering real-time, twenty-four-hour financial information, news, and analysis to some 250,000 subscribers through proprietary terminals that rent for about $1,200 per

month. Several other global operations have flourished around
this core business: the syndicated Bloomberg News service,
with 80 bureaus and over 450 reporters; Bloomberg Television,
offering twenty-four-hour news broadcasts in seven languages,
and three other magazine shows in the US; Bloomberg News
Radio (via 100 affiliates worldwide); *Bloomberg* magazine,
circulated to Bloomberg system subscribers; the monthly
Bloomberg Personal; Bloomberg Press books; and the www.
bloomberg.com website. These media are all spearheaded from
a few floors of an otherwise unremarkable black glass office
tower in midtown Manhattan.

————

At the front desk, a security badge is issued while-u-wait, thus adding visitors to the vast pool of surveilled data that is Bloomberg.
The fifteenth-floor reception is visually anchored by a large
aquarium, in which tropical fish meander in leisurely disregard
of the Dow's current status. Men and women with full briefcases
schmooze in twos and threes, or talk on their cell phones—the
adrenalized chatter of stock exchanges and conventions. Beyond,
employees help themselves from a cornucopia of snacks at a vast
and conspicuously positioned commissary—a pit stop on the
Information Highway, fueling round-the-clock work.
    A bank of glass-walled rooms intervenes between this
lobby and the main newsroom, offering a tantalizing peek
into the company's throbbing heart. Beyond the assortment of
miscellaneous meetings in the immediate foreground, a TV
anchor is sitting at her podium, enunciating with that earnest
radiance of a person addressing multitudes, but actually talking
to a teleprompter. The architectural transparency not only
facilitates working relations, but also serves as a metaphor
for the fungibility of media content at Bloomberg. In the main
newsroom, a person may digitally edit the sound wave of their

voice for radio, then step over snaking cables, and hop into an elevated chair in the floodlit corner of the same room to record a portion of Bloomberg Television. TV anchors operate the teleprompter and robotic cameras, and upload video segments and financial graphics from the Bloomberg terminal via a battery of customized keypads. Bustling and humming with many phones and purposeful voices, the newsroom is strangely improvisatory, as if the people have retrofitted themselves to the technology, which has grown like kudzu—a far cry from the sanitized *2001*-style vision of futuristic environments. Here, desks are piled high with equipment, keyboards, and miscellaneous personal mementos. Intermittent super-brightness emanates from the television studio corner, but otherwise the ambience is crepuscular, the walls sandbagged with a solid flank of computer servers (the main system computers, the "Data Generals," are sealed in their own glass-fronted clean rooms on each floor). Like in a military bunker, the outside world is relayed primarily via clocks that tell the time in several cities around the world, and live action caught on various monitors. In contrast to the maze of screens, joysticks, and buttons in this main newsroom, the view from one of the corner television interview studios—a straight vista up Park Avenue—is almost surreally beautiful.

———

True to his company philosophy, Michael Bloomberg doesn't have a private office. But he does have a glass-fronted antechamber behind his desk, where interviews are conducted in some measure of acoustic, if not visual, privacy. A glass-encased wooden gavel from Johns Hopkins University (where Bloomberg is chairman of the board of trustees) shares the coffee table with a pile of Bloomberg publications. Talking with Bloomberg is like a rodeo ride, with the split-second buy-sell vehemence you might expect from a former equity trader turned financial data nabob. He speaks in the same short, pit bull sentences and rhetorical questions that make one laugh out loud, cheering his relentless chutzpah, when reading his recent autobiography. *Bloomberg by Bloomberg* tells how he turned his $10 million payoff from Salomon Brothers into his own media empire.

Mike—as his security badge declares him—is impatient about questions regarding his design philosophy. Like many entrepreneurs, he sees design as an ornamental gloss on the real business of making money. Bloomberg L.P. is marked by a mixed array of design expressions—some of which work service-ably well, while others clearly sacrifice elegance (and perhaps usability) to utility. Still, Bloomberg as a company is significant not because it embraces a traditional policy of "good design," but because—by virtue of the sheer speed and diversity of media with which it delivers information—it has such widespread impact on daily mass communication.

———

In his book, Bloomberg writes that "transparency produces fair-ness," and refers several times to the way that the computer's dissolution of traditional barriers to information—for example, by giving buyers and sellers access to the same data—has revo-lutionized the financial services industry. The absence of parti-tions or private offices throughout Bloomberg's global empire seems the physical corollary of this philosophy, as do the lack of formal titles and traditional job descriptions. Still, Bloomberg brushes off such intellectualizing. "It isn't that transparency does anything," he replies. "It's that the alternative prevents. Barriers inhibit transparency. This doesn't suit the person who wants to have their corner office and isn't willing to give that up. But the more the rest of the world builds impediments to communica-tion, the happier I am, because they're competitors."

For years, the proprietary terminal known as the Bloomberg Box was oddly self-effacing. Bulky, squat, and PC-like, it was criticized by subscribers for taking up precious desk space and adding another keyboard to the gamut of data-entry devices required to operate in financial services. The Box was recently transformed into a sleek pair of gunmetal gray flat-screen monitors that perch at eye level on a vertical bracket. From a clunky box, it has evolved into something that would not look out of place in the Sharper Image catalogue, its styling and slim proportions projecting decidedly more fetish value than its predecessor. Hence, perhaps, *New York Times* reporter Mark Landler's remark that the device "has become almost a totem on Wall Street, like owning a desktop BMW."

The redesigned Box uses flat-screen technology. "CRTs kill you," Bloomberg says categorically, when asked what led to the new model. "Flat panels take a lot less desk space, generate a lot less heat and a lot less radiation. They do cost more. But once you get over the science and major engineering problems, then volume brings the price down." The new paired screens can be mounted side-by-side (like an open book) or vertically, at an adjustable height. "There are a lot of cases where you want to monitor something while doing work," says Bloomberg. "Under Windows, if you display two screens one under the other, it's a lot harder. We are giving you the ability to put two screens next to each other physically."

The new design of the Box was done in-house, but Bloomberg declines to specify by whom. "We don't have a team—we don't formalize those things that way. We may have used an outside guy to design the bezel, but fundamentally we do all this stuff ourselves." He seems genuinely amazed that anyone would be interested in the external characteristics of something that is prominent in so many people's daily work environments. "How much time can you spend looking at a bezel for a flat panel?" he asks. "This isn't rocket science…"

The Bloomberg terminal carries text and numbers in various colored fonts on a dark blue background. It can perform various analytic functions and generate on-the-fly graphs and charts from its deep trove of data, collected and archived by some 1,000 Bloomberg employees based in Princeton, New Jersey. Data search is conducted via a specially designed keyboard that future ethnographers may interpret as the Rosetta Stone of late twentieth-century information society. Along with a circular loudspeaker on the right-hand side (for accessing radio news) are several groups of color-coded buttons, whose capitalized abbreviations describe a universe of financial instruments and indices including equities, money markets, municipal bonds, and currencies. Most important among these buttons is the big green "GO" command, allowing the user to feel like they've just launched a nuclear warhead when they're actually just punching in a request for information. "The mouse has really very little utility for us," Bloomberg explains. "When you have a long list of alternatives, typing in a number makes a lot more sense than moving a mouse. Most human beings today still find it easier to press keys for the number seven and 'GO' than bringing the mouse over onto seven and double clicking. If we had a business where everything could be identified with an icon, that would be a different story. But our clients have to see it spelled out in words then pick it. We have a hundred thousand different securities on this system. We have one and a half MILLION municipal securities. To have an icon for each municipal security? *C'mon.*"

On the subject of information graphics, I ask what he thinks of three-dimensional data display. "A nice gimmick, but it doesn't add anything," Bloomberg quickly informs me. "People don't think in three dimensions. It's hard enough plotting X versus Y. 3D is the kind of thing to keep people at the MIT Media

Lab occupied and to give you something to write about. But in the real world, it's about as useful as 3D movies. Remember those days?"

Still, he concedes that even if it has limited relevance in the business world, 3D has a significant role to play in entertainment. "If you could make your television in 3D, people would love it." Asked to expand on a pithy statement in his book, that "the data most people desire is entertainment," Bloomberg swiftly responds with another mantra from the same tome: "Entertainment is nice but not necessary." Not necessary at all? "It's fungible. If the price of a movie went to $100 from $7, would I prefer to go to the Hoops or the Pucks, or buy a book, or go lie in the grass in Central Park? They're all different things. But any specific form of entertainment is very fungible with any other form of entertainment. In the aggregate they probably really are necessary. But if you didn't see the World Cup in the US, or the Super Bowl, your life would go on."

So what defines something as *information* as opposed to *entertainment*? "Information is necessary to do your job. Or lead your life. Information's what you need." This may be one reason why, as he asserts, newspapers "will be around for an awfully long time. They're random-access, have multiple displays like our TV screen, and are very portable. You'd have to replace those characteristics electronically before you could replace a newspaper."

Bloomberg Television's segmented screen is his attempt to overcome the fact that TV, like radio, is a sequential-access medium. A few minutes spent watching this channel is enough to appreciate its addictive potential. Despite its cluttered surface, garish palette, and wild profusion of typographic and numerical data, the Bloomberg TV screen is absolutely riveting, because keeping up with its changing contents is akin to a game—like watching a manic advent calendar, or an animated bento box. In vain I set myself the challenge of writing down an entire screen's worth of information before one story cycles to the next. The system repeats major stories at thirty-minute intervals, but the individual departments—statistical gauges of quotidian culture such as weather, time, and sports, plus financial headlines, general news and trivia, and stock quotes—turn at different rates. Upcoming topics are flagged with a cut like those on manila file folders. Highlights, bevels, and shadows endow the screen with the appearance of a hyperactive clock radio: one with lots of buttons to press, bulging with novelty, but whose plethora of functions is probably more symbolic than actually useful.

"The problem with sequential access is that if you want a specific kind of information you've got to wait until it comes up," says Bloomberg. "We've tried to cut the wait by a factor of four, by having four different things going on at the same time."

What determined the factor of four, as opposed to five, or seven? "The physical space the eye can see. There's a technical limitation to the number of characters that can be resolved on a television. Then you try to lay it out." Evidently, there is still some way to go with this particular art, since text breaks are often very clumsy, leaving a jagged rag and lots of empty space—especially in the middle-left compartment, where lifestyle and trivia appear. Asked whether much usability testing has been done with the on-screen graphics, Bloomberg replies, "I watch it myself, all the time. I designed it. Why would I ask anybody else?"

Does he think there's an end goal of technology that will make things ultimately convenient? "As technology gets better, as you have more bandwidth, faster chips, and smaller battery technology, you will have much more complex systems internally, and the external interfaces will become simpler. That's why I think kids studying computers in elementary schools is one of the great frauds of all time. There's nothing a kid is going to learn in elementary school that's going to be remotely useful by the time they get out of high school, much less out of college."

Instead, Bloomberg argues that schoolchildren should be taught "reading, writing, arithmetic, social skills, personal hygiene, logic." And he's equally adamant about how these skills should be imparted. "Well, you don't do it by computer," he insists. "We invented a device to do this a long time ago: it's called a human teacher. The more technology we have, the more the world is a meritocracy, and the more obvious it becomes whether you have the basic skills: the ability to reason, to absorb information, put it in context, know about history and geography. One thing that's becoming less important with time are the technological skills, because it's those things that get automated."

So how exactly would he characterize the design attributes of the media that Bloomberg L.P. puts out?

"I think they're less important than the content. I didn't say they were unimportant, I said they are less important. I don't want this company to be fighting battles with press releases and pizzazz and image. We should be fighting the competitive battles with substance. It isn't that I don't care about production values. But I don't believe for one second that the presentation is anywhere near as important as the content. Other companies may. That's what they're supposed to do. Life is not a zero-sum game."

———

Returning to Penn Station one summer weekend I encounter the pair of gigantic Bloomberg TV screens that project from a concave wall heralding the main entrance to the Amtrak ticket hall. Between them, the word *Bloomberg* looms against a backlit background, forming precisely the kind of grand triumphal archway that New York City lacks at all its termini. This giant advertisement is reminiscent of the dioramas in world's fair pavilions, dazzling in their scale and technological artillery. A stranger descending from the taxi drop-off might be forgiven for thinking

Daddy Wouldn't Buy Me a Bauhaus

that this was, in fact, Bloomberg Station. And that's not entirely beside the point.

A mutant descendant of Charles and Ray Eames's multi-screen presentations (most memorably at IBM's Information Machine in its pavilion at the 1964 New York World's Fair), the Bloomberg Television interface is an archetype of our times: the visual manifestation of a society gorging itself on information. The USA Today of TV, it is an object lesson in simultaneous perception, or possibly, displaced attention. The sheer quantity and immediacy of the data transmitted take precedence over one's ability to absorb it. Whether or not one agrees with the implicit values of such a service, the success of Bloomberg L.P. requires us to recognize that terms of the design debate have changed—and to start considering what new criteria now apply. The company's prolific and multifarious output serves notice that design, in the information era, is no longer just a matter of how things look or even how they work, but is, more often, the raw expression of an ever-changing nexus of speed, electrons, and global capital.

The Choreography of Site-Specific Media

Lisa Strausfeld

Profile: Pentagram Design, 2004

Pentagram made a very shrewd move when it brought Lisa Strausfeld on board in January 2002. With her appointment, the firm brought into its ranks an alumna of the 1990s-era Visible Language Workshop (VLW) at MIT's Media Lab, and thus one of the elite corps of graduates from a program whose influence is already proving disproportionate to their actual numbers and relatively youthful careers. (Her VLW classmates included David Small, Grace Colby, Suguru Ishizaki, and Yin Yin Wong.)

Strausfeld's résumé includes a hybrid education encompassing art history and computer science at Brown University, followed by a master's degree in architecture from Harvard. Only then did she move down the block to the MIT Media Lab. It was there that I first encountered her in 1994, while I was conducting what turned out to be the last interview with her professor, Muriel Cooper, the eccentric but brilliant director of the Lab's Visible Language Workshop (see pages 209–26 in this volume). Strausfeld's use of very clean, mostly sans-serif typography and an elemental color palette worthy of Johannes Itten reflects both her architectural training and the abiding graphic influence of Cooper, who (as head of the media department at the MIT Press in the 1970s) designed the authoritative textbook on the Bauhaus, and disdained the curlicues of postmodernist graphics as she reared a new generation of visual (interactive) designers.

Strausfeld's arrival at the Media Lab coincided with the donation of several powerful new Silicon Graphics computers capable of generating three-dimensional information spaces. "There was a serendipitous convergence: we got the first batch of SGIs, so it was the first time anyone in the VLW had worked in three dimensions," something which, fresh from architecture grad school, made perfect sense to her. She became interested in the structure of information and the abundant spatial metaphors we employ to denote our daily activities, and their possible computational equivalents.

Strausfeld has continued to work at the frontiers of interactive design, through several career phases. After graduating from MIT, she established Perspecta, a San Francisco–based software-development company with two fellow Media Lab graduates, Earl Rennison and Nicolas Saint-Arnaud. She decided to leave that company even before the dot-com bubble burst, to join Quokka Sports, where, as director of its research arm, Quokka Labs, she developed prototypes for new ways of presenting live sports information on the Web. Shortly before Quokka's collapse in 2000, she moved to New York, and went solo under her own banner of Informationart, working as a consultant to Pentagram to design a media wall for the new Pennsylvania Station in the renovated Farley Post Office building in midtown Manhattan.

In all these phases, Strausfeld has demonstrated an abiding concern for the relationship between architectural space and information space, and for the reinterpretation and reapplication of the precepts of architectural modernism to the realm of data. Recently, she has begun to turn back to architectural space per se, with commissions to embed information into actual buildings: the aforementioned Penn Station; a transportation hub at the World Trade Center (commissioned by the Port Authority of

New York and New Jersey before Studio Daniel Libeskind won the Ground Zero rebuilding commission); and the expansion of the Walker Art Center in Minneapolis, designed by the Swiss architects Herzog & de Meuron. Of these, the first two were designed as speculative prototypes and are now unlikely to be built; the third is slated for implementation in 2005.

In these three projects, Strausfeld demonstrates a methodological approach markedly in contrast to typical "information architecture," a term she hates using because of its connotations of commercial interactive design. Imbued with her architectural training, she treats each commission as a problem, and information as site specific—to be experienced bodily, rather than just through the eyes (and fingertips).

The clues to this structural approach are revealed in a diagram she developed at Quokka: a grid showing the different degrees of immersive experience offered by different display devices. Screen dimensions are charted against durations of engagement and their various social contexts: from the individual experience of the handheld device or desktop computer, to the more convivial group setting in an arena, beholding Jumbotron or other large-scale display. The diagram pinpoints Strausfeld's concern with the physical as well as the emotional dimensions of experience. "The idea of embodying information has always been interesting to me. I like the idea of merging these two worlds — the world of abstract and intangible ideas and the world of physical things."

At Perspecta, she and her partners developed information structures that allowed viewers to "fly through" information so that, as you moved closer to a particular piece of information, more and more detail, or related articles, came into view. While Perspecta's clients were mostly in the technology news sector, she and Rennison also developed a more contemplative demo, the *Millennium Project*, which arrayed early twentieth-century landmark events in science, art, and politics as information objects suspended in black virtual space according to their longitude, latitude, and date. When these seemingly neutral colored specks were approached, explanatory text would come into focus, like wall labels hanging free of their walls. The resulting "ride" was reminiscent of trailers for movies set in outer space—implying an infinite depth of knowledge available for discovery.

Moving to Quokka, Strausfeld, a self-confessed non-sports fan, made it her goal "to capture every emotion of live sports events through data" rather than through the typical pictorial means: photos of vanquished or triumphant athletes. "It was about giving the driest data an emotional content." Here, instead of using implied three-dimensional deep space to contain rich troves of data, Strausfeld and her team concentrated on montaging different species of information, in variegated bands and boxes, across the plane of the Web page. Bucketloads of numbers (the nutrients on which sports fans nourish themselves) offered every conceivable measurement—racers' positions, times, distances, and route cross sections, for example. Syncopated against these statistics, several windows of livestreamed video from the racecourse (cameras mounted on, say, a Tour de France bicycle or Grand Prix race car) offered a dizzying multiplicity of vantage points. Compounded by techno sound tracks and interviews with the heroes themselves, reliving their own first-person experience in replay mode, the choreography of time and space had a vertiginous, seductive beauty.

The overall effect of these dense but riveting charts was to elevate sports to the status of medical emergency—trauma as entertainment—with patients' vital signs urgently and anxiously monitored. With options to toggle between alternate synoptic views, users gained a sense of pseudocontrol over the data—a panoptic position more akin to that of a sports producer in a

TV control room, deftly selecting which sources of live feed to broadcast.

For Strausfeld, though, it's not just numbers that count. Just as the *site* is of critical significance in generating architecture, so is the *siting* of information within a physical landscape: not for her the gigantic one-size-fits-all electronic display board, indiscriminately blaring out public information and advertising. Instead, she analyzes the architectural environment and makes site-specific interventions, modulating the support structures on which media will be presented so they become kinetic sculptures that just happen to deliver information—from the necessary but banal (train times), to the apparently vital but largely ritualistic (stock-market figures), to the sublime but usually underfunded (public art projects, to whose presentation the off-hours on the Penn Station and WTC media walls were earmarked).

If constructed, this monumental two-hundred-foot-long video screen would have been the dominant focus of this gigantic train-station concourse, one of our few remaining archetypes of public gathering spaces, besides the sporting arena and the airport. In lectures, Strausfeld frequently shows archive images of crowds in Times Square and Grand Central Station, assembled to watch epochal events like the first space shot: she is particularly interested in how the *collective* experience of news shapes social space. The Penn Station Media Wall is an expression of a (perhaps nostalgic) desire to create an information hearth that could connect myriad strangers, momentarily joined by their need to reach assorted destinations; here, however, multiple storylines deliberately disperse the viewers' attention, rather than focusing them on a commanding single narrative.

On the dominant upper proportion of the screen, train departure times alternate with vast dynamic graphs of stock-market data. A sliding-panel effect allows one type of information to give way to another or, concertina-like, to expand outward to fill the full real estate, in a gliding motion reminiscent of shuffled theatrical flats. Talking-head interviews are relayed upper left at Gulliveresque scale, while the obligatory stock-market ticker chatters away on the lower margin, and several smaller video feeds are shown lower right. Giant letters, spelling NASDAQ and other totemic acronyms, appear now and again on the main body of the wall, scrolling right to left over static data in smaller point sizes. Diaphanous curtains of information glide over one another, transparent, hierarchical, and strenuously factual but somehow also mirage-like, dreamy, and intangible—befitting the (numerical, and predominantly financial) content.

Perhaps this is why the Penn Station Media Wall has become a canonical work without ever having been built: it is, in the nicest sense, vaporware, a work of paper (information) architecture whose dynamic, dancing data and kaleidoscopic dazzle incarnate the Zeitgeist fantasy of an endless upward stock market—a visible representation of the frenzied advances of technology—importing the adrenaline rush and sensory overload of the floor of the New York Stock Exchange to the hall of a major transit hub. It perfectly captures the boomtown mood of late 1990s dot-com New York—a theme park, as one E*Trade advert of the time unapologetically put it, in which "The Theme Is Money."

Postcrash and post-9/11, the attitude to technology has changed. Pentagram was invited by the Port Authority of New York and New Jersey to develop an information system for a transportation terminal on the World Trade Center site. Here, the data have slipped their moorings on the Big Board: Strausfeld threads a ribbonlike "media stream" (an eighteen-inch-wide, high-resolution LED display) through the terminal's spaces, winding, bending, and curving along walls, overhead, or potentially even on floors. Moving at different speeds and in different directions, the interactive text and graphics accompany people walking through the space, and anticipate their needs (providing imminent transit

departures; distances to food concessions; weather advisories
followed by ads for nearby rainwear stores). For consistency, each
category of information is kept in the same type size and horizontal position within the "stream."

A grove of slim seventy-foot-high obelisks rises from the
floor of the main terminal hall toward the upper retail balconies.
These are positioned in the space, in conjunction with three low,
rectangular video partitions, with the spare, space-making intent
of minimalist sculpture (Strausfeld is particularly admiring of
Richard Serra's work). Branchless trees or dynamic totem poles,
these programmable towers might, depending on the time of
day, display the sound waves of arriving trains; carry local, civic,
and national affairs, weather, or financial news; or simply serve
as a bar-chart floor directory. Approached by visitors, the low-
est six feet of each tower act as an interactive terminal, with further information about the actively displayed content or sponsor;
after peak hours, when most "eyeballs" have caught their trains
home, the towers would be released for public art presentations.
Programmed collectively, advertisers might allow slivers of luxury
brands to climb all five towers in sync, or show catwalk models in
teasing partial glimpses that encourage the viewer to fill in missing information. Instead of revealing all, Strausfeld plays with
the metonymic possibilities of commercial messages, sliced and
diced as visual spectacle.

Indeed, her interests are increasingly turning toward the
choreography of content. A diagram in Pentagram's WTC project documentation confirms this: an at-a-glance score of all the
types of content that might be displayed during a typical twenty-
four-hour schedule, it looks just like digital film-editing or
music-authoring software, with multiple bands synchronized
in a horizontal array. This chart flattens out the spatial differences between, say, the content in the West Concourse and the
Media Walls in the Terminal Hall, and strips away the semiotic

complexities to reveal how much the meaning—the cognitive effect—of this system results above all from the syncopated *disjunctures* between different types of content, both horizontally (changing over time) and vertically (relative to one another, at a given moment). While Strausfeld recognizes the discrete iconic significance of different species of information (e.g., commercial advertising versus news, versus public art images), the elegance and economy of this diagram suggests that, for her, what really matters is the overall orchestration of these media channels in time and space as a dynamic site-specific system: that herein lies the relatively untapped potential of media in public spaces.

In the Walker Art Center proposal, Strausfeld takes an even more subtle and adventurous step toward her ambition eventually to "break free of the constraints of display. I'm interested in the work becoming independent of technology at some point: informed by it but not necessarily delivered by it."

Working with/in response to Herzog & de Meuron's architecture, Strausfeld eschews display panels in obvious places in favor of a hierarchy of information outlets. Whether these are gigantic letters projected onto a translucent exterior facade, or flat-screen monitors in the reception, or interactive wall panels announcing an artist's talk, or small, stealthy baseboard-level room-label displays, these nevertheless speak with a consistent institutional authority. "I like the idea that people think of the information as independent of any display, as a voice—the voice of the Walker—that's pushing information toward you, whether outside as you're driving to it, or inside. It's the difference between designing a banner for an institution and designing a sequence of banners that vary depending on where you are in the building, the time of day, and the kind of work on show."

Strausfeld sees herself moving toward editorial content development, through the application of rule-based systems that "encode some kind of ambiguity in the best sense." Lately, teaching in the graphic design master's program at the Yale University School of Art, Strausfeld has instructed her thesis students to study the communication landscape along Route 22 in New Jersey, the suburban environment where she grew up. And she has inevitably found herself revisiting the work of Robert Venturi, Denise Scott Brown, and Steven Izenour, whose *Learning from Las Vegas* of 1972 became a kind of holy writ about media in the urban environment, one now sorely due for updating.

Cognizant of Venturi et al. but (thirty years on) with new tools, new densities of data, and the added dimension of interactivity to contend with, Strausfeld aims to create information experiences that have the lean but implicit richness of certain kinds of architecture—imbued with "moments of clear ambiguity," as she paradoxically describes it. "Before I even studied architecture formally, I was into the aesthetics of programming software. The most elegant solution to coding an algorithm was the shortest, the one with the fewest lines. There's a connection with architecture, where you design this artifact that doesn't move, this fixed thing that has to accommodate all these activities over time. Designing that elegant piece of code, designing a building that's the most essential form to accommodate all those activities: there's a certain design ethic about that, and an aesthetic that I admire."

Julie Snow: The Rugged and the Refined

Julie Snow Architects, 2005

A luminous white aerie on the twenty-fourth floor of the Rand Tower in downtown Minneapolis, commanding a rare, Manhattan-worthy view of the surrounding skyscrapers: the HQ of Julie Snow Architects. The red dot matrix of the TCF building's clock pierces the nighttime panorama. In the far left corner sits the principal of the firm, at work on her G4 laptop—all the toys are black, white, or silver. She's talking on the phone, but periodically, instead of finishing a sentence, she'll throw back her head and emit a voluptuous chuckle—a vocal signature that elides language and laughter, erupting frequently in conversation.

You might not guess this aspect of Snow's personality from her buildings, which tend to be on the abstemious side, not playing for laughs. But the chortle gives it away: underneath it all, she's a playful person. It's just that the game is serious, and Snow has a taste for the tough stuff—engineering, construction, the rigors and logic of building assembly—and architecture is, even in this first decade of the twenty-first century, still considered (effectively) a man's world.

———

Snow's buildings are spartan—at least, they may strike one as such at first glance—but also luxurious in their austerity, in a way that recalls seventeenth-century Dutch still-life paintings, with their contradictory surface expressions of frugality and abundance. Her concern seems to be with creating a taut, precise framework for the enactment of daily life rituals, enabling them but not overdetermining them by imposing a heavily stylized environment in which the user feels obliged to conform to the behavioral dictates of the architect. There is a reticence to her architecture that some may find too astringent, wishing for a more explicit voice or more forceful personality. Snow resists, in favor of establishing finely detailed environments wrought out of structural and social necessities and a relish for the crafts of building engineering and assembly: a glass wall that appears to hang free of its support structure in the Great Plains Software project, a turnbuckle that pulls together the weight of a roof in an inner-city police station, the tracery of stellar constellations on a transit stop's glass canopy. Her aesthetic—wresting elegance out of prefabricated parts and industrial assembly systems—has developed through close collaboration with contractors, building-component manufacturers, and most particularly with engineers: Arup, the international engineering firm, is a regular collaborator. "I'm not an engineer," she volunteers. "But I'm really good at talking to engineers, listening to them." (She's also married to one: Jack Snow.)

———

Spot the black speck making steady progress across a vast, flat, arable landscape. Zero in and the speck turns out to be a BMW 530i driven at high speed across the Great Plains. In the driver's seat is a woman dressed in monochrome, focused on the far horizon, Philip Glass at full blast on the stereo. Destination: maybe Fargo, North Dakota, or perhaps this time it's Sioux Falls, South Dakota. Who can tell these states apart? The plains are the plains after all. A police car appears in pursuit, pulls up beside the car, which, even in the midst of a grit-strewn Midwestern winter, is immaculately shiny. The driver's window rolls down; she lowers her tortoiseshell glasses and pleads, "Officer, I had no idea I was going that fast." With a caution, he lets the Emma Peel of architecture go.

Fargo is an unlikely spot on Earth for a cutting-edge software development company. But the freedom and openness of the landscape inspires the corporate ethos of Great Plains Software, and hence its desire for an uninterrupted creative environment for its growing workforce—expanded from 10 people to 650 in fifteen years. Two long bars are mutually offset to maximize views, especially through the south bar's glass facade, and interspersed by equivalent slabs of landscaping, emulating the shelterbelts that protect crops from the climatic savagery of the open plains.

> People think of the plains as unarticulated bland space. But to me it's extremely profound. There isn't a topographically determined path across it, so you have to make a decision about where you want to be. This is a particularly American quality: a vast, unrestricted democratic country in which everyone has opportunity. There was no program, no org chart for the Great Plains Software project. They simply said, "We want the building in eighteen months. GO!"

So Snow gathered the clients and engineers in her office for a three-day charette to design the building systems and the ubiquitous IT, developing program and landscape in tandem. Together they devised the most efficient way to span forty-eight feet without interruption—rolled I-sections bolted to round columns. The undivided floor space echoes the seemingly limitless terrain of the Dakota Plains while meeting the software developer's needs for spatial flexibility and fast telecommunications throughout, accommodating their fluctuating cycles of individual and group activity.

> The buildings create a dialogue with the landscape. This huge plain of space allows the users to reconfigure their work environment and navigate it in as free a way as possible. It's like the deck of a battleship, but the tools are there to connect the team members to the broadest bandwidth.

———

Transparency, clarity of vision, landscape, and light—these are the principal subjects of Snow's architecture, though not always explicitly so. Her buildings are often taken to be exercises in minimalism. Lest that seems simply reductive, here's the real aim: the stripping back of architectural noise to achieve a state of quietness in which a building's occupants can perceive the quality of the landscape in which their building is set, notice the quotidian passage of light through all the shades of daytime, into dusk, evening, night. Asked when she herself experiences these moments of repose, Snow responds, "When I'm taking the dog for a walk in the morning, around the lake."

Introspection. Reflection. Meditation. These are the states of calm that her buildings induce and which her clients seek her out to create. She talks of her aspiration toward creating "transformative" architectural experiences, those that still the mind. Spaces that invite you to "just start breathing a little more slowly."

> I look at architecture as a playing field on which people operate. It's all about making connections between places and activities, site and architecture. Our work is not reductive. It's inclusive— but not overly complete or complex, so it has room for other things. In a really beautiful room, an unmade bed looks good.

———

There are characteristic tropes: the insistent rectilinear forms and horizontal massing; low-rise buildings that seem to hug the ground, grow long and thin out of their locations, their proportions and facades reminiscent of Dutch modernism; buildings as vessels for the harvesting of light.

Snow grew up in Michigan, as Julie VandenBerg, in a Dutch-Reform household whose spiritual strictures and disdain for frippery or material flamboyance seems to have had an enduring impact on her aesthetic sensibilities. John Dinkeloo, founding partner in the architecture firm Roche Dinkeloo, was a high-school friend of her father's. Yet it was her mother who—impressed by the diversity of Dinkeloo's activities and travel opportunities—encouraged her daughter to take up architecture. Snow began her studies at the University of Colorado at Boulder, where she experienced a different kind of luminosity:

> In Colorado the light is intense. The light in Michigan is like the plains: it's very uniform and has almost a spatial quality. You're in a bowl of light—it's diffuse rather than coming from a source. It's spatial rather than directional.

Leaf through this monograph and you will see buildings that glow, especially at night—twinkling despite their conspicuous lack of architectural rhinestones. Snow's Minneapolis light rail transit stations should perhaps be called *rail light transit* stations, since she uses light and structure to create urban beacons, using an elemental structural grid—rib-like bays that delineate rather than enclose space—to confer brief instances of aesthetic coherence on the new transit system. (Ultimately, overall unity is defeated by the transit authority's determination to commission "context-specific" designs for the different stops, from a range of architect/artist teams.)

Of the three stations Snow was commissioned to design, two were realized in collaboration with artist Tom Rose, and the third was lost to the scrum of metropolitan design politics. At the Cedar-Riverside station, in a modest neighborhood that has become home to many of Minneapolis's East African immigrants, the station canopy is glass and decorated with the celestial constellations that might be seen through it. At the Lake Street/Midtown stop, astride a junction beset with big-box retailers, franchise foods, and parking lots, the station is like a candelabra for a less-than-glamorous part of the city. On this filigree bridge, linear bands of pastel-colored light cling to its illuminated ribs, high and beckoning, offering an ethereal palette against the night—a taste of Mies-meets-Dan-Flavin on a $1.75 transit ride.

Perhaps it has something to do with the CAD-rendering software Snow's firm uses that her buildings often seem to bask in an impossibly sharp and delineating sunlight—the kind that gives each figure in the scene an intensely etched outline, as if we, too, must be as firm and precise around our edges as her buildings aspire to be. Perhaps this is too much to ask of mere mortals.

Take the University of South Dakota Business School, for example. A competition entry (alas, not to be realized), this building would have had an extraordinary shimmering facade. A set of clear, rectangular volumes pierce the ground-hugging main structure—all the better to emphasize the gorgeousness of its surface, crystalline and seductive in its variegated translucencies. There's a comment here about the deceptive allure of the shiny (albeit not metal but glass), perhaps befitting an academic department dedicated to the dissemination of techniques for making and managing money.

———

Snow speaks of always trying to find a place within the conditions of a project or its site that suggests "a contradiction that architecture has to resolve"—the programmatic grit in the oyster, so to speak—"not really to resolve it, but to articulate it, by detailing it intensely." Often, this point of abrasion has to do with apparently irreconcilable needs: for shelter *and* exposure, for visual accessibility *and* physical security, for the pleasure of effulgent light *and* the comfort of penumbra.

In the Fifth Precinct police station in Minneapolis's Lyndale neighborhood, for example, the task was to make a building that would convey openness and congeniality to the surrounding community while maintaining a sense of security, yet without turning it into a fortress. Here the solution was in "districting" the two main components by creating a large transparent community room at one end and a wing of brick-faced offices for the police officers at the other. Their windows and, thus, everyday work are visible from the street but protected by a low brick wall enclosing a light well.

In the Koehler House, on the dramatic coastline of New Brunswick, the challenge was to reconcile the simultaneously threatening and fragile aspects of the environment. Here, on the savage coast of the Bay of Fundy, the choreography of physical experience—alternating rhythms of tight and open spaces—accentuates the drama of the remarkable site.

> It was so loud in the wind we could hardly talk. But as soon as you walk down off the high point of the site, it becomes quiet and warm, and the landscape just holds you. You want both of those experiences in the house. As you come up the staircase, slotted between twelve-foot-high walls, you're very contained. Then suddenly you're connected physically and visually to the bold ocean view. It's a trajectory, this idea of projecting yourself into the landscape. You want to be both protected and connected, to huddle next to the fireplace, or to stand up on the top deck and exult.

Snow expresses a preference for sensual and spatial juxtapositions, which she tends to articulate in evocative catch phrases. *The thick/thin thing*: pairing of solid and light structures. *The cave and the agora*: sharp contrasts of dark, contained spaces with open, luminous expanses. *The rugged and the refined*: natural textures and materials paired with high-tech industrial components—architecture as protection from harsh conditions, whether social or environmental.

———

Snow began designing factories at $90 per square foot. She has cut her teeth on utilitarian structures out in the middle of nowhere, industrial plants for the postindustrial economy—the Short Run Production facility in New Richmond, Wisconsin (a fast-order manufacturer of small, highly engineered parts); the Origen Center in Menomonie, Wisconsin (a business incubator-cum-corporate training facility); QMR in River Falls, Wisconsin (a fabricator of molded plastic parts). These buildings gain dignity from the relationship of inside to outside: the interiors are flooded with light so as to humanize them, and the prosaic, repetitive activities that go on within them are linked to the ever-changing moods of the natural landscape.

> We started out with very pragmatic building types, and we made a strategic choice between exploring more extravagant forms, or exploring details and assembly. You can't do both: you cannot do something interesting with the skin and the structure and still have a great deal of formal manipulation. We're a little techie at heart. I just really love construction—the way buildings are made—taking the assembly and refining it. I've always said: When I master Ninety Degrees, I'll move on.

Now she is on the cusp of change, from work that has been predominantly concerned with accommodating pragmatic functions, toward an architecture that is "magnetic." From the days of ultra-minimalism, working on tight budgets to create new industrial spaces, Snow has progressed to making luxury homes out of former industrial structures along the Minneapolis riverfront. Her latest completed project combines conversion and new construction, turning the former Gold Medal milling complex along the Mississippi River into loft condominiums for the city's wealthiest denizens and adding a brand new nine-story building that holds its own between the renovated historic facades of the Mill District (including the neighboring Mill City Museum) and the new Jean Nouvel–designed Guthrie Theater.

The oddities in Snow's portfolio—the SecurePet ID Collar and the Telematic Table proposal for the Walker Art Center— signal her ambition to transcend the boundaries between architecture and other design fields, such as product design and interactive media. Working with experts in other fields, from veterinary science to computer software, her firm has begun to address architecture at scales very different from that of buildings. Whatever the form or purpose, the work is always graced with precision, attention to detail, a sensitivity to the play of light and transparency, and a seductive shimmer.

Ge(ne)ography

Ben Fry

*Else/Where: Mapping—New Cartographies
of Networks and Territories*, 2006

They look like hybrids of architecture, theatrical flats, and musical notation: isometric structures whose banded vertical panels are interlaced by grey filaments, crisscrossing as if spun by a slightly crazed spider. In successive frames, the view shifts and the panels start to resemble skyscrapers, or city blocks reimagined by a muted-palette Mondrian.

But in fact these abstract representations are maps of a new kind: Haplotype Maps, visualizations of clusters of nearby genetic variants that tend to occur together along a given stretch of a chromosome. They were produced by Ben Fry as part of his PhD in Media Arts and Sciences, which he completed at Massachusetts Institute of Technology (MIT) in 2004. Fry specializes in visualization of data whose structure and content are undergoing continuous change, with a focus on the burgeoning field of genomics.

Now working at the Broad Institute of MIT and Harvard (formerly the Whitehead/MIT Center for Genome Research) effectively as its first resident information designer, Fry is developing new programming and visualization tools that enable genomics researchers to see what they are discovering in a highly abstract landscape. It is a landscape characterized by dramatic shifts in scale, massive quantities, constantly updated information, and critical variants yielded by tiny modifications in the arrangement of basic units. Sounds like a place you'd like to visit? Could be your own body, since the landscape under consideration sometimes happens to be the human genome.

Dr. Eric Lander, director of the Broad Institute, hired Fry upon completion of his doctorate, recognizing that he was charting important new terrain, in which the quantity of data being generated has, thus far, been almost inversely proportional to the quality of information design available to represent it.

"Biology is undergoing a remarkable revolution right now, from being a laboratory discipline in which people studied their own particular problem, to becoming an information science," Lander explains. "A decade or two ago, a biological scientist typically worked on a specific component: one protein, one gene. It was as if they were studying the earth from ground level, by looking around them.

"But in the last ten to twenty years, with the advent of genomics, biologists have been able to pull up to the 100,000 feet level and see the entire world of biology in one glance. We now know the whole sequence of the human genome, so we're presented with the two million genetic variants of the human population, and their correlation in hundreds of people; all the patterns by which genes are turned on and off in diverse tissues in the body; all the mutations that occur in cancer; all the networks and pathways by which signals are sent to the cell. The field is suddenly coming to grips with how to deal with all this data."

Fry became involved with the Broad Institute during his doctoral thesis, when he worked closely with its biologists on ways to represent the intricate pattern of correlation between nearby genetic variations in the human genome. "Ben came along and was very rapidly able to develop five or six ways of communicating different and important aspects of the data," says Lander. "There's just no substitute for visualizing data: you see patterns in it that you won't be aware of any other way."

―――

An alumnus of the MIT Media Lab's Aesthetics and Computation Group (ACG), headed by John Maeda, Fry is clearly influenced by Maeda's emphasis on intellectual "dual processing": to gain admission to this highly selective graduate program, students must demonstrate competence not only in graphic design, but also in software design; they develop these skills in tandem. Fry's portfolio includes numerous experimental software studies and, in collaboration with Casey Reas (a fellow ACG alumnus, now assistant professor in the Design|Media Arts program at UCLA), he has developed Processing, a new programming environment for learning computational design that has already attracted a tribe of twelve thousand alpha-testers.

In his PhD thesis, Fry drew an analogy between genomic cartography and conventional cartography, which synthesizes illustration, information design, and statistics, and uses technological tools for implementation. "It was a useful way to frame things. In doing this new stuff on computer, people tend to presume it's completely different than what anyone else has done. But when I went to look for books and resources, I found there isn't nearly as much good material in the interactive work as in cartography." Over centuries, cartographic skills have been honed for tackling complexity and establishing hierarchy, to present rich information in a limited space. "Then the question is: How do you make cartography dynamic, and what happens when you apply it to genetics?" In his PhD dissertation, Fry writes:

Rather than focusing on a final outcome, genomic cartography should be a flexible process around a dynamic diagram that can handle change. To attain this flexibility, software presentation methods must be grounded in variability—the positioning of elements must be semi-automatic, based on rules set by the cartographer. Rather than simply applying rules of graphic design, the designer must be able to abstract some of these rules, and implement them as active software elements.

The creation of visual tools for expressing ideas is not a matter of merely garnishing scientific findings, argues Fry. "I try to explain [to the scientists] that rather than seeing the visual thing as the icing put on top, to ornament a paper, it's much closer to the writing they're doing. You couldn't get away with a writing style of the kind that they use in the images; you'd get laughed out of the review process. So they recognize they need to have a certain degree of skill. Even among the 'priesthood,' they need to be able to talk to each other. You can only move things along in a field as fast as you can communicate."

Standard genomics representations are barely decipherable, unless one is trained to read them. Produced using a small range of software visualization tools made by scientists, they suffer from lack of awareness of basic principles of information design. At best, they are cluttered, dense, and confusing; at worst, they are actively misleading. "How do you even start *looking* at one of these images?" Fry asks. "If you look at an enormously complex map of a city, you get some immediate understanding of where the streets are, what its features are. That's what's missing from this complex diagramming."

Fry's work in genomic visualization has so far tackled several different levels, from single chromosomes (human chromosomes 13, 14, 20, 21, and 22) to an entire genome, with side excursions into contexts of use, such as a prototype PDA Genome Browser that would enable scientists to read data on handheld devices. He has tried out various aesthetic approaches to mapping massive amounts of known data, while also depicting the terra incognita of genes not yet identified, from the deep-space planetary orbit of his 2002 Genome Valence (a 3D view of BLAST, the algorithm most commonly used for genome searches) to the architectonic lattice of Chromosome 13 (done in 2001). These studies are marked by a certain visual astringency: a translation, perhaps, of the Bauhaus design legacy inherited via Maeda's Media Lab predecessor, Muriel Cooper, inflected by Maeda's Japanese-inspired purism.

———

In one virtuoso section of his dissertation research, Fry painstakingly unpacks the map of the human genome as represented in gff2ps—the software program created to read General Feature Format (GFF), a standard file format for annotating genomic sequences. He demonstrates how poor use of basic visual elements—such as color, line thickness, sizing and spacing, category indication, and alignment of data tracks—conspire to render this widely used diagram far less legible than it might be. He then proposes a cleanup and a way to implement the improved design as a software tool (developed using Processing) that could be applied to various genomic data sets.

Part of the challenge in reading such diagrams is that one needs a basic grasp of the terminology (arcane, at least to a layperson) used to describe the different categories of genomic information. First there are the building blocks of a genome, the set of bases represented by the letters A, C, G, and T, which stand for the lengthy names of chemicals. C, for example, is the abbreviation for cytosine, which is short for deoxycytidine triphosphate. Chromosomes are made up of DNA, each a long polymer molecule composed of many such bases. The shortest human chromosome, Chromosome 22, comprises about 50 million letters; the longest, Chromosome I , about 250 million. A genome— the collective name for a particular organism's complete set of chromosomes—may be composed of anything from a few thousand letters to billions of letters. To give a sense of scale, the 3.1

288 Daddy Wouldn't Buy Me a Bauhaus

billion letters that make up the 24 unique chromosomes comprising human DNA would extend over five thousand miles if printed out as a single line of 12-point Times Roman.

––––––

At the Broad Institute, Fry takes part in weekly group meetings with its team of computational biologists and has clearly learned to speak biology fluently enough to participate meaningfully in their discussions. "Our biggest issue," Fry explains, "is how to compare the genomes of different species in a really clear picture. So we can say: 'Here's an evolutionary tree, here's the data for all the animals.' If you look for the differences between the human genome and the mouse genome, the mouse has over ten times as many olfactory genes as the human. By contrast, we share the HOX region of genes—which is involved in the development of our limbs and structural core—with a striking number of species. Right now, scientists are looking at the area around CFTR, the gene tied to Cystic Fibrosis: a region of 1.7 million letters in the human genome. The task is to find that region in the chimp, dog, mouse, fruit fly, zebra fish, etc., and compare with all those organisms."

Fry is currently creating interactive maps for browsing individual genomes and comparing those of different species, as part of the International Haplotype Mapping Project, a $100-million research venture involving six countries, in which the Broad Institute is a major partner. The project attempts to show, at a glance, variations between people, families, and populations.

Fry's interactive visualizations—which allow data comparisons from multiple viewpoints—have already proved "incredibly useful in helping to digest the data," according to Dr. Eric Lander, who explains: "These kinds of visual representations become memes—cultural units that spread very rapidly when they click for people."

Most of the variation between the genomes of two individuals comes down to Single Nucleotide Polymorphisms (SNPs, pronounced "snips"), single-letter changes that occur once every thousand or so letters of genetic code. Fry's Haplotype mapping visualization takes data for 103 SNPs in a population of 500 different people, and offers a quick visual way to grasp patterns in connections between sets of SNPs, and adjacent clusters. His interactive application allows the user to move between alternate views of the same data, prioritizing different aspects as needed. Shuttling between them enables "a tight coupling between the qualitative—useful for an initial impression and getting a feel for that data—and the quantitative—necessary for determining specific frequencies of haplotypes of interest for specific study."

When the important thing is to be able to read the individual letters on a chromosome, a view can be selected that gives each letter (or SNP) equal spacing; a thin grey line links to a real scale at the base of the diagram, showing its true position along the chromosome. By clicking a button, the diagram shifts to show SNP columns once again in their correct proportions, giving a sense of their pattern of relatedness.

The definition of a block is still under debate, so Fry's software lets users modify the mathematical parameters that determine block boundaries, by tweaking the algorithm via an on-screen slider. Block transitions can be emphasized by shifting the view from 2D to 3D, and by offsetting the blocks along the z-axis. For those who like their data quantitative, another view shows just raw letters and their respective percentages.

Given the exponential scale of the data being navigated, it might seem tempting to devise a means to travel visually from millions of letters down to the individual letters of a genome. But as Fry points out, "What gets missed in *Powers of Ten*–style continuous zooms are the plateaus along the way where interesting things are happening. You need to design for each of those plateaus, where you see very different phenomena, at the relevant scale. When you look at the 1.7 million letters around the CFTR gene, there are seven different genes to consider within that region, and the first thing to figure out is just where they start and stop. At the 250,000-letter scale, there are other kinds of things to consider. At the 150-letter scale, you can read all the letters in one go." In Fry's recent Genome Comparison chart (2005)—a prototype interface for comparing the genomes of several species, from human to zebra fish—these exponentially different scales of data are presented in linked horizontal bands.

He makes an analogy to designing type for different scales of reading. "When you take a 12-point font and blow it up, it's not the same as a typeface designed at 72-point. It's like the difference between a headline face and a book face, optically."

———

There are pluses and minuses to being a pioneer in a field, Fry notes. "The downside is that I don't have many people to compete with. At conferences, there isn't a visualization section, but I suspect that's going to change." (One of the few other designers working in this area is David Small, who also earned his PhD at the MIT Media Lab, and is working on another user interface design commission for the Broad Institute.) Fry anticipates building a team with another designer and software engineers, to expand the Institute's representation capabilities.

Meanwhile, its director, Dr. Lander, feels that "some of this just involves a creative wandering and exploration that has an aspect of individual creativity. I want to give Ben the chance to turn the data over in his mind, take various people's problems, and come up with really unusual, quirky, and insightful ways to visualize them."

Asked how he chooses what to work on, Fry says "it's a combination of me speculating and asking the scientists: 'What do you care about at this level?' Then saying to them, 'Actually, you need *this* level, and *this* set of features.' The scale of the projects is very big. You go region by region, half-a-million letters of code at a time."

Postscripts

Arquitectonica

Laurinda Spear (1950–) and Bernardo Fort-Brescia (1951–) are the principals of Arquitectonica, the Miami architecture firm that they cofounded with Andrés Duany and Elizabeth Plater-Zyberk in 1977. Arquitectonica has built dozens of residential, corporate, and government projects, the majority of them in Florida but also in China, Indonesia, Peru, Brazil, and various European cities. Among their recent buildings are the Bronx Museum of the Arts and the Westin New York at Times Square, both in New York; Microsoft Europe's headquarters in Paris; the East Los Angeles College arts campus; the Thomas P. Murphy Design Studio Building at the University of Miami School of Architecture; and the Brickell Heights residential complex, also in Miami. In 2005, Spear launched ArquitectonicaGEO, which focuses on sustainable landscape architecture.

Reyner Banham

Peter Reyner Banham (1922–1988) was an architecture and design historian, journalist, educator, and critic. A professor at London University's Bartlett School of Architecture from 1964 to 1976, he then moved to the States, where he taught at SUNY Buffalo and University of California, Santa Cruz. He had been appointed Sheldon H. Solow Professor of the History of Architecture at New York University's Institute of Fine Arts shortly before his death.

Theory and Design in the First Machine Age (1960), Banham's first book, was based on his Courtauld Institute doctoral dissertation (under Nikolaus Pevsner). His later books include *The Architecture of the Well-Tempered Environment* (1969), *Los Angeles: The Architecture of Four Ecologies* (1971), and *A Concrete Atlantis: U.S. Industrial Building and European Modern Architecture* (1986).

In the 1972 BBC documentary *Reyner Banham Loves Los Angeles*, he toured the city guided by an imaginative precursor of GPS navigation: an eight-track tape player he dubbed the "Baede-Kar." His writings are collected in *Design By Choice* (1981) and *A Critic Writes: Essays by Reyner Banham* (1997).

Michael Bloomberg
Michael Bloomberg (1942–) is a businessman, philanthropist, politician, and the CEO and cofounder of Bloomberg L.P., the global financial, software, data, and media business headquartered in New York. He served three terms as mayor of New York City (2002–13). In 2020, he ran as a Democratic candidate for president of the United States.

When I asked Bloomberg, during this interview, about the potential of three-dimensional representation of financial data, I had in mind *Financial Viewpoints*, a project by erstwhile MIT graduate student Lisa Strausfeld. He dismissed the concept as "a nice gimmick…the kind of thing to keep people at the MIT Media Lab occupied and to give you something to write about."

In 2001, Bloomberg L.P. hired Strausfeld—by then a partner at Pentagram—to design the digital media installations for its New York headquarters. She later joined Bloomberg L.P., spending three years there, first as its global head of data visualization and later as creative director of Bloomberg View.

Muriel Cooper

Muriel Cooper (1925–1994) is now recognized as a seminal figure in digital design, as well as an influential educator and book designer. This profile was originally commissioned as a report on new projects at the MIT Media Lab's Visible Language Workshop, of which she was director. It changed, overnight, into an in-depth survey of her entire career.

On the Friday of Memorial Day weekend in 1994, Chee Pearlman, *I.D. Magazine*'s editor-in-chief, called me into her office and told me to take a seat. Then she dropped the bombshell: Cooper—whom I had just visited in Cambridge, Massachusetts, for the second of two interviews—had died of a heart attack the previous day.

I was bereft. I'd been meaning to call Cooper to thank her for her time but, preoccupied with other assignments, had put off doing so until I'd listened to the tapes and formulated some supplementary questions. Now it was too late.

When we met, Cooper was sixty-eight, exactly twice my age; I could see my own potential future reflected in her working life. She had switched professional contexts at several points and her work resisted easy categorization but, in fact, she pursued a constant thread of inquiry throughout her career: into "static" versus "dynamic" media.

In 1994, Cooper posthumously received the AIGA Medal and a Chrysler Award for Design Innovation, whose $10,000 prize was put toward an endowment for a professorship in her name at MIT. David Reinfurt and Robert Wiesenberger co-curated a 2014 exhibition of her work, *Messages and Means*, at Columbia University, and later co-edited the catalogue raisonné *Muriel Cooper* (MIT Press, 2017).

Coop Himmelb(l)au

Founded in 1968, Coop Himmelb(l)au is an architecture, urban planning, and design studio headquartered in Vienna, Austria, with offices in Los Angeles, Frankfurt, and Paris. Wolf D. Prix (1942–) has been CEO and design principal since the retirement and departure of cofounder Helmut Swiczinsky (1944–).

This article was published shortly after Coop Himmelb(l)au came to international attention with its rooftop remodeling on the Falkestrasse, Vienna, and the firm's inclusion in the 1988 *Deconstructivist Architecture* exhibition at the Museum of Modern Art, New York, curated by Philip Johnson and Mark Wigley.

Since then, Coop Himmelb(l)au's influence and portfolio has expanded to include completed buildings such as BMW Welt in Munich (2007); Akron Art Museum in Ohio (2007); Central Los Angeles Area High School #9 for the Visual and Performing Arts (2008); Busan Cinema Center in Busan, South Korea (2011); the European Central Bank headquarters in Frankfurt (2014); and PANEUM: House of Bread II, Asten, Austria (2017).

Duany Plater-Zyberk & Co.

Andrés Duany (1949–) and Elizabeth Plater-Zyberk (1950–) are husband-and-wife partners in DPZ CoDesign (formerly Duany Plater-Zyberk & Co.), which they established in 1980, having left Arquitectonica, the practice they cofounded with Bernardo Fort-Brescia and Laurinda Spear in 1977.

DPZ became widely known for its design of the urban code for the new town of Seaside, Florida, discussed in this volume; the firm has since developed form-based urban codes for several hundred new towns and urban redevelopments.

Duany and Plater-Zyberk cofounded the nonprofit Congress for the New Urbanism in 1993 with the goal of "transforming the built environment from ad-hoc suburban sprawl toward human-scale neighborhood development."

Awarded the 2001 Vincent Scully Prize by the National Building Museum, their books include *Suburban Nation: The Rise of Sprawl and the Decline of the American Dream* (2000, with Jeff Speck) and *Garden Cities: Theory and Practice of Agrarian Urbanism* (2011). Plater-Zyberk has taught at the University of Miami School of Architecture since 1979, and she served as its dean from 1995 to 2013.

Peter Eisenman

Peter Eisenman (1932–) is an architect, educator, and principal of Eisenman Architects, based in New York. He was the first director (1968–81) of the Institute for Architecture and Urban Studies—a radical experiment in architectural pedagogy that emphasized the history and theory of architecture alongside design. He has taught at Princeton, Harvard, Cambridge, Ohio State, and Yale Universities.

Eisenman's built works include the Wexner Center for the Arts in Columbus, Ohio, as the Visual Arts Center at Ohio State University was later named (1989); the Aronoff Center for Design and Art at the University of Cincinnati (1996); the Monument to the Murdered Jews of Europe, in Berlin (2005); and the University of Phoenix stadium, in Glendale, Arizona (2006). His books include *Houses of Cards* (1987), *Eisenman Inside Out: Selected Writings 1963–1988* (2004), and *The Formal Basis of Modern Architecture* (2006), a republication of his 1963 Cambridge University doctoral dissertation.

This piece was my first in-depth profile for *Blueprint*. When it came out, I saw that an overzealous copy editor had mistakenly added an "i" to the word *genus* in the first paragraph, such that it read: "Eisenman is the archetype of the genius." Not what I'd intended (and duly rectified in this edition), but given how much of our conversation had been about error, misreading, "not-truth," and lying, this mistake was strangely apposite.

Michael Eisner

Michael Eisner (1942–) was chairman and CEO of the Walt Disney Company from 1984 to 2005, a period in which he spearheaded a transformative phase of growth, hiring renowned architects to design buildings for its US and European properties.

In fall 1990, *Blueprint* sent me to the States to report on Disney's patronage of contemporary architecture. Nervous about making it to my morning meeting with Eisner in rush-hour freeway traffic, I did a test run the day before to Disney's Burbank corporate headquarters—recently completed to Michael Graves's design, with Seven Dwarfs caryatids. Halfway through the interview, I looked at my tape recorder, and saw to my horror that I hadn't pressed the record button. Thankfully, I'd been taking notes in shorthand. I hit record and pretended I hadn't just had a minor heart attack.

From Disneyland, I flew to Walt Disney World in Florida to see Graves's new Swan and Dolphin hotels and Robert A. M. Stern's Newport Beach Club hotel. Wandering their freshly carpeted hallways, I felt a familiar sense of dislocation: the loneliness of the long-distance architecture critic. I'd traveled halfway around the world to a theme park—not for fun, but *on business*.

Euro Disneyland opened outside Paris in 1992; it was renamed Disneyland Paris in 2009. In 2006, the Burbank headquarters was renamed the Team Disney—Michael D. Eisner Building.

Ben Fry

Ben Fry (1975–) is an American information designer and software developer, and the founding principal of Fathom, a consultancy in Boston. This piece took me furthest from my familiar territory in architecture and design, to the frontiers of genomic research. It was no simple task to translate Fry's sophisticated data visualizations for the Broad Institute into words. But, in doing so, I came to comprehend the scale of information with which genomic scientists customarily contend, and the work ahead for a new class of designers: those capable of producing dynamic tools that allow scientists to visualize both *quantity* and *complexity* of data, identify significant patterns within it, zoom in to specific regions, and manipulate the data as if it were a plastic material.

Fry is co-creator, with fellow Media Lab graduate Casey Reas, of Processing, an open-source programming language, first developed in 2001, that allows artists and designers to program animations, images, and interactive media designs, and to teach these skills. Processing 1.0 was released in 2008, and has since developed into a meta-language with a worldwide community of users and educators. Fry and Reas are coauthors of *Processing: A Programming Handbook for Visual Designers and Artists* (MIT Press, 2007; second edition, 2014).

Fry received the 2011 National Design Award for Interaction Design from the Cooper Hewitt, Smithsonian Design Museum.

Frank Gehry
When *Blueprint* asked me to interview Frank Gehry (1929–) in 1988, he was just starting to become known outside the United States; thirty years later, he is a household name, and arguably the world's most famous living architect. He founded his practice in Los Angeles in 1962; Gehry Partners LLP was established in 2001 and is based in Marina del Rey, California.

His buildings include the Vitra Design Museum, in Germany (1989); Weisman Art Museum, in Minneapolis (1993); Guggenheim Museum Bilbao (1997); Walt Disney Concert Hall, in Los Angeles (completed in 2003, fifteen years after Gehry was first shortlisted for the project); Fondation Louis Vuitton, Paris (2014); and the West Campus for Facebook, in Menlo Park, California (2015). Current projects include the Battersea Power Station development in London and the Dwight D. Eisenhower Memorial in Washington, DC.

In addition to honorary doctorates from nineteen universities, Gehry's awards include the 1989 Pritzker Prize, 1992 Praemium Imperiale, 1999 AIA Gold Medal, 2015 J. Paul Getty Medal, and 2016 Presidential Medal of Freedom.

Michael Graves

By the time this essay appeared, American architect Michael Graves (1934–2015) was both celebrated and derided for his championship of postmodernism, represented by hallmark works such the Portland Building, in Portland, Oregon (1982); Humana Building, in Louisville, Kentucky (1985); and Team Disney headquarters, in Burbank, California (1991). He was also a prolific designer of consumer products for mass retailers Target and JCPenney, as well as for Alessi, for which he created the best-selling Whistling Bird Teakettle (1985).

I got to know Graves over many years, both as an architectural journalist and as a graduate student, crossing paths with him regularly at Princeton's School of Architecture, where he taught for thirty-nine years.

Following decades of success, tragedy struck in 2003: Graves became paralyzed from the waist down following an infection. I visited him in rehab in New Jersey while he was beginning physical therapy and learning to use a wheelchair, and in 2005 I interviewed him at Pantages Theatre in Minneapolis, in his first public appearance since his paralysis. Graves's disability shaped his design outlook in his final decade: he became an accessibility advocate, designing hospitals, hospital furnishings, and housing for disabled veterans.

Before his death in 2015, at age eighty, he helped establish the Michael Graves College at Kean University in New Jersey, and gifted his Princeton home to the school. Among dozens of awards,

Graves received the 2001 AIA Gold Medal, 2012 Driehaus Architecture Prize, and 2015 Cooper Hewitt National Design Award for
Lifetime Achievement (awarded posthumously). Michael Graves
Architecture & Design continues to operate from its Nassau Street
offices in Princeton.

April Greiman
One of the earliest adopters of the Macintosh computer as a tool
for experimental design, American graphic designer and artist
April Greiman (1948–) is a pivotal figure in digital communication, renowned as a leader of California New Wave typography.
She trained at the Kansas City Art Institute and at the Basel School
of Design in Switzerland, where she studied with Wolfgang
Weingart and Armin Hoffmann. In the mid-1970s, she established her studio, Made in Space, in Los Angeles. In 1986, she
produced issue number 133 of the Walker Art Center's *Design
Quarterly* entitled *Does it make sense?*, which famously included a
life-size naked self-portrait produced using MacVision software,
and printed on a three-by-six-foot foldout poster.

In 1998, Greiman received both the AIGA Medal and the
Chrysler Design Award; a decade later, the Society of Typographic
Arts honored her with its Lifetime Achievement Award. Her work
appeared in the 2018–19 exhibition *West of Modernism: California
Graphic Design, 1975–1995* at the Los Angeles County Museum of
Art. She was head of visual communication at CalArts from 1982
to 1984 and is currently professor of design at the Roski School of
Art and Design, University of Southern California.

Philip Johnson
American architect Philip Johnson (1906–2005) was one of the
leading arbiters of twentieth-century architecture, and curator of
two landmark exhibitions at New York's Museum of Modern Art
that bookended his career: *Modern Architecture: International*

302   Daddy Wouldn't Buy Me a Bauhaus

Exhibition (co-curated with Henry-Russell Hitchcock, in 1932) and *Deconstructivist Architecture* (co-curated with Mark Wigley, in 1988).

Among his best-known buildings are his own Glass House, in New Canaan, Connecticut (1949), which he built two years after his MoMA exhibition on Mies van der Rohe's Farnsworth House; the New York State Theater at Lincoln Center (1964); Pennzoil Place, Houston (1976); Crystal Cathedral, Garden Grove, California (1980); and the AT&T Building in New York (1984).

I interviewed Johnson twice for *Blueprint*: in his eightieth and ninetieth years. Meeting him for the first time was daunting, given his reputation as the Godfather of a cabal of prominent architects and his history as a fascist sympathizer. Johnson was charming, as expected, but also skillfully evasive—something I took pains to convey in the eventual profile.

At the end of our first conversation, Johnson asked me to introduce him to the "Children"—he wanted to know what the next generation was thinking about. I gathered a dozen fellow students of architecture and architectural history, then in our twenties and early thirties (including Stan Allen, Barry Bergdoll, Douglas Darden, Keller Easterling, Alexey Grigorieff, Taisto Mäkelä, and Mark Stankard), and, a few weeks later, we joined Johnson and his then-partner John Burgee for supper and conversation around a huge circular table in their offices. When he asked whose work we found interesting, Daniel Libeskind's name came up; Johnson was intrigued but apparently not that familiar with him.

The following year, when Johnson co-curated the *Deconstructivist Architecture* exhibition at MoMA, Libeskind's work was featured alongside that of Frank Gehry, Rem Koolhaas, Peter Eisenman, Zaha Hadid, Coop Himmelb(l)au, and Bernard Tschumi.

Meeting Johnson again shortly before his ninetieth birthday, I asked him to autograph my copies of *The International Style* and the *Deconstructivist Architecture* catalogue. "Ah! The Old Days!!" he wrote, in swirling handwriting, in the former. "Ah!! The New Days!" in the latter.

Johnson received the AIA Gold Medal in 1978 and the Pritzker Prize (the first bestowed) in 1979. He is the subject of two major biographies: Franz Schulze's *Philip Johnson: Life and Work* (University of Chicago Press, 1996) and Mark Lamster's *The Man in the Glass House: Philip Johnson, Architect of the Modern Century* (Little, Brown and Company, 2018). The Glass House, which he bequeathed to the National Trust for Historic Preservation, is now open to the public.

Rem Koolhaas

This piece was written when Dutch architect Rem Koolhaas (1944–), founding partner of Office for Metropolitan Architecture (OMA) and its research arm, AMO, was on the cusp of change: from influential theorist to internationally famous practitioner. He had just completed his first buildings, in the Netherlands, having returned to his native country after studying at the Architectural Association in London, and Cornell University, and spending time at the Institute for Architecture and Urban Studies in New York, where he wrote *Delirious New York: A Retroactive Manifesto for Manhattan*, published in 1978.

Koolhaas coauthored *S,M,L,XL* with Bruce Mau (Jennifer Sigler, editor) in 1995. He is a professor at the Harvard Graduate School of Design, where he runs the Project on the City, a research program that has yielded several publications: *Mutations* (2001), *The Harvard Design School Guide to Shopping* (2002), and *Great Leap Forward* (2002).

Among OMA's buildings are the Seattle Public Library (2004); China Central Television Headquarters, Beijing (2008); Fondazione Prada, Milan (2018); and UCCA Center for Contemporary Art, Beijing (2019). Koolhaas's awards include the 2000 Pritzker Prize, 2003 Praemium Imperiale, 2004 RIBA Gold Medal, 2010 Golden Lion for Lifetime Achievement from the Venice Biennale of Architecture, and 2018 Commander of the Ordre des Arts et des Lettres. *Countryside, the Future*, an exhibition organized by Koolhaas/AMO, opened at the Guggenheim Museum, New York, in February 2020, shortly before the museum was closed temporarily due to the coronavirus pandemic.

Phyllis Lambert

A Canadian architect, urban design activist, and philanthropist, Phyllis Lambert (1927–) is founder-director emeritus of the Canadian Centre for Architecture (CCA) in Montreal. In *Building Seagram* (Yale University Press, 2013), she details her role in persuading her father, Samuel Bronfman, to commission Mies van der Rohe to design the iconic New York skyscraper—one of the most compelling chapters in twentieth-century architecture.

During a stint working at the CCA from 2011 to 2012, I came to appreciate lesser-known aspects of Lambert's personality: her love for her bear-size Bouvier de Flandres dogs; her hospitality, with splendid formal dinners in her town house in Vieux-Montréal; and her sheer stamina, evidenced by her decades-long career in architecture, historic preservation, and affordable housing.

Lambert is the recipient of the 2014 Golden Lion for Lifetime Achievement from the Venice Biennale of Architecture, and the 2016 Wolf Prize in Arts. She is a fellow of the Royal Architecture Institute of Canada and recipient of its Gold Medal, and an honorary fellow of both the American Institute of Architects and the Royal Institute of British Architects.

Berthold Lubetkin

Berthold Lubetkin (1901–1990) was a Soviet émigré architect who arrived in England in 1931 and quickly gained acclaim for modern works such as the Finsbury Health Centre, the penguin pool at the London Zoo, and Highpoint I and II apartment towers. He had long abandoned architecture and vanished into obscurity when he won the RIBA Gold Medal in 1982.

I was then a junior reporter at *Building Design*. Out of sheer curiosity, I rang directory enquiries and asked if there was a listing for a B. Lubetkin in Bristol—his last known residence. There was indeed. I rang the number; an old man answered, and he agreed to an interview.

Entering a dark, cluttered apartment in a Georgian mansion, I felt the privilege of youth meeting age—I was twenty-two, he was eighty-one—tempered by melancholy that this pioneer of modern architecture was living his final years in a cramped space devoid of the luminosity of his own buildings.

Inside my signed copy of *Lubetkin and Tecton: Architecture and Social Commitment*, I recently found a letter dated soon after the publication of this interview. "You either have a phenomenal memory or you have hidden surreptitiously a tape recorder," Lubetkin wrote. "Next time I will have to frisk you!"

There was no next time. Lubetkin died in 1990. In her 1995 memoir, *In This Dark House*, his daughter Louise Kehoe revealed another side to him: a tyrannical father who isolated his family on a farm he dubbed World's End. Kehoe learned of her father's Jewish identity, and the loss of his parents in Auschwitz, only after his death.

Lubetkin's work was the subject of John Allan's *Berthold Lubetkin: Architecture and the Tradition of Progress* (1992) and was included in the 1999 exhibition *Modern Britain 1929–39* at the London Design Museum.

Andrée Putman

Andrée Putman (1925–2013) was a French interior and product designer. The year before this profile was published, she had completed the project that catapulted her career: the interior design of Morgans Hotel New York, the first boutique hotel (which closed in 2017). Putman went on to design the interiors for hotels around the world, museums including the Bordeaux contemporary art museum, and flagship stores for Balenciaga, Karl Lagerfeld, Azzedine Alaïa, and Guerlain.

Her namesake Studio Putman, launched in 1997, specializes in interior design, furniture and product design, and perfume creation, for clients such as Veuve Clicquot and Louis Vuitton, as well as private homes. Among many awards and honorary doctorate degrees, Putman received the 2005 Veuve Clicquot Prize and was appointed Chevalier de la Légion d'honneur, Officier des Arts et des Lettres in 2008. A retrospective exhibition, *Andrée Putman: Ambassador of Style*, was shown at the Hôtel de Ville in Paris in 2010.

Paul Rand

Paul Rand (1914–1996), born Peretz Rosenbaum, was an American graphic designer, art director, author, and educator. He was renowned for his logos for leading corporations, including IBM, UPS, and Westinghouse, and for his influence as a professor at Yale University, where he taught for nearly twenty years.

This was my first article for *I.D. Magazine*, and my first profile of a graphic designer. Shortly after its publication, angry letters started to arrive at the magazine's offices from various of his professional confrères, protesting my effrontery at questioning Rand's opinions, and offering fulsome testimonials of why he should be treated as a design deity. Debate over Rand's reputation has continued long after his death: Michael Bierut's 2004 article

"The Sins of St. Paul," on Design Observer, generated vociferous reader comments.

Rand's work has been the subject of numerous exhibitions; the most recent, *Everything Is Design: The Work of Paul Rand*, was presented at the Museum of the City of New York in 2015. As an author, Rand published numerous books, including *Thoughts on Design* (1947), *A Designer's Art* (1968), *Design, Form, and Chaos* (1993), and *From Lascaux to Brooklyn* (1996). Among the publications on his work are Jessica Helfand's *Paul Rand: American Modernist* (1998), Steven Heller's *Paul Rand* (2000), and *Paul Rand: Modernist Design (Issues in Cultural Theory)*, edited by Franc Nunoo-Quarcoo (2003).

David Rockwell

David Rockwell (1956–) is an American architect and president of the Rockwell Group, a 250-person practice based in New York, known for its designs for the hospitality, entertainment, cultural, and performing arts sectors.

Founded in 1984, its projects include the Mohegan Sun casino, in Connecticut; Nobu restaurants, in New York and elsewhere; the National Center for Civil and Human Rights, in Atlanta; the Shed and Fifteen Hudson Yards, in New York (with Diller Scofidio + Renfro); and set design for numerous Broadway productions, including *Hairspray* and *The Rocky Horror Show*.

Rockwell Group developed Imagination Playgrounds, a kit of blue foam blocks that encourages children to invent their own play environments. Originally developed for playgrounds in New York, the kit has been provided to thousands of children in Haiti and Bangladesh through UNICEF's P.L.A.Y. program, in partnership with Disney.

Rockwell Group received the Cooper Hewitt, Smithsonian Design Museum's 2008 National Design Award for Interior

Design and a Tony Award for scenic design in 2016. Its publications include *Pleasure: The Architecture and Design of Rockwell Group* (2002), *Spectacle* (with Bruce Mau, 2006), and *What If…? The Architecture and Design of David Rockwell* (2014).

Julie Snow

Julie Snow founded her architecture firm in Minneapolis in 1995. Since the publication of this essay in Snow's monograph, the firm has been renamed Snow Kreilich Architects, with Matthew Kreilich's appointment as partner. Snow Kreilich received the 2018 American Institute of Architects' Firm Award; its numerous completed projects include the US Land Ports of Entry in Warroad, Minnesota (2010), and Van Buren, Maine (2013), and numerous private residences. A 22,500-seat soccer stadium in downtown St. Louis is currently underway, in collaboration with HOK.

Snow received the 2014 AIA Minnesota Gold Medal for distinguished achievement and a 2011 Arts & Letters Award in Architecture from the American Academy of Arts and Letters. She has taught at Harvard Graduate School of Design, Yale University, University of Southern California, and University of Minnesota, where she received the Ralph Rapson Award for Distinguished Teaching.

Bob Stein

Bob Stein (1946–) is an American digital media publisher. In the mid-1980s, he cofounded the Voyager Company, the first commercial publisher of educational CD-ROMs, and the Criterion Collection, which published some three hundred classic films on various platforms, including laserdisc and DVD, during his tenure. (Today, under different ownership, Criterion offers movies via online streaming and the Criterion Channel subscription service.)

In 1997, Stein launched Night Kitchen, a developer of authoring tools for experimental electronic publishing. From 2005 to 2010, with significant funding from the MacArthur Foundation, he ran the nonprofit Institute for the Future of the Book, whose mission was to explore "the evolution of intellectual discourse as it shifts from printed pages to networked screens." IFB developed Sophie, an authoring environment (which, since Apple's OS change in 2010, is now accessible only on emulators), and CommentPress, a blog-based publishing engine that allowed readers to comment in the margins of texts. Stein then spent four years trying to build a company called Social Book, which aimed to develop an environment for social reading.

He recently donated his archives to Stanford University, including materials from his time in China during the Cultural Revolution, and from working at Atari and Voyager.

Stirling Wilford
James Stirling (1926–1992) was a British architect whose notable design credits—working in partnership with James Gowan (1956–63) and then with Michael Wilford (1971–92)—include the History Faculty building at Cambridge University (1968); Neue Staatsgalerie, Stuttgart (1984); Fogg Museum Sackler Galleries at Harvard University (1984); and Clore Gallery extension to the Tate Gallery, now Tate Britain, London (1987).

No 1 Poultry, the retail-office complex that occasioned this article, was completed in 1997, long after the glow of postmodernism had faded (if indeed it had ever really captured the imagination of the British public). The development was listed by Historic England in 2017, but was also voted Fifth Worst Building in London by readers of *Time Out* in 2005. The project was developer Peter Palumbo's second attempt to build on the site: his first, a tower by Mies van der Rohe, commissioned in 1969, was decried by Prince Charles as "yet another giant glass stump." The long controversy was explored in the 2017 RIBA exhibition *Mies van der Rohe + James Stirling: Circling the Square*. Awarded the Pritzker Prize in 1981, Stirling died at age sixty-six, days after the announcement of his knighthood. The RIBA renamed its top award for architecture the Stirling Prize in 1996. Michael Wilford (1938–) now practices as Michael Wilford Architects in England and as Wilford Schupp in Stuttgart.

Lisa Strausfeld

Lisa Strausfeld (1964–) is an American information designer and data visualization entrepreneur based in New York and Portland, Oregon. I first met Strausfeld at the MIT Media Lab in spring 1994; she is one of several graduates of its Visible Language Workshop who went on to become influential designers of the contemporary information landscape.

Strausfeld was a partner at Pentagram from 2002 to 2011, when she left to launch Major League Politics. In 2012, she joined Bloomberg LP as its global head of data visualization, later becoming creative director of Bloomberg View.

In 2017, she was appointed a senior research fellow at the New School in New York, where she developed a virtual-reality prototype for navigating a three-dimensional networked timeline of women's history, working with historian Gina Luria Walker and development studio Glowbox.

Strausfeld's projects include Sugar, the graphical user interface for One Laptop Per Child, created with Nicholas Negroponte, cofounder of the Media Lab; multimedia installations for the Walker Art Center, Minneapolis; and websites for numerous arts, educational, and cultural organizations. She received the 2010 National Design Award for Interaction Design from the Cooper Hewitt, Smithsonian Design Museum and currently runs her own firm, Informationart.

Sir Christopher Wren

Sir Christopher Wren (1632–1723) was a British architect, astronomer, mathematician, and geometer whose greatest works include St. Paul's Cathedral in London and the Royal Naval College in Greenwich.

I'm still amazed I got away with publishing this piece, which appeared on the arts page of *The Independent*. But with the mounting absurdity of the proposals for new commercial schemes along the banks of the River Thames, it seemed reasonable to consult *the* most celebrated architect in the city's history (albeit long dead) for his opinions. I quoted Wren using direct statements from the *Parentalia*, the Wren family memoirs published in 1750.

Today, Renzo Piano's Shard, currently the tallest building in the city (complete with tourist gift shop and sixty-ninth and seventy-second floor observation decks), stands a few blocks from one of the sites we discussed on our boat ride: London Bridge City. A multibillion-dollar mixed-use redevelopment is underway on the Battersea Power Station site, master planned by Rafael Viñoly, with phases designed by Gehry Partners, Foster + Partners, and WilkinsonEyre, and due for completion by 2025.

Sir Christopher Wren must surely be chuckling in his grave.

Richard Saul Wurman

Richard Saul Wurman (1935–) is best known as the founder and chair of the TED (Technology, Entertainment, Design) Conferences (1984–2002) and the TEDMED conferences (1995–2010). In 2001, he sold TED to a nonprofit organization run by publisher Chris Anderson, who developed it into a global media enterprise; online viewership of TED talks is now taken as a gauge of an individual's influence.

Wurman received his BArch and MArch degrees from the University of Pennsylvania, where he studied with Louis I. Kahn.

Among his ninety published books are *The Notebooks and Drawing of Louis I. Kahn*, co-edited with Eugene Feldman (1963); *What Will Be Has Always Been: The Words of Louis I. Kahn*, editor (1986); *Information Anxiety* (1989); and *Information Anxiety 2* (2000). Access Press, which he founded in 1981, produced travel and culture guides whose color-coded thematic organization prefigured the navigational structure of websites. His most recent book is *Understanding Understanding* (2017).

Lately, Wurman has been working with ESRI and Radical Media on a website, Urban Observatory, that allows viewers to compare and contrast data from cities around the world.

Wurman's awards include the 1996 Chrysler Design Award, the 2004 AIGA Gold Medal, and the 2014 Lifetime Achievement Award from the Cooper Hewitt, Smithsonian Design Museum. He is a fellow of the AIA and of the World Economic Forum, Davos, and has been inducted into the Art Directors Club Hall of Fame.

Acknowledgments

I am grateful to many people for their roles in commissioning and publishing the pieces in this collection, and to long-standing friends for their stalwart support and encouragement through the distinct phases of my idiosyncratic career. Sadly, several are no longer with us, but I acknowledge them here with much fondness.

My greatest thanks are to my editors, fellow writers, designers, and production editors at the various publications in which these articles appeared.

At *Building Design*: editors Paul Finch and Martin Pawley, and my erstwhile news editors Hugh Pearman and Ian Martin.

At *Blueprint*: founding editor Deyan Sudjic, publisher Peter Murray, and art director Simon Esterson; the 1980s–early 1990s editorial team, including Stephen Coates, Liz Farrelly, Luke Hayman, Rick Poynor, Caroline Roux, and Vicky Wilson; and my fellow contributors, especially Brian Hatton, Robin Kinross, Sarah Miller, Rowan Moore, Martin Pawley, John Thackara, and James Woudhuysen.

Special thanks to Deyan—my good friend, editor, and esteemed colleague for over thirty years—for writing the Foreword.

At *The Independent*: Tom Sutcliffe, arts page editor in the paper's early years, and my fellow arts writers, including Philip

Core, Ian Irvine, Kevin Jackson, Mark Lawson, Tom Lubbock, Judith Mackrell, and Mark Steyn.

At *I.D. Magazine* in the 1990s: editor-in-chief Chee Pearlman; art director Tony Arefin; assistant art directors Andrea Fella and Luke Hayman; editorial team members Andrea Codrington Lippke, Melissa Dallal, Peter Hall, Phil Patton, and Bonnie Schwartz; and Julie Lasky, editor-in-chief from 2002 to 2009.

Steven Groák supervised my Project X essay collection in my final year at the Bartlett School of Architecture, and gave me the confidence to envisage a possible career as a writer on architecture and design. For early opportunities to flex my critical muscles (sometimes under a pseudonym), I am grateful to Haig Beck and Jackie Cooper, founder-editors of *International Architect*, and to Suzanne Stephens, editor of *Skyline* in the early 1980s.

My undergraduate classmates at the Bartlett—especially Jane Cowan, Tom Croft, Ros Diamond, Jaimie Shorten, and Peter St John, and Snehal Shah, who was then studying down the road at the Architectural Association—all remain close friends despite time and distance, always game to join me for dinner at short notice whenever I manage to cross the Pond.

At Princeton University's School of Architecture, professors Alan Colquhoun, Robert Maxwell, Chester Rapkin, and Tony Vidler all turned a benevolent blind eye to my off-campus pursuits as an architectural journalist. In other departments, professors James Beniger, Gary Gerstle, and Michael S. Mahoney opened my eyes to the social, economic, and cultural dimensions of technological change, and led me to my dissertation topic, through their enlightening courses in sociology, communications theory, American social history, and history of science.

My thanks to three fellow alumni: Alexey Grigorieff (MArch *86) for sneaking me into Michael Graves's studio to use the fax machine, saving me time and anxiety about getting my *Blueprint* copy to London; Jonathan Ames '87 for numerous taxi rides to

Newark Airport in his jalopy, as I set off to review buildings and interview architects around the US; and Raymond Gastil (MArch *91) for reconnecting me with Abby Bussel, my editor at Princeton Architectural Press, when she visited Santa Fe in late 2018.

On mentioning that I'd been looking for a way to gather these pieces and bring them back into circulation as a book, Abby spontaneously recited the title of my Frank Gehry profile—"Call That a *Fish*, Frank?"—as if she'd been carrying it in her head since its original publication in 1988. Her enthusiasm for this project has been unstinting through all the months of hard work in selecting the pieces from my archive, and writing new material to contextualize them. I am grateful for her judicious but always generous editorial hand. Sara Stemen has guided this book through the production process with accuracy, levity, and sparkle, revealing to me only recently that she had been among my students in Yale University's MFA Graphic Design program in the 1990s. Thanks as well to Lynn Grady, Lia Hunt, Jessica Tackett, Wes Seeley, Paul Wagner, Natalie Snodgrass, Janet Behning, Valerie Kamen, and Stephanie Holstein at Princeton Architectural Press, to Cora Siedlecka at Abrams & Chronicle Books, and to proofreaders Laura Didyk and Tanya Heinrich.

In Santa Fe, I have been blessed with the support of a group of marvelous women—Rose Driscoll, Portia Franklin, Barbara Mehlman, Bonnie Schwartz, Joan Stango, and Julia Wirick (my erstwhile Princeton roommate, rediscovered here in the High Desert decades later)—who have kept me going through the myriad challenges of building a studio practice as a sculptor alongside continuing work as a writer and editor. Around the US, Barbara Bloemink, Cheryl Hornstein, Ann Komara, Lisa Krohn, Eve Lerman, Felicia Molnar, and Lisa Strausfeld have provided emotional anchorage through my many changes of residence and professional identity. In the UK, I have relied on Nancy Stewart and my fellow "Paulinas" Annabel Arden, Tamsin

Mitchell, Sue Prevezer, and Gina Russell, for their friendship, guidance, and love.

Finally, Marc Hacker and Kenny Schwartz deserve special mention for their hospitality and for reading through a big pile of archive Xeroxes, then giving helpful feedback on which pieces to include in this collection. I am indebted to Marc for his kindness, practical advice, and sheer wisdom, which I have cherished— throughout this and all my other projects—since our days as fellow members of Atelier 43 at the Bartlett in the late 1970s.

Credits

All articles are © Janet Abrams except where otherwise noted. The author is grateful for permission to republish her articles, which originally appeared in the following publications:

39–45 / Berthold Lubetkin: "Lubetkin Speaks," *Building Design* (*BD*), March 12, 1982

47–60 / Peter Eisenman: "(Mis)reading Between the Lines," *Blueprint*, February 1985

61–64 / Andrée Putman: "My Tea with Andrée," *Blueprint*, October 1985

65–73 / Bernardo Fort-Brescia and Laurinda Spear/Arquitectonica: "Miami Vice Versa," part 1, "Of Vice and Vixen," *Blueprint*, September 1986

73–79 / Andrés Duany and Elizabeth Plater-Zyberk: "Miami Vice Versa," part 2, "Town Kriers," *Blueprint*, September 1986

81–96 / Philip Johnson: "Now We Are 80," *Blueprint*, March 1987

97–108 / Rem Koolhaas: "Delirious Visions," *Blueprint*, February 1988

109–113 / Reyner Banham: "Reyner Banham: A Past Master," *Blueprint*, April 1988

115–122 / Frank Gehry: "Call That a *Fish*, Frank?," *Blueprint*, September 1988

123–128 / Coop Himmelb(l)au: "When the Sky Falls In," *Blueprint*, December 1988–January 1989

129–134 / Sir Christopher Wren: "A Tale of the Riverbank," Janet Abrams © *The Independent*, January 5, 1989

135–139 / James Stirling and Michael Wilford: "Britischer Architekt," Janet Abrams © *The Independent*, June 26, 1989

141–145 / Phyllis Lambert: "Phyllis's Choice," *Blueprint*, April 1990

147–157 / Michael Eisner: "The World According to Mickey," *Blueprint,* February 1991

159–173 / Paul Rand: "'This Must Be Progress'—The Master of Modernism on God, Graphics, and Other Devotions," *I.D. Magazine*, September–October 1993

175–182 / April Greiman: "Woman and Her Symbols," in *it'snotwhatyouthinkitis/cen'estpascequevouscroyez* (arc-en-rêve centre d'architecture/Artemis, 1994)

183–193 / Michael Graves: "*Gesamtkunstwerk*: Coming Home to Rome," in *Michael Graves: Designer Monographs 3*, Alex Buck and Matthias Vogt, eds. (Ernst & Sohn, 1994)

195–207 / Richard Saul Wurman: "Richard Saul Wurman Gets What He Deserves," *I.D. Magazine*, March–April 1994

209–226 / Muriel Cooper: "Muriel Cooper's Visible Wisdom," *I.D. Magazine*, September–October 1994

227–238 / Bob Stein: "A Man for All Media," *I.D. Magazine*, March–April 1995

239–244 / Philip Johnson: "When We Were Very Young," *Blueprint*, July–August 1996

245–252 / David Rockwell: "Best of All Possible Worlds," *I.D. Magazine*, September–October 1996

253–262 / Michael Bloomberg: "Information Overlord," in *Rethinking Design 4: Medium* (Mohawk Mills, 1997)

263–271 / Lisa Strausfeld: "The Choreography of Site-Specific Media," in *Profile: Pentagram Design*, Susan Yelavich, ed. (Pentagram Design/Phaidon, 2004)

273–281 / Julie Snow: "Julie Snow: The Rugged and the Refined," in *Julie Snow Architects* (Princeton Architectural Press, 2005)

283–291 / Ben Fry: "Ge(ne)ography," in *Else/Where: Mapping—New Cartographies of Networks and Territories*, Janet Abrams and Peter Hall, eds. (University of Minnesota Design Institute, 2006)

Photography of original print publications: Kim Richardson

Janet Abrams is an artist and critic whose essays on art, architecture, and design have been published internationally, in books and periodicals including *Archis*, *Blueprint*, *Ceramic Review*, *frieze*, *I.D. Magazine*, *The Independent*, *Metropolis*, and the *New York Times*. Among her previous books, she has explored the shift from analog to digital culture in *If/Then: Play—Design Implications of New Media* (editor) and *Else/Where: Mapping— New Cartographies of Networks and Territories* (co-editor with Peter Hall). She has served as director of the University of Minnesota Design Institute, Minneapolis; editor at the Netherlands Design Institute, Amsterdam; and associate director for research at the Canadian Centre for Architecture, Montreal. She holds a PhD in architectural history, theory, and criticism from Princeton University, and an MFA in ceramics from Cranbrook Academy of Art. Winner of SITE Santa Fe's 2014 SPREAD 5.0 competition for New Mexico artists, she practices as a sculptor, mainly working in ceramics and bronze, from her studio in Santa Fe. *www.janetabrams.com*

Deyan Sudjic was born in London. He has worked as an editor in Milan and as a curator in Seoul and Istanbul, among many other cities. Sudjic was the founding editor of London-based *Blueprint* magazine and served as the director of the Venice Architecture Biennale. He is a former director of the Design Museum in London. His most recent book is *The Language of Cities*.

Published by
Princeton Architectural Press
202 Warren Street
Hudson, New York 12534
www.papress.com

Printed and bound in China
24 23 22 21 4 3 2 1 First edition

ISBN 978-1-61689-951-6
Library of Congress Control Number: 2020939152

Editors: Abby Bussel and Sara Stemen
Designers: Paul Wagner and Natalie Snodgrass